The State, Politics and Health: Essays for Rudolf Klein

B

The State, Politics and Health: Essays for Rudolf Klein

Edited by Patricia Day,
Daniel M. Fox,
Robert Maxwell,
and Ellie Scrivens

BLACKWELL
Publishers

First published 1996

Blackwell Publishers, Inc.
238 Main Street
Cambridge, Massachusetts 02142
USA

Basil Blackwell Ltd.
108 Cowley Road
Oxford OX4 1JF
UK

Library of Congress Cataloging-in-Publication Data
State, politics and health: essays for Rudolf Klein / edited by Patricia Day ... [et al.].
    p. cm.
Includes bibliographical references and index.
ISBN 1-55786-868-9 (HC)
1. Medicine, State. 2. Medical policy. 3. Klein, Rudolf, 1930-
    I. Klein, Rudolf, 1930- . II. Day, Patricia.
RA394.S73 1995
362.1–dc20
                                  95-36573
                                      CIP

British Library Cataloguing in Publication Data
A CIP catalogue record for this book is available from the British Library

Composition by Megan H. Zuckerman

Printed in the USA by Book Crafters

This book is printed on acid-free paper

Contents

Acknowledgements

This book, and its companion, *Only Dissect: Rudolf Klein on Politics and Society* began with conversations among the editors in the fall of 1993. The King's Fund and the Milbank Memorial Fund supported the project. Staff members of the two funds, especially Carmel McColgan of the King's Fund and Gail Cambridge and Katharine Ristich of the Milbank Memorial Fund, managed editorial details. The diplomacy of Rolf Janke, executive editor of Blackwell Publishers' North American branch, facilitated this transatlantic effort.

Introduction

These essays celebrate the achievements of Rudolf Klein, an exemplary colleague in the study of politics and policy, especially of health and health services. Rudolf Klein's work continues to defeat conventional labels after more than four decades of prolific publication. He is an historian, a journalist, a political scientist, a policy analyst, a social scientist, an academic, and an adviser to public bodies. But none of these labels, or even all of them together, accurately describes this intensely detached and warmly impersonal practical intellectual purist whose sixty-fifth birthday offered this occasion for flattery and emulation.

A companion book, *Only Dissect: Rudolf Klein on Politics and Society,* arrays articles and papers he wrote throughout his career, selected by Rudolf and Patricia Day. These works survey the policy and politics of his times with his characteristic wit and insight. Rudolf frequently says that he is at his best in articles and short pieces, the most perishable of formats.

Perhaps a brief survey of Rudolf's curriculum vitae provides some clues to his broad-ranging output of work. He was born in 1930 in Prague where he lived with his medically trained parents until all three left Czechoslovakia to live in England and Scotland in 1939. After an education on the hoof at a variety of schools in towns and cities where his father was working, he went up to Merton College, Oxford. There he studied medieval history and won the Gibbs Memorial Prize. After Oxford, he spent 20 years in Fleet Street as a leader writer and home affairs editor.

In the early 1970s Rudolf moved from journalism to academic research on politics and public policy. At the end of the 1970s, he became Professor of Social Policy at Bath University where he founded (and directs) the Centre for the Analysis of Social Policy.

Rudolf has written extensively across a range of what other academics see as discrete specialisms, from health and medicine to politics and public expenditure. An additional measure of the diversity of his work was his role as a specialist advisor to the Expenditure Committee and Social Services Committee of the House of Commons. He has also sat on a variety of Economic and Social Research Council Committees and has been a consultant to the Department of Health, the Cabinet Office, and the Organisation for Economic Cooperation and Development. From 1981 to 1987 he was co-editor of *The Political Quarterly*.

Style and substance are inseparable in Rudolf's work. He presents his ideas and evidence to support them in prose that creates the illusion of effortlessness. He is a master of the art of making insight appear to be self-evident, hard-won evidence seem to be casual observations of a normally attentive observer.

The essays in this book aspire to Kleinian standards of rigor and coherence, although his elegance and originality are hard to match. His originality lies especially in the way he comes at issues and the questions that he asks. Frequently he chooses to explore a paradox and through doing so gives a new insight that sticks in the reader's mind and will not go away. He never has fitted neatly into any conventional categorisation, despite working in the university world, which is based on academic specialisation, and living in a country that is still profoundly riven by distinctions of class and occupation. Rudolf is a natural free spirit driven by curiosity and enjoyment. He simply moves across such boundaries, not only with apparent effortless, but with a quizzical puzzlement that anyone should take them seriously.

Contrary to the convention of celebratory volumes, we assigned a topic to each author. A few invitees declined, others dropped out; but most of them are here. Rudolf contributes a concluding comment.

Three of the four broad subjects on which we invited essays are major topics in the politics and policy of health affairs. These subjects are the profession of medicine in the making of health policy, the allocation of scarce resources to produce health care, and the role of the state in health policy. The fourth subject is policy analysis itself: the variety of skills and disciplines with which people study such questions as the changing role of the professions and the state in the provision of health care.

The essayists take note of Rudolf's contribution to scholarship. They celebrate him by striving for rigor, by paying attention to historical tensions and fictitious versions of the past, by exploring the diversity of ideas as well as the vested interests that contribute to policy, by emphasising uncertainty in policy making – the unexpected and unintended consequences of policy and the inappropriateness of tidy solutions, especially those favoured by ideologues – and by demonstrating the value of comparative analysis across countries, the public and private sectors, and public sector organisations.

Moreover, the essayists demonstrate that policy analysis is a craft, carried on for its own sake as well as for its practical value. For each of them, as for Rudolf, the exploration of health and social policy reveals broader themes in politics and policy making.

Each essayist chose a different way to honour Rudolf. Most of them make explicit reference to his work. A few bear witness to his roles as counsellor, critic and mentor. Each strives to meet Rudolf's high standards of timeliness, rigor, clarity and humour. Each took seriously our admonition to avoid dullness.

We hope the essays collected here and those by Rudolf Klein himself in the companion volume are read by people who care about politics and policy whether or not they specialise in health affairs. We particularly commend these books to those considering or beginning careers in policy analysis, because Rudolf has been an effective mentor and a model of excellence. He claims that he learnt his trade from Lord Beaverbrook who showed him how to write and that is the model he prefers to use in handing his craft on. He has been there to listen, to comment and to console.

Rudolf is acutely aware of the aspiring author's need for an immediate response to a newly written piece. He has helped many students and colleagues transform incomprehensible text into something readable by pulling out the central arguments and spelling them out clearly. He has demanded 'elegant prose' but his advice has been 'keep it simple' and 'when in doubt, leave it out.'

His two most significant pieces of advice have typically been 'you don't have to be right all the time, if necessary just be interesting' and 'whatever you do, make sure it is something you are interested in — and have fun.'

— Patricia Day
— Daniel M. Fox
— Robert Maxwell
— Ellie Scrivens

Part I

Theory
and
Policy

1

The Life You Risk
Should Be Your Own

Albert Weale

Rudolf Klein's work is marked by the virtues of at least three academic disciplines: the attention to the role of political values found in the social philosopher; the understanding of comparative institutions found in the political scientist; and the appreciation of the role of accident, luck and contingency found in the historian. Since I could not possibly hope to emulate Klein by making a contribution in all these three fields, I shall confine myself to an exercise in the field of social philosophy.

The problem I shall examine concerns the principles upon which it is ethically desirable to design the institutions by which a society can allocate health care resources. I shall argue that the idea of equality of citizenship is a meaningful and justifiable basis upon which we can design institutions and practices, and I shall suggest that if we take this approach seriously it has implications for our evaluation of how institutions like the National Health Service (NHS) are governed. In particular, I shall suggest that, although the principles of democratic citizenship call into question the typical practices of the Westminster system of government in respect of health care, they also establish a firm intellectual foundation for the socialisation of health services.

I have a personal reason for pursuing this agenda. One of my early forays into this territory was in my PhD thesis, published as

Equality and Social Policy (Weale 1978). Young men who write books, even rather self-confident young men, can easily be blown off course by a poor review. I am pleased to say that Rudolf Klein's review in *Political Studies* was positive (not all of them were). I took great comfort from Klein's opinion since I had already become an admirer of the work that he had been doing on the public expenditure process at the Centre for the Analysis of Social Policy. But there was a hint of reserve in his review because it concluded that the book was, if anything, too short. In retrospect, I think this an accurate assessment, but it was so partly because I could not complete the argument at the time. I now think that the argument I was trying to mount then got off on a wrong foot, though I still maintain that the central insight had some point. I should like to take this opportunity, therefore, to rectify the earlier shortcoming by presenting an argument that I think will work. But, since I know that Rudolf Klein delights in the pleasures of controversy, I suspect it is an argument with which he will disagree.

In what follows, then, I shall argue for three propositions:

First, there is an intellectually justifiable principle of political morality to the effect that there should be a public responsibility for providing high-quality health care across a common range of conditions to all members of a political community. The basis of this principle rests upon an appeal to the ideas of political equality and democratic citizenship, and I shall summarise it in a slogan that is the title of the present chapter and that I have adapted from a famous article by T. C. Schelling: the life you risk should be your own (Schelling 1968).

Second, the present structure of the NHS does not implement the ideals of democratic citizenship as well as it might, not because of the basis of its provision but because of the basis of its financing. In particular, the financing of the NHS does not incorporate the principle of what I shall term democratic responsiveness.

Third, one way of achieving greater democratic responsiveness would be to introduce earmarked taxation or a scheme of compulsory social insurance for health care, and such a system of financing can be defended against some obvious objections.

In seeking to develop this argument, I shall at crucial points have to rely upon appeal to the idea of equality. However, the ideal of equality that I have in mind is not equality of moral respect as found in the tradition of Kantian ethics nor equality of welfare found in socialist thought. It is, instead, the idea of political equality, understood in the spirit of the remark attributed by John Stuart Mill to Bentham that everyone should count for one and no one for more than one (Mill 1861). But first, to understand this point, we need to consider the idea of democratic citizenship.

The Idea of Democratic Citizenship

The key idea in the theory of democratic citizenship is that societies are to be seen as schemes of co-operation among their members to the common advantage. The reasoning leading to this conception of society is as follows. Social co-operation produces a large surplus of advantages over and above a hypothetical scheme of nonco-operation. The principal means by which it does this is through the division of labour in large-scale societies. This is, of course, the great insight of Adam Smith, as recorded in the opening sentence of The Wealth of Nations: 'The greatest improvement in the productive powers of labour, and the greater part of skill, dexterity, and judgement with which it is anywhere directed, or applied, seem to have been the effects of the division of labour' (Smith 1776).

The thought here is a simple but powerful one. Human beings acquire their productive capacities through practice and specialisation, and in order for this specialisation to take place a certain scale of social organisation is necessary.

However, in order for social cooperation of this scale to take place, certain institutional conditions must be met. Most importantly, there must be, *inter alia*, systems of property, and the institutional arrangements that accompany them, for example, developed institutions of contract law and public schemes for registering and controlling economic activity, including such legal practices as corporate personality, accountancy devices, and rules of liability.

Institutional arrangements of this sort serve a number of functions, including the co-ordination of individual behaviour, the provision of security against risk, and the partitioning of the span of responsibility for outcomes. The co-operative surplus created by well-functioning systems of social co-operation is so large relative to the surplus that would be generated by, say, a Hobbesian state of nature, that there is no point in trying to track the relation between current social practices and some hypothetical baseline of nonco-operation. In particular, there is no point – in the way that some social philosophers have attempted – in making the baseline of nonco-operation somehow criterial for what happens within societies with highly developed institutions facilitating the division of labour.

So far I have simply provided the rationale for a system of social cooperation. Can we get a rationale for democratic citizenship to govern such schemes of cooperation? Here the argument turns on the last point of the previous paragraph. Since the nonco-operative baseline cannot provide a point of reference for the allocation of the benefits of the co-operative surplus, we have to turn to an alternative forward-looking criterion. One such criterion is that of the general advantage, understood, as John Stuart Mill insisted it should be, in such a way that we define it to contain a strong version of the principle that everyone is to count for one and no one for more than one. The relation of the equality principle to the principle of the general advantage is controversial since one can see it either as implied by the requirement that the advantage be general, which was Mill's own position, or instead as an independent principle of justice, which is the position of critics of Mill's utilitarianism. Either way, the essence of the principle is that we should base our policies on the test of the general advantage, subject to the constraint that each potential beneficiary is to be respected as an equal participant in the determination of what the general advantage is to be. This is a principle of political equality.

The essence of political equality in this sense is that one is to understand one's fellow members of society as engaged in a co-operative enterprise to common advantage. This does not mean that all purposes are public purposes, but it does require that we think of social organisation as involving more than a modus vivendi among individuals, all with their own distinctive purposes. Instead, we have to realise that if any individuals are going to pursue satisfactorily their private purposes, this can only be done within the context of social institutions, the shape of which is a collective responsibility to be fulfilled within the constraint of respecting other members of the community as equals.

Democratic Citizenship and Health Care

So far the argument has been conducted in general terms, without specific reference to health care. Is it possible to apply this understanding of democratic citizenship to the design of health care institutions in such a way that we can identify clear implications? In particular, it would seem that given the stress upon the institutions associated with the division of labour in society the most natural implication would be a free market in health care as the way to promote the general advantage.

At this point we simply need to invoke the familiar arguments about market failure in health care. These have all been well summarised in Nicholas Barr's *The Economics of the Welfare State* (1993). Although, in general, markets are the principal way in which schemes of social co-operation can work to the general advantage, there are well-known problems in the health care sector connected with asymmetries of information, the high transactions costs of monitoring by insurers, and the problems associated with adverse selection and moral hazard. These features of the production of health care lead to market failure not just in the colloquial sense that markets often fail to produce outcomes of which good-natured observers approve, but also in the precise sense that the market will not produce an allocation of resources in which no one can be made better off without making anyone else worse off. Put in less abstract terms, the theoretical expectation is that a free market in health care will lead to cost escalation, defensive medicine, and absence of cover for large segments of the population. If anyone is not convinced that this theoretical expectation is borne out in practice, all they have to do is to take a trip to New York – ensuring of course that they have adequate insurance coverage.

Given these market failures, it is necessary, in order to avoid the problems inherent in private insurance, to devise a scheme of medical care that is based upon the principle of collective insurance. Put more strictly, the point is that all schemes of insurance are collective since they all rest on devices for pooling risks among individuals. In many cases, the emergence of this collective protection can be by and large left to the market. But there are certain areas, of which the market in health insurance is one (another is private pensions, as revealed in recent fiascos), where the market does not work well. In particular, the problem in the case of medical care is to devise collective insurance arrangements that avoid, as far as possible, the problems associated with asymmetries of information, transactions costs, and inadequate coverage. I shall call any such scheme a socialised scheme of medical care.

It is important to remember at this point that political control over such a scheme is not a consequence of its being socialised but a cause. On the principles of democratic citizenship all social institutions are to be judged by the forward-looking criterion of whether they work to the general advantage. We substitute socialised schemes in place of private markets because of a political judgement about the inefficiencies of the latter. Hence, political control – even where it only to take the form of establishing the institutions of laissez-faire – is presupposed in any account of justifiable social practices.

At this point we need to introduce one further element of the problem, namely, the idea that health care resources are limited. We have to be careful in considering this idea. In the first place, I for one take seriously Robert Evans's claim that civilised health care systems do not need to confront the citizens of affluent countries with the dilemma of 'your money or your life' (Evans 1986). Certainly, the coverage provided by the Canadian system as compared with the US system suggests that organisational arrangements are a crucial variable in making good use of resources, as Rudolf Klein himself once noted in an article written jointly with Theodore Marmor (Klein and Marmor 1986). However, I think it has to be true in some sense that health care resources are limited, if only because at any given level of technology the members of a society could decide to invest in more research and development.[1] What we should not do is accept, from the fact of limited resources, the fallacy so beloved of successive secretaries of state for health in the United Kingdom that, since we could in theory spend an indefinitely large amount on health care, the amount that we actually spend is right, and all we should do is focus on the questions of the cost effectiveness of those resources that have been allocated.

The situation then is one in which we need to make a collective decision about the health risks that are to be covered by the scheme of collective insurance (socialised medicine), acknowledging that not all health risks can be fully covered. Moreover, since the process of collective choice presupposes the principle of political equality, we need to incorporate into our notion of collective decision making respect for the principle that each person is to count for one, and no one is to count for more than one.

The proper way to do this, I propose, is to adopt the principle that the range of health risks covered for all persons be the same (making obvious allowances for differences of sex and ethnic group) and that the total volume of resources be determined by a collective judgement about how much of a society's productive output be taken in health care as against other forms of consumption. In essence, this would amount to making collective provision to prevent or treat a specified range of clinical conditions that can be expected statistically to arise in the population of which one was a member.

That this conclusion is not empty can be seen by listing some of the principles of health care allocation that it excludes. Among these are the following: willingness and ability to pay; a decent minimum below which no one should fall; historic entitlement; and the moral status of individuals. All of these principles have been used in some health care systems at some time, and some of them are present, implicitly or explicitly, in a number of current systems.

To highlight the contrasts here, consider one example, namely, the political practices associated with Oregon's attempts to move the rationing of medical care in its Medicaid programme on to a more rational basis. The operative principle in Oregon's programme appears to be that of the decent minimum. The aim of the reforms has been to improve the provision of health care for the poor and those unable to provide cover for themselves. A great deal of sophistication has gone into the development of lists of clinical procedures and their effectiveness. Indeed, much of the original impetus behind the policy developments in Oregon arose out of a concern with the ineffectiveness of the organ transplant programme and a desire to put more resources into ante-natal care. But, from the point of view of the principles of democratic citizenship, the problem with the Oregon procedure is that political representatives are not taking decisions on services that could be expected to affect them. Whosoever's needs are being met, they are not the needs, even in a statistical sense, of the decision makers themselves. Thus, when decision makers are risking lives, it is not their own lives they are risking. The practice thus violates the principles of political equality as understood within the theory of democratic citizenship.

By contrast, the method of allocation that would be favoured by the theory of democratic citizenship would be one in which individuals collectively decided the range of conditions for which they would make provision. Individuals, treating one another as equals, would therefore include or exclude in their scheme of mutual insurance certain clinically defined conditions or certain clinical procedures from which all would stand to gain or lose. The reason why this would be the basis of decision making is that it is these characteristics that can be treated as effectively being random with respect to individuals. Rationing care by ability and willingness to pay or by historic entitlement, by contrast, would not be random with respect to individuals since when these decisions were made individuals would know into which risk category they fell. No doubt, under the principle of political equality, some individuals could have a reasonable guess that their rationing decisions would not affect them, but there would always be a margin of uncertainty, and for this reason they would always be acting in accordance with the principle: 'the life you risk should be your own.'

So the general picture that we arrive at can be summarised as follows. In deciding what is to the common advantage, individuals have to select institutions that serve their interests. Familiar objections from welfare economics on grounds of market failure suggest that a free market in health insurance will not serve the common interest. The fact of scarce resources means that some rationing will have to be done. And the theory of democratic citizenship suggests that the collective choice about health care provision should not only be responsive to popular preferences about the balance between health care and other forms of consumption but should also respect the constraints implied by the principle of political equality.

Democratic Citizenship and the Westminster System

These normative propositions are still at a high level of generality. But this is an advantage. It means that we have not so far foreclosed on arguments about the relative merits of institutional arrangements. There is nothing in these propositions that says, for example, that hospitals have to be collectively owned or that doctors have to be salaried employees. The principle that needs to be respected is that the allocation of health care resources should correspond to what would be agreed through a process of collective deliberation by agents seeking to promote the common advantage, subject to the constraint of political equality. What institutional and organisational arrangements are best suited to bring this outcome about is in large part a matter for empirical enquiry.

Moreover, to have laid the stress upon the idea of democratic citizenship is not to claim that there is any particular political system in which collective decisions about health care are taken according to the principle that the life you risk should be your own. Someone might think, for example, that the principles that I have so far derived from the theory of democratic citizenship justified the structure of the UK's NHS with its principles that care be free at point of use and that the rationing of treatment be a product of the way that clinical judgement interacts with the constraints of public expenditure allocated on the basis of cash limits (that's a funny meaning to give to the notion of 'comprehensive,' I know, but that is in practice what it does mean, I think). But to seek to justify the UK's NHS directly from the principles of democratic citizenship would be a mistake since we need to take into account the extent to which the British system of government provides an adequate institutionalisation of the principle of democratic equality.

Consider, in this context, how we might define the Westminster system of government. Here I shall use the approach of social choice theory (Arrow 1963). Within social choice theory, political institutions are one means for arriving at judgements about matters of collective concern. The essential feature of democratic institutions is that they make the collective choice responsive to the preferences of individuals within a society. Different systems of democratic governance can be characterised by reference to the rules they implicitly use for aggregating individual preferences into a social or collective choice and thereby the way in which they make public policy responsive to the preferences of citizens.

Thus, the Westminster system is the name for a particular set of institutional rules for aggregating individual preferences into a social choice. These rules include the following: decisions are to be made by representatives elected in geographically based constituencies; these representatives are typically organised into parties in turn organised around principles and programmes; the ability to make collective decisions is decided by competition between political parties for the right to govern according to their announced programmes; political authority is highly centralised so that there is little constraint, at least by comparison with other liberal democratic systems, on what the governing party can implement within its programme of action; and the allocation of public expenditure is undertaken from a consolidated fund in which the government has the constitutional freedom to reallocate expenditure between programmes, even if, as Rudolf Klein reminded us in his earlier work, in the short term it is constrained to marginal adjustments (Klein et al. 1974; Klein 1975; Hofferbert and Budge 1992).

However, behind the rules of the Westminster system there is also a set of norms and principles providing its rationale. If we examine these norms and principles, we can see that they have typically rested upon a claim about the ability of the Westminster system to implement democratic preferences. Hugh Berrington (1964) characterised it well when he said that the rationale of the British constitution was no longer in the twentieth century based on the idea of checks and balances but on the assumption that a political system needed to combine highly centralised authority with democratic responsiveness.

Democratic responsiveness, I want to argue, is a value that is at the heart of the theory of democratic citizenship. I think that we can see what it means by considering two different ways in which it might be institutionalised. One way would be to follow an idea of what we might call 'referendum responsiveness,' according to which important public decisions should be made by citizenship-wide referenda. There are obvious practical and political objections to this approach, although my own view is that these objections are too often accepted as being decisive. Direct referenda do not need to have the pathologies that are often associated with them, and they do at least go some way towards maintaining collective control over government decision making (Budge 1993; Cronin 1989).

However, it is not my intention in this chapter to defend the idea of referendum responsiveness as an interpretation of democratic responsiveness. Instead, what I want to argue for is democratic responsiveness as tracking. What I mean by tracking is that government decisions should not be indefinitely free of the constraint of popular opinion. If there is a firm body of opinion that over time moves in a particular direction, then a government that was acting in accordance with the principle of democratic responsiveness understood as tracking would seek to implement policies that followed that movement of opinion. So tracking is a rather vague and indeterminate relationship. It does not require that governments follow every twist and turn of public opinion, but it does mean that governments should not systematically ignore public opinion and that over a period of three to four years should adjust their policies according to the movements of public opinion.

How well in practice do the rules of the Westminster system provide a method of preference aggregation that is responsive to the preferences of citizens in this tracking sense? Such empirical evidence as we have suggests that the system of rules that define the Westminster system do not make the system at all responsive. The clearest case in which this feature has been revealed is over the total volume of resources going into the NHS in the 1980s. The three election victories of 1979, 1983 ,and 1987 might lead one to infer that the electorate had become Thatcherite and favoured a low-tax/no-welfare-state society. But, as Ivor Crewe (1989) has pointed out, Mrs Thatcher's pursuit of Victorian values was 'a crusade that failed.' On the basis of poll evidence, Crewe was able to conclude that after 'nine years of Thatcherism the public remained wedded to the collectivist, welfare ethic of social democracy' (Crewe 1989).

Even more striking than this general conclusion is the evidence about public attitudes on the balance between the priority to be given to tax cuts and the priority to be given to social services. Forced to choose between cutting taxes at the expense of services like health, education, and welfare and extending these services even at the cost of increased taxes, public opinion was only balanced evenly between the two in May 1979; as the 1980s went on, increasing majorities came to favour the alternative of extending services even if that meant raising taxes, to the point where the expanders outnumbered the contractors six to one (Crewe 1989).

Of course, it might well be argued that this says more about the inaccuracy of public opinion poll sampling than it does about the state of popular preferences, and it could always be, as the French say, that people have their heart on the left and their pocket-book on their right – with their voting being determined by their pocket-book. But we should also at least entertain the thought that the problem is to be found as much in the institutions of the Westminster system as in the deficiencies with which popular preferences have been estimated. If we take this second route, then the inference is clear. On the crucial question of how much by way of resources was going into health care, the Westminster system failed to translate popular preferences for increased expenditure into policies.

Why should this be so? The obvious explanation is that in choosing between political parties who present themselves as offering coherent programmes for implementation when they come into office, voters are effectively denied a choice over the levels of public expenditure in particular programmes. Voters are choosing over policy bundles rather than separate dimensions of public policy, and it is rather as if, when you did your weekly shopping, instead of picking goods off the shelf you had to choose between competing trolley loads of goods made up by the respective store managers of Sainsbury or Tesco.

Thus, it is at least arguable – to put the matter no more strongly – that the Westminster system has increasingly failed to provide an adequate institutional mechanism by which government policies could track popular preferences, and it is plausible to think that this failure is due to the fact that Westminster systems only work well when most policy issues can be reduced to a single left/right dimension and not when there is more than one dimension of difference in politics.

The conclusion I come to therefore is rather like the conclusion that I came to in *Equality and Social Policy* (Weale 1978) though on the basis of rather different assumptions (proof no doubt that political theorists think that it is the journey, not the arrival, that matters). This is that there is a case for seeking to ear-mark certain tax revenues so that it would be easier for voters to see what exactly was at stake in the spending plans of different parties. If the model is that of collective insurance, then it would be worth making this clear in the fiscal arrangements that are made. By itself this would not be sufficient to rectify the lack of democratic responsiveness within the Westminster system of government. Other, even more far-reaching changes are needed to do that. But it would go some way to creating the conditions under which a collective decision could be made on health care spending that was both prudent and conformed to the principle of political equality.

I now turn to consider some of the objections that have been raised against this conclusion.

Ear-marked Taxation: Some Problems

I am going to assume that the disadvantages of ear-marked taxation should be set in the context of the principle of the general welfare. There are some bodies and persons for whom ear-marked taxation would be a disadvantage, but I discount objections from that quarter unless they can be shown to work to some general disadvantage. For example, ear-marked taxation would be a problem for the Treasury – as it is for finance ministries the whole world over who dislike it intensely – because, as Samuel Brittan (1994) has pointed out, such taxation makes it more difficult to control the overall volume of public expenditure by setting one spending ministry against another. It is of course essential to control the overall volume of public expenditure, but this should not be at the expense of a rationally defensible system of allocation within particular programmes. Thus, one serious objection to the present situation is that, since the demise of volume planning, there is no procedure within the public expenditure process forcing those making the crucial decisions to spell out what they think these sums will buy in terms of real services. If ear-marked taxation moves us away from that situation, then it will be a benefit.

There is the disadvantage that changing the present funding of the NHS from general revenues to an ear-marked tax or social insurance premium would narrow the tax base from which funds are drawn by excluding revenues from indirect and corporate sources. But this would be a price well worth paying for the gain in democratic accountability (after all, there are plenty of other good causes on which indirect and corporate revenues could go).

One argument against ear-marking used both by the Labour Party's Social Justice Commission (Commission on Social Justice 1994) and in a recent article in the *Journal of Social Policy* is that whilst 'a health tax on earnings is much more buoyant [than a property tax], aggregate real earnings tend to rise and fall with the national economic cycle. Hence, the NHS may face periodic funding crises' (Bailey and Bruce 1994). Now I may not be alone in feeling that periodic funding crises would not be an entirely novel phenomenon in the history of the NHS, and in moods in which I am feeling especially bullish about ear-marked taxation I am inclined to say to this argument that it is better to face periodic funding crises than chronic under-funding, which is what arguably characterises the present system. In fact, I am not really sure that Bailey and Bruce believe their own argument since later in the same article they say that one of the general problems with ear-marked taxes is that they will lead to an over-expansion of services. But let me try to take the argument about periodic funding crises on its merits.

It is, I think, an implication of a greater use of ear-marked taxes that in periods of economic recession expenditure has to be reduced. There is of course no need to make the financing of any service exclusively depend upon ear-marked revenue, so that other sources of revenue could act as a cushion. But one has to say in honesty that a drop in income will lead to a drop in expenditure. My own view is that if that is life, then that is life. Everyone is born into a community at a particular time, and you just have to take the luck of the generational draw. If you live through periods in which there are relatively few recessions, or the recessions are not deep, as occurred between 1945 and 1973, then you are just lucky. Problems of fairness and justice arise only in respect of those matters that organised social action can control, and if aggregate economic activity cannot be controlled over long cycles, then principles of fair distribution cannot arbitrate between members of different generations.

A second argument, of a quite different character, is also used by those like Bailey and Bruce who are opposed to ear-marked taxation: namely, that its use makes it difficult to avoid the argument for using them for other public services (Bailey and Bruce 1994). They argue – in a passage that seems to me to be very obscure – that such a development would restrict public accountability. The very opposite seems to me to be true. The reason why party competition in the Westminster system can be democratically unresponsive is that issues are wrapped up together in programmatic opposition. Unpacking issues leads to greater democratic control, not less. There is in fact a theorem in social choice theory that shows how the issue-by-issue median is a majority rule equilibrium, which further strengthens the argument (Weale 1995).

I conclude therefore that the arguments against ear-marked taxation are not as strong as some of its opponents suppose, and therefore that the proponent of democratic responsiveness should not be embarrassed by the thought that democratic responsiveness implies a greater use of earmarked taxation.

Conclusions

The rationale that I have offered for the construction of publicly justifiable health care institutions departs of course from the historical evolution of the NHS. This should be no surprise. As Rudolf Klein has made clear in his history of the NHS, the wartime consensus within which the institutions were constructed was based upon rationalist and paternalist assumptions on the part of managers and clinicians rather than upon an articulated theory of political equality (Klein 1989). Nevertheless, since the NHS has been in operation it has come to attract other ideas, and the rationale that I offer is not intended necessarily to indicate the need for radical change in the basis of operations rather than greater reform in the government machine that is ultimately responsible for it.

Second, I have not said anything about the internal market. This is deliberate. I do not see how any considerations of political principle can bear decisively on the evaluation of the internal market by comparison with the previous administrative structure. It may well be that the internal market will have consequences that undermine arrangements that would be agreed in a situation of political equality; but that is a matter for careful empirical investigation. We cannot deduce a preference for or against the internal market as an administrative arrangement solely from arguments of principle, although from arguments of principle I think we can deduce pretty directly a failure of democratic accountability in refusing to test the assumptions about how the internal market would work before putting it into full-scale operation.

Third, I do not want to claim that democratic responsiveness as tracking exhausts our understanding of democratic accountability since, as Rudolf Klein pointed out in his study of the concept undertaken with Patricia Day (Day and Klein 1987), the idea of accountability is a complex one subject to many shades of interpretation in theory and in practice. But I would want to argue that policies based on the principle of democratic citizenship will require the hard-headed understanding of the ambiguities of political choice that Rudolf Klein has done so much to demonstrate to us in his work.

Notes

1. Would they want to? There are tricky questions here about the wisdom and rationality of investing in technology to prolong life indefinitely since the prospect of an indefinitely long life is arguably grossly unattractive – as Bernard Williams once pointed out in an article named after Janacek's opera 'The Makropulos Case' (Williams 1973). Fortunately, I can leave these complex metaphysical issues aside.

References

Arrow, K. J. 1963. *Social Choice and Individual Values.* 2d ed. New Haven and London: Yale University Press.

Bailey, S. J., and A. Bruce. 1994. Funding the National Health Service: The Continuing Search for Alternatives. *Journal of Social Policy* 23(4): 489–516.

Barr, N. 1993. *The Economics of the Welfare State.* 2d ed. London: Weidenfeld and Nicholson.

Berrington, H. B. 1964. *How Nations Are Governed.* London: Sir Isaac Pitman and Sons.

Brittan, S. 1994. Time to Know What You Pay For. *Financial Times,* 15 December.

Budge, I. 1993. Direct Democracy: Setting Appropriate Terms of Debate. In *Prospects for Democracy: North, South, East and West,* ed. D. Held, 136-55. Cambridge, MA: Polity Press.

Commission on Social Justice. 1994. Social Justice: *Strategies for National Renewal.* London: Vintage.

Crewe, I. 1989. Values: The Crusade That Failed. In *The Thatcher Effect: A Decade of Change,* eds. D. Kavanagh and A. Seldon, 239-50. Oxford: Oxford University Press.

Cronin, T. E. 1989. *Direct Democracy: The Politics of Initiative, Referendum and Recall.* Cambridge, MA, and London: Harvard University Press.

Day, P., and R. Klein. 1987. *Accountabilities: Five Public Services.* London and New York: Tavistock Publications.

Evans, R. 1986. The Spurious Dilemma: Reconciling Medical Progress and Cost Control. *Quarterly Journal of Health Service Management* 4(1): 25–34.

Hofferbert, R. I., and I. Budge. 1992. The Party Mandate and the Westminster Model: Election Programmes and Government Spending in Britain, 1948–85. *British Journal of Political Science* 22(2): 151–82.

Klein, R. 1989. *The Politics of the NHS,* 2d ed. London and New York: Longman.

——. 1975. *Priorities and Inflation.* London: Centre for Studies in Social Policy.

——, and T. Marmor. [1989] 1994. Cost vs. Care: America's Health Care Dilemma Wrongly Considered. *Quarterly Journal of Health Service Management* 4(1): 19–24. Reprinted in T. R. Marmor, *Understanding Health Care Reform.* New Haven and London: Yale University Press.

——, et al. 1974. *Social Policy and Public Expenditure.* London: Centre for Studies in Social Policy.

Mill, J. S. [1861] 1991. Utilitarianism. Reprinted in John Stuart Mill, *On Liberty and Other Essays,* ed. J. Gray, 129-201. Oxford: Oxford University Press.

Schelling, T. C. 1968. The Life You Save May Be Your Own. In *Problems in Public Expenditure Analysis,* ed. S. B. Chase Jr., 127-62. Washington D.C.: Brookings Institution.

Smith, A. [1776] 1979. *An Inquiry into the Nature and Causes of the Wealth of Nations,* eds. R. H. Campbell, A. Skinner, and W. B. Todd. Oxford: Oxford University Press.

Weale, A. 1995. Democracy and Disagreement. In *Party, Parliament and Personality: Essays Presented to Hugh Berrington.,* ed. P. Jones. London and New York: Routledge.

——. 1978. *Equality and Social Policy.* London: Henley and Boston: Routledge and Kegan Paul.

Williams, B. 1973. *Problems of the Self.* Cambridge: Cambridge University Press.

2

Is There a Cake to Divide?

Samuel Brittan

Touching Base

I first came across Rudolf Klein when he was in charge of the leader page of the *Observer.* Then as now he was an influence for reason, calm, and cool observation untinged by wishful thinking. In those days, many commentators suffered from illusions about the capacity of the diminished post-war Britain to run the world – either in terms of power and diplomacy or by giving a so-called moral lead. Rudolf would have none of this. But there was never any danger of excessive coldness or detachment because of the genial sense of humour with which he observed people and events.

Unlike some who came to recognise the hubris of the political establishment, Professor Klein has never gone in for navel-gazing exercises about the supposed crises of Britain. He has seen this country's problems as examples typical of middle-sized European mixed economies. Although he has carried out international comparisons, he has achieved an international dimension mainly by the analysis of issues, which are enlivened by national detail but have many common features throughout the developed industrial world.

It would have been uncharacteristic of Rudolf to have spared me completely from his kindly, critical gaze. Always practical, he was keenly aware of my tendency not only to excessive length but also to excessive abstraction. He will no doubt feel the same over this contribution, where I have the temerity to suggest that discussion of some recent theoretical work can shed light on public policy questions, both in the health service and in the public sector generally – areas where he has made such distinguished contributions. At any rate, I have the double task of making my own assessment of some recent ideas and of convincing Rudolf that the arguments stemming from them are worth pursuing.

Mutual Advantage versus Impartiality

The period since 1970 has seen a revival of normative political theory: an attempt to work out consistently how individuals ought to behave towards each other in the macrosphere where the compulsive agency of the state is involved. It is part and parcel of the revival of interest in theoretical ethics and cannot be divorced from views of right behaviour in the microsphere among individuals or between voluntary groups.

One presupposition of this revival is that the principles of right conduct – whether between individuals or in the political sphere – are not always apparent and repay theoretical investigation. This is in contrast to the common belief that the principles are obvious – embodied in the great religious teachings or their secular equivalent – and that the only worthwhile problem is how to persuade or force human beings to conform to them more closely.

The revival has come at a price. Whereas an important minority of the educated public at one time had a smattering of the teachings of Aristotle, Locke or John Stuart Mill, the present-day successors to these writers are of interest mainly to academics – and a small minority among them, mostly American or American–educated. Modern writers like John Rawls and the early Robert Nozick have an obvious passion for public affairs. But much of the discussion has centred on the minutiae of their arguments and has been the preoccupation of a handful of postgraduates in the discipline of political philosophy.

The matters raised are, however, too important to be left to so-called professional philosophers or to be ignored by 'behavioural political scientists.' A good place at which to take the plunge is

Professor Brian Barry's *Theory of Justice* (1989), which is volume one of a projected trilogy entitled *A Treatise of Social Justice*. It is decidedly not just a tract for the times; but part of the driving force is nevertheless an attempt to rescue egalitarian ideas from the neglect or hostility the author believes them to have suffered in the Thatcher-Reagan period and its aftermath.

Barry follows the modern tendency to narrow the discussion of justice to 'social justice' and of the latter to the distribution of income and wealth. Some philosophers quite reasonably object to this narrowing of the subject matter, which precludes discussion of a vast range of questions – for example, the meaning of a just trial, or how to assess whether a child has been justly treated at an institution or whether the law concerning property rights for divorced parties is just. But I want to avoid semantic arguments (except in one case where they seem unavoidable) and also to avoid criticising writers for failing to have written books on different subjects from the ones they have chosen.

In principle, Barry's book takes off from the work of both the English eighteenth-century philosopher David Hume and the twentieth-century Harvard philosopher John Rawls. But in practice it is first and foremost an interpretation and defence of Rawls's principles of justice. It is none the worse for that. For Rawls has thrown up more material for other writers to chew over than anyone else in the revival of normative political philosophy (Rawls 1972; 1992).

Barry aims to distinguish the notion of justice as rational prudence from justice as impartiality or fairness. Under the first conception, agreements and rules are allowed to reflect the fact that some people have more bargaining power than others. Under the second, 'justice should be the content of an agreement that would be reached by rational people under conditions that do not allow for bargaining power to be translated into advantage.' (Since this essay was written, the second volume of Barry's trilogy, entitled *Justice as Impartiality* [Clarendon Press 1995], has appeared.)

He seems to me to succeed in this aim. It is indeed prudent to be constrained by certain principles in dealings with others and to try to have some at least of these principles enforced against backsliders. Otherwise life is indeed nasty, brutish, solitary and short. But that does not end the matter. Many men and women do, at least at times, want to behave justly, even if they are not observed or even if they are playing in an endgame and not subject to retaliation. People do discuss what would happen if everyone behaved in a certain way or how they could justify their conduct (or their vote or their political behaviour) to an impartial spectator. Justice, whether in the Rawls sense or a wider one, is not the only virtue and may conflict with other virtues. But to brush aside the concern for just conduct is as unrealistic as to hope that benevolence alone will abolish the need for government.

Barry argues convincingly that Hume and Rawls alike operate with both a mutual advantage and an impartial view of justice, which are intermingled in their writings. But why does Barry himself spend so much time on mutual advantage problems, given his strong commitment to fairness and impartiality? Indeed, the first part of his book is devoted to discussion of a standard problem first posed by R. B. Braithwaite (1955) in his inaugural lecture as Professor of Ethics in Cambridge in 1954. (I was actually present at that lecture and in common with the many members of the Cambridge establishment present failed to comprehend Braithwaite's solution, a fact that influenced my later choice of career.)

The problem is constructed around the dilemma of a pianist named Luke and a trumpeter named Matthew who live in adjacent rooms and can only practise on their musical instruments at the same hour each day. Each finds it distracting to practise while the other is playing. Given some additional information about the detailed preferences of the two men, how should the playing time be divided between them? Numerous solutions have been suggested, some based on fairness but others being simply the best bargaining solution that two might agree upon themselves without a superior authority to enforce a solution.

It would be sufficient to say that such problems and their more realistic equivalents do occur and generate quasi-mathematical problems that Barry wants to try his hand at solving. But a more interesting justification for his preoccupation, which he does not mention, suggests itself to me. That is that even a person committed to a fairness approach towards justice can go quite a long way towards making the world less brutish by relying on the rational pursuit of long-term mutual advantage. Impartiality comes in to enable human beings to go that extra mile where mutual advantage is not enough. To put it another way: the human instinct for justice exists, but it is not strong or universal enough to place sole reliance on it. Or as the economist D. H. Robertson once remarked: the economist economises on love; that is, he has to make it go the furthest possible way without wasting it in spheres where lesser or baser motives would do.

Principles of Just Distribution

Nevertheless, Barry's main concern is with the impartiality aspect. He develops this mainly by interpreting and defending Rawls's two principles of justice. Having in an earlier work attacked Rawls as a Gladstonian defender of property rights, Barry now emerges as a strong supporter of the Harvard philosopher's famous two principles of justice (famous at least among those who discuss that type of thing). Briefly, they are:

1. Equal rights to the most extensive scheme of equal basic liberties compatible with a similar scheme of liberties for all;
2. Social and economic inequalities must:
    a) work to the benefit of the least advantaged and
    b) be attached to offices open to all.

Rawls himself derives these principles from what he calls the 'veil of ignorance.' The idea is to work out the principles on which free and rational people concerned to further their own interests would desire their community to run if they did not know their own social or economic place, the market value of their own talents, and many other actual features of their own situation.

The bulk of the discussion has been on principle 2a, which Rawls calls the Difference Principle, but which many economists and game theorists prefer to call *the maximin*: maximising the position of those with the minimum. The balance of learned discussion points to the conclusion that these particular principles, and in particular the Difference Principle, do not necessarily follow from the veil of ignorance. I observed myself in a work published at a very early stage of the debate (Brittan 1973) that 'the different hypothetical distributions for which people would vote, would reveal differences in their attitude to risk and uncertainty. Somebody with a taste for gambling would be interested in seeing that there were some really big incomes just in case he came out on top.'

This objection has been much elaborated in the subsequent academic debate. Barry does not attempt to re-open the argument; and he makes comparatively little use of the veil of ignorance in his own book. Instead, he argues for the two principles directly, adding that a similar argument can in his view be extracted from an early chapter of *A Theory of Justice*.

Barry starts off from the principle of equality of opportunity, which has widespread intuitive appeal. He goes on to argue that it is not only advantages of inherited wealth or education that load the dice against some people and in favour of others. Qualities such as intellectual ability or manual dexterity or artistic gifts have a large inborn element and may owe little to merit, effort, or application. People are also affected by changes in the market for different kinds of ability that have little to do with their own efforts. The idea of a level playing field in which people compete for unequal prizes is thus a chimaera. Barry is of course right, although he may not like to be reminded that that arch-antiredistributionist F. A. Hayek made the point with great eloquence many years before:

> The inborn as well as the acquired gifts of a person clearly have a value for his fellows which do not depend on any credit due to him for possession. There is little a man can do to alter the fact that his special talents are very common or exceedingly rare. A good mind or a fine voice, a beautiful face or a skilful hand, a ready wit or an attractive personality, are in large measure as independent of a person's efforts, as the opportunities or experiences he has had. (Hayek 1960)

Barry concludes that a natural or fair state of affairs is equal distribution. He then arrives at Rawls's principles by asking what could upset the presumption in favour of equality. If every person or household received exactly the same – or even the same adjusted for the degree of pleasantness or unpleasantness (disutility) of his or her work – there would be no incentive for people to move to posts where their talents were most in demand, and total wealth would therefore suffer. Even the poorest would thus gain from some departure from pure equality. But these departures should be no greater than the minimum that can be justified on incentive grounds. Neither Rawls nor Barry is at all convincing on what should determine the rewards of those who are neither at the bottom nor at the top. They both rely on the so-called lexical principle: that if the poorest derive benefit from a more just organisation of society so will the decile above it, and so on into further deciles.

We are then left with the left-of-centre principle of most working social scientists and economists. Equality is the ideal; but to make the world work we require the kind of differentials that benefit the academic classes and salaried professionals but not the dreadfully high rewards gained from business or inheritance.

Against Equality

I resist the temptation to go into the many questions begged by the lexical principle and instead take issue with the basic presumption in favour of equality. Barry himself focuses on the key issue in a few crucial pages (238-41) easily missed. Assume that there are two Robinson Crusoes, A and B, on separate islands, who know of each other's existence. (Barry talks of Crusoe and Man Friday who have become separated; but the nomenclature does not affect the argument.) A turns out to be prosperous, and B turns out to be living in penury because, for instance, A's island is much more fertile. Neither is the cause of the other's good or bad fortune. Barry would say that the situation is unjust and that the richer A should make transfers to the poorer B to reach as near to equality as is consistent with improving B's welfare. That is, the redistribution should only stop where the disincentive effect on A is so great that B ceases to gain.

There are many things that could be said about the disparity in welfare of the two Crusoes. One might say it is undesirable or that A should transfer something to B if he has any fellow feeling. But 'unjust' is hardly the word to describe the initial state of affairs, brought about neither by A nor by B nor by a third person but by the fertility of their respective islands. If A refused to help B he might be called hardhearted, or lacking in compassion or even callous and inhuman, but not unjust. Terminology apart, it is hardly the duty of A either to equalise conditions or (allowing for the Difference Principle) to make B as nearly well off as himself as possible. To my way of thinking, A's duty is only to raise B to something approaching the conventional minimum that both would have recognised before they were shipwrecked, plus some additional amount depending on A's generosity, which cannot be determined by any a priori principle.

Is this the point at which Barry and I have different bedrock 'ought' principles and on which we simply have to part company? A little more can be said before this point is reached. Those who believe, as Rawls and Barry both do, that the distribution of resources is ultimately a collective decision will understandably have a presumption in favour of equality, from which departures have to be justified. Those who, in the tradition of Locke, emphasise the importance of people's own efforts in creating resources that did not exist before and that are not at the expense of anyone else, have an equally understandable presumption in favour of market rewards and even inherited holdings. The model of the Locke school is the frontier pioneer who has carved his holding out of the wilderness.

Modern society is inextricably compounded of both elements. Many people do add to total wealth by their ingenuity and efforts. But they do so against a background of laws, property rights and police protection, as well as general customs, which could be different from what they are and do indeed vary from place to place. The two pictures are useful correctives to each other. But neither – nor any mixture of them – is much help on distributional issues.

Does that mean that practical social scientists – which most contributors to this volume will probably be – can relax and just accept the normative principles of the government of the day (assuming that some can be discerned) or follow their own hunches?

In Defence of the Veil

Not quite. For in contrast to Barry I find that the veil of ignorance is a more convincing starting point than either the two principles of justice that Rawls derives from that veil or Barry's own modified egalitarianism.

The veil of ignorance has suffered from attempts to make it too precise. One can go too far in suggesting attributes of which the subject of the thought experiment has to imagine himself or her-

self be ignorant. In some formulations, he is supposed to be ignorant not merely of his own personal economic and social position
but even of the society or century to which he belongs. And Rawls
himself suggests that he is not supposed to know his own attitude
to risk. To deprive someone of one attribute after another in quest
of a perfect veil of ignorance is to come near to asking him or her
to imagine him- or herself divested of all qualities, in which case
he or she would hardly be a person able to engage in discourse on
just rules.

In his later work, Rawls goes some way to conceding that his
principles are not eternal verities but embody the values of
Western liberal democracies. But he still opposes actual experiments, and he insists that the issue is 'philosophical' – by which he
means purely one for armchair ratiocination by the analyst. The
more general approach, of which the Rawls system is only one
example, is known as contractarianism. In place of the historical
social contract of authors like Locke and Rousseau, modern con-
tractarians would derive the basic rules of society from a hypothetical contract that it would be rational for everyone to accept.
Although the Rawls version is the best known, there are many
other contractarian doctrines. If we try to avoid excessive abstraction and excessive precision, the veil remains a useful device for
dramatising this point of view.

However specific the veil of ignorance is made, it is unlikely to
provide one indisputable set of principles for action, whether
Rawls's principles of justice or any other. My own first desire
under the veil of ignorance would be to make sure that everyone
had a minimum income, defined not in absolute terms but in relation to the wealth of my society. This would be a safeguard in case
I drew one of the unfortunate cards and found myself at the
bottom of the pack. In addition, I would want to ensure a large
area of personal freedom where I could make my own decisions
and to ensure political, social, cultural and economic opportunities that could not be literally equal all round but should be free of
barriers of privilege and irrelevant entry qualifications.

For what they are worth, some experiments made with students
point to similar conclusions (Frohlich, Oppenheimer and Eavey
1987). When uncertain of their position they would favour maximising average income or welfare subject to a 'floor constraint':
that is, provided there is a minimum below which no one can fall.

This is of course not a single solution but a family of solutions governed by the choice of floor.

Thus, what contractarian reasoning can do is to help narrow – but not remove – differences on emotive subjects such as the distribution of income, wealth and power. To the extent that we can make the imaginative leap, it is a way of removing obvious bias, although not all differences of opinion.

Postscript on Health

I had intended to leave the revival of political ethics at this point, but further reflection suggests that a few desperately brief remarks on health policy, where Rudolf Klein has made such an outstanding mark, might throw some light on the nature of the post-Rawls debate.

The justification of state involvement in at least the finance of health is not very different for a Rawlsian than it is for a mainstream economic analyst of the social services such as Nicholas Barr (1987). The issues relate to the difficulties of insurance as a method of financing health provision such as moral hazard and nonavailability of insurance for certain risks except on prohibitive terms.

The justification of state provision, as distinct from finance, is the practical one of the inflation of medical costs if the state or insurance company meets the bills. If these difficulties can be overcome, for example, by health trusts, then there is no particular reason why a follower of Rawls should insist on the state providing medical services. Meanwhile, however, the cost effectiveness of the British system of health delivery is celebrated by no less a 'Tory Radical' than Nigel Lawson (1992) who had as chancellor to cope with the likely financial consequences of suggested changes. Many other issues, such as whether there should be some area of everyday modest expenditure where the citizen should pay for his or her own treatment or make a contribution such as prescription charges are also essentially practical ones.

Many left-wing Rawlsians might feel unhappy with the idea of the availability of private medical treatment. But there can be no convincing objection if the elasticity of supply of medical services is fairly high, as it almost certainly is in the long run. The right to pay more for a private room or for a consultant of one's choice is just as much a part of basic liberties as the right to choose between an expensive holiday and a top-class CD player.

Can the Rawls principles of justice give even a faint clue about how much of the national income or the government budget should be spent on health? Barry insists that the most disadvantaged representative person must be seen in terms of the lowest of the five or six groups into which society might be divided. But if we look at the worst off of these groups we do not get much of a handle on the question. Members of the bottom group will vary both in their state of health and in their preference for medical treatment compared with take-home income or other state services.

But going back to the veil of ignorance is much more helpful. A good way for a voter to focus on his preferences for health versus other expenditure is to ask him how much expenditure on health he would favour if he had no idea of his age or state of health. Of course, not one voter in a hundred would be able to come out with any figure in billions of pounds or as a proportion of gross domestic product (GDP) that had any meaning. But he could make use of his own experience and casual knowledge at least in answering incremental questions. Moreover, a hypothecated tax to pay for the NHS might give some seriousness to stated preferences and reduce the tendency to speak as if the health service should absorb the whole national income several times over.

Finally, let us take a classic microquestion in the allocation of scarce resources within the NHS. Should a rare and expensive treatment, when a choice has to be made, be provided for an old person in indifferent health, for a high-earning professional or businessperson, or for a healthy young man with a modest income who has most of his life ahead? The normal health economist would say 'no' to the first category and might want to argue the toss between the other two cases, perhaps bringing in the notion of utiles of satisfaction. (The question to be considered about the middle-aged professional is whether he or she has an earning capacity that will provide spillover benefits to others via his or her tax payments).

A literal-minded Rawlsian might go for the old and infirm person as the most disadvantaged. But if properly trained to think in terms of broad social economic groups (as Barry advocates) he or she might be more stuck for a reply. If, however, the analyst goes straight to the veil of ignorance the problem becomes clearer. If I did not know which of these three people I was most likely to be, I would favour the healthy young person, as in that position I would derive most benefit from the treatment.

Conclusion

So my conclusion is 'Three cheers for the veil of ignorance,' but let us downgrade the maximin principle and still more the egalitarian presumption. Although Barry takes an opposite stand, he has clarified what was in danger of becoming a more and more unfocused and untidy debate, and he has done so for far more subjects than the few I have had the time, space, and competence to cover here.

Finally, empirical public policy students and new-style political theorists would both benefit if they knew a little more of each other's activities. This would not pave the path to the millennium. What it might provide is a better basis for seeing across ideological chasms and for discussing constructively the disagreements that remain.

References

Barr, N. 1987. *The Economics of the Welfare State*. London: Weidenfeld and Nicholson.

Barry, B. 1989. *Theories of Justice*. London: Harvester-Wheatsheaf.

Braithwaite, R. B. 1955. *The Theory of Games as a Tool for the Moral Philosopher*. Cambridge: Cambridge University Press.

Brittan, S. 1973. *Capitalism and the Permissive Society*. London: Macmillan.

Frohlich, N., J. A. Oppenheimer, and C. L. Eavey. 1987. Laboratory Results on Rawls's Distributive Justice. *British Journal of Political Science* 7(1): 1–21.

Hayek, F. A. 1960. *The Constitution of Liberty*. London: Routledge and Kegan Paul; Chicago: University of Chicago Press.

Lawson, N. 1992. *The View from No. 11*. London: Bantam Press.

Rawls, J. 1992. *Political Liberalism*. New York: Columbia University Press.

———. 1972. *A Theory of Justice*. Oxford: Oxford University Press.

3

Quasi Markets: The Answer to Market Failure in Health Care?

Julian Le Grand

Ever since the new internal or 'quasi' market was introduced into the British National Health Service (NHS) in 1991, Rudolf Klein has been among the most prominent of those considering its impact and analysing its effects (Klein and Redmayne 1992; Klein, Day and Redmayne 1993; Klein and O'Higgins 1983; Challis, Day, Klein and Scrivens 1994[1]). It seems appropriate, therefore, to include in any volume celebrating his achievements some further reflections on this innovative form of welfare provision. Klein's work has always been characterised by a commitment to rigorous analysis; it therefore seems appropriate for those reflections to have something of an analytic flavour.

This chapter tries to meet both of these requirements by addressing a crucial analytic question with respect to the NHS quasi market. It is probable that, save for a few inhabitants of the furthest shores of the New Right, most social scientists, politicians, and civil servants who have reflected on the issue at all believe that to allow a 'pure' market to operate in health care would be a disaster. This view is based not so much on empirical evidence, for empirical examples of pure health care markets in operation in health care are difficult to find. Rather it is based on more analytic considerations: some drawn from the economic theory of market failure and some from other theoretical perspectives.

Now, quasi markets share many common features with 'pure' markets: competition, self-seeking behaviour, the use of financial incentives, and the like. Should not the same theoretical considerations that lead these social scientists to reject pure markets in the case of health care lead to a similar rejection of quasi markets? Or is there something about the 'quasi' nature of these markets that enables them to escape these problems? It is these questions that this chapter is trying to resolve.

The chapter begins with a short run-through of the arguments from economics and elsewhere for market failure in health care. It then considers the extent to which these same arguments apply to quasi markets. There is also a brief conclusion.

Before the main discussion begins, a point about terminology – which, as is the case with many such points, is actually about rather more than terminology. One of the very few areas where I part company with Klein concerns the preference he has expressed on occasion for the term 'mimic' markets instead of quasi markets to describe these new types of organisational arrangements. 'Mimic' implies imitation or shadowing; and, in theory at least, these markets should not be imitations or shadows of real markets. The phrase 'mimic markets' reminds me of the old idea of Lange–Lerner market socialism where a central planning authority attempts to mimic the operations of a competitive market by setting up planning tools (input/output matrices and the like) that endeavour to replicate the outcomes of a competitive market in a command economy setting. The incentives in such a system remain essentially managerial (state enterprises fulfilling the commands of the central planning authority) and are not those of the market. Now it is true that, as I shall discuss shortly, in practice the grip of the planners on the British NHS has proved difficult to shift, and in that sense, at least in the early years, the quasi market was shadowy in its impact. Nonetheless, the policy intention is clearly to introduce a form of proper market, with market incentive structures and some freedom to exploit those incentives; and it is with the success or failure of this 'ideal type' of quasi market that I am concerned here[2].

Markets in Health Care

The operations of markets offend all kinds of people. They offend the planner and those with a penchant for simplicity and order, for they are unstructured and apparently anarchic. Their individualistic nature offends the communitarian. They upset the moralist because they appear to pander to, indeed actively to encourage, some of the worst aspects of human nature, including greed, suspicion, and mistrust. Perhaps most damaging of all, they distress the egalitarian, for they are seen as generating massive inequalities and therefore promoting grave social injustice.

All of these criticisms are reinforced in the case of markets in health care. There is seen to be an even greater need for planning in the case of health facilities than in other areas of economic or social life. The community has health needs that the market will ignore. The delivery of quality health care is perceived as depending heavily on relationships involving trust, particularly those between doctor and patient; if market-type incentives undermine those relationships, there is no alternative guarantee of quality. And inequalities in health care, particularly, are seen as unacceptable; a society where the poor cannot get the health care they need is unjust indeed.

Economic theory amplifies and extends some of these arguments (Barr 1993; Le Grand, Propper and Robinson 1993). It echoes the communitarian objection by pointing to the existence of 'external benefits' from health care: that is, benefits from certain kinds of health care (notably immunisation and other treatment from infectious diseases) that accrue not only to the individual in receipt of care but to the wider community and that will not be taken into account in the normal operations of the market.

Economic analysis also points to the problem of poor information by consumers. If markets are to work effectively as engines of efficiency, rewarding good quality providers and penalising bad quality ones, consumers have to know what constitutes quality – a condition manifestly at odds with the normal situation with respect to patients and doctors. In addition, some economists note the problems of 'transactions costs': the management and administrative costs of actually running a market (Williamson 1985). A related point concerns the need to preserve competition and the consequent need to regulate the market (Propper 1993). Finally, economists draw attention to the difficulties of markets in private health insurance, notably those associated with moral hazard and adverse selection.

So the case against the use of markets to allocate health care is a formidable one. Small wonder that even Nigel Lawson, Mrs Thatcher's longest-serving Chancellor of the Exchequer and, on his own admission, an 'arch-promoter of privatisation,' acknowledges in his memoirs that medical care should not be privatised and that it is sui generis (Lawson 1992). Lawson, however, clearly did not believe that *quasi* markets were subject to the same problems as pure markets since he was one of the very small group who formulated the proposals for the NHS reforms.[3] Was he right? Cannot these criticisms of the pure market be applied with equal force to health care quasi markets? Or are quasi markets a partial (or even complete) solution to the problem of market failure?

Quasi Markets in Health Care

It is probably easiest to describe a quasi market by comparing it with a conventional or pure market. A quasi market differs from a pure market on both the demand and the supply sides (Bartlett and Le Grand 1993). On the demand side, the finance for purchasing comes from the state, not from the individual consumer's own resources. Moreover, the purchaser is not the consumer him – or herself; rather, the state appoints an agent to act on the consumer's behalf. So, in the case of the British NHS reforms, there are two types of state-appointed agents involved in using state funds to purchase health care: the District Health Authority (DHA) or Health Commission[4] and the General Practitioner (GP) fund holder. The DHA purchases hospital and community services on behalf of the population resident in its district; the GP fund holder receives a budget or fund from the state out of which he or she purchases selected hospital and community services on behalf of the patients on the practice's list.[5]

On the provider side, providers are generally not-for-profit organisations of some kind, although they may also include some conventional for-profit firms. In the British case, although there is some contracting with private hospitals, the vast majority of providers take the form of 'trusts'; units that are still formally owned by the state but that have been given some freedoms over services, contract prices and input mix.

From this brief description, it should be clear immediately that some of the sources of market failure that have been identified would still apply to quasi markets (Robinson and Le Grand 1994). In particular, the transactions costs problem and the need for pro-competitive regulation remain (UK Department of Health 1994; Le Grand 1994). Conversely, it is equally obvious that some of the criticisms do not apply. The use of state funds instead of private health insurance for financing health care means that moral hazard and adverse selection are not relevant, at least in their standard forms. State finance also helps take care of the problem of external benefits for it reduces the 'price' of obtaining health care below that which would pertain in the market and hence stimulates use beyond the market level.[6] However, the issues concerning market anarchy and planning, equity, information, and the morality of market behaviour are not so clear-cut and need more attention.

Market Anarchy and Planning

There are few that would now subscribe to the view that markets always create anarchy and hence that rational planning is required properly to allocate all goods and services. A market economy is not anarchic; for most of the myriad of goods and services that are produced in the modern economy, markets are the best way of bringing supply and demand in line with one another, of eliminating shortages and queues, and of encouraging invention and innovation. As the recent dismal experience of the command economies in Eastern Europe and the former Soviet Union testifies, in these respects markets commonly operate better than any planned economy can hope to do. Adam Smith's invisible hand is now almost universally acknowledged to work more efficiently than the visible hands of planners.

I say 'almost' because, whatever its record elsewhere, a belief in the necessity of rational planning often still seems as prevalent in the NHS as it ever was. It fuels one of the major criticisms of the new quasi market in the NHS: that its operations frustrate the planning process (Paton 1992). This criticism is often focused on GP fund holders, whose activities are viewed (especially by DHA) as loose cannons in the system, disrupting the carefully laid schemes of the planners.

This attachment to planning is perhaps not so surprising. The NHS was born of a climate of wartime planning; its creation was, as Klein has said in his seminal study of the development of the NHS, 'one in which paternalistic rationalists within the civil service and medical technocrats. . .played a leading role' (Klein 1989). Its subsequent history was as a planning organisation; its administration was – and indeed still is – heavily staffed by planners. Even now, the staff of some health authorities are finding it difficult to break the habit of thinking of themselves as planners rather than purchasers.

But is this faith in the need for state planning of health services justified? There are a number of reasons why it might be. First, it could be argued that some medical facilities require large capital investments; and these must be planned if they are to be undertaken in the most appropriate way. Second, there has to be some authority that takes account of the needs of the 'community,' something that markets, being based on the decisions of individuals, can never do. Third, even if the economic case for planning is weak, there are political reasons why the quasi market cannot be left to sort things out on its own. Market adjustments, such as those that are leading to the closing down of hospitals, inevitably involve distress for all those involved; even worse, they generate enormous political unpopularity.

However, none of these arguments are very robust. Of course, on occasion, large capital investments may have to be made by providers; but this is true of most modern industry. In making those decisions, providers will have to forecast the likely demand for the services the supply of which the investment concerned is designed to increase; but there does not seem to be any particular reason why this should be more difficult in the health care field than in any other. Moreover, the providers themselves are better placed to make that forecast than any state planner can hope to be; they are much closer to the service concerned, they have much better information about what their users might want or need, and they understand the investment required.

The argument concerning community 'needs' is also suspect. Outside the conventional external benefit argument (dealt with by state finance), it is far from clear what these needs are. Put more precisely, what does the community need over and above that which GP fund holders, for instance, will not supply on behalf of their patients? Health promotion programmes? But it is in the interests of fund holders (and indeed DHAs) to encourage their patients to look after their own health since this will reduce the demand on the fund holders' budgets. More general public health measures? But most of these fall outside the remit of the NHS and would not be part of the NHS planners remit in any case. Until there is a clearer idea exactly what community needs are (and why they will not be met by existing purchasers), this argument will lack conviction.

Finally, the political argument. Here again, the criticism seems misplaced. In many ways planning decisions are more likely to attract public hostility than markets for in the former case there is a villain that can be identified, whereas in the latter there is only the workings of an impersonal agency. This is illustrated by the government's suspension of the quasi market in London. This was a measure brought about by anxiety over the consequences of the market operations for excess capacity in the major London teaching hospitals; but it is one that arguably has fuelled rather than damped down political controversy and, moreover, has left the issue unresolved.

However, all that said, if there remains some need for planning, it should be noted that quasi markets do offer a greater opportunity for planning interventions than pure markets do. For in a quasi market, the state retains control of the methods of financing health care. This gives it a variety of levers through which to influence purchasing and hence to implement its policies. Quasi markets probably obviate the need for most planning; however, the mechanisms are there if required.

Equity

The biggest source of inequity that affects pure markets arises from the fact that, in such a market, the amount of a service that anyone can purchase will depend on his or her own resources. Since people come to the market with different levels of resources, they will receive unequal levels of service, not because they value the service differently or because they have different 'needs' for the service but because they have unequal purchasing power.

This should not be a problem for quasi markets. For, in a quasi market, the state is the purchaser and therefore can organise purchasing on the basis of need. Or, to put it another way, it can equalise purchasing power between users so that no one user has an advantage over another. So, for instance, if a DHA or GP fund holder is funded on a simple capitation basis, this is equivalent to equating purchasing power for all the users concerned. Alternatively, people with higher need could receive more through adjusting the capitation payments, so that purchasing power can directly follow need.

In practice, there is some doubt whether the state has actually equalised purchasing power, at least between the different purchasers. It has been claimed that GP fund holders have been more generously funded than DHAs (Dixon et al. 1994); however, this has been challenged (Bowie and Spurgeon 1994). In any case, such inequalities, if they exist, are not intrinsic to the idea of quasi markets and can be rectified without affecting the principle.

The same is true of a related equity problem that has purportedly arisen from the operations of the quasi market: the development of an alleged two-tier service, where patients of GP fund-holders receive preferential treatment over those of nonfund-holders (Whitehead 1994; see also Coulter 1994). Again, if this is indeed a problem, it is not intrinsic to the notion of quasi markets. For it arises from a rather peculiar feature of the British case: the simultaneous existence of two types of purchaser, DHAs and GP fund holders. If one were abolished, the two-tier problem would disappear, but the quasi market would still exist.

However, there is another form of inequity that can arise more directly from the operations of a quasi market: that created by 'cream skimming' (Bartlett and Le Grand 1993). Cream skimming, sometimes known as patient-dumping or adverse selection, occurs when either purchaser or provider has an incentive to select patients on the basis of cost rather than need. This will occur if, for some reason, the 'price' of treatment for a particular patient does not accurately reflect the actual cost to purchasers or providers. So, for example, GP fund holders, the size of whose funds are currently determined by their past referral practices, have an incentive to keep potentially expensive patients off their lists. Similarly, providers who have a block contract with a purchaser (that is, a contract that simply purchases a service at a specified price but an unspecified quantity) have an incentive to try to deflect potentially expensive patients to some other provider.

But again cream skimming is not a necessary feature of a quasi market. There are a number of ways of dealing with the problem. One is to offer an insurance scheme to purchasers or providers. In effect, this approach has been taken by the British government with respect to GP fund holding, whereby the fund holder is not responsible for the cost of treating a patient above a certain limit (currently £6,000). It is perhaps because of this that there has been little evidence found of cream skimming by fund holders in practice (Glennerster et al. 1994).

Alternatively, funding can be adjusted in such a way so as to align price more accurately with cost. So, for instance, a risk-adjusted capitation formula for determining fund holders' budgets could be devised that compensated (or even more than compensated) fund holders for the risks involved in accepting potentially expensive patients on their lists (Glennerster et al. 1994; Matsaganis and Glennerster 1994).

Imperfect Information

Quasi markets overcome the difficulties created by ill-informed consumers for pure health care markets by using better-informed agents as the actual purchasers. In the British NHS case, the agents are DHAs, who purchase health care on behalf of all the people living in their district, or GP fund holders, who purchase health care for all the people on their list.

The use of agents as purchasers is not unproblematic. First, there is the question of how well informed the agent actually is, both in terms of medical knowledge and with respect to the condition of the patient on behalf of whom the agent is purchasing. Of the two kinds of purchaser, in the British case the GP fund holder seems to have the edge over the DHA, being more knowledgeable both about the patient's condition as well as the appropriate treatment for the condition.

A second problem is that there has to be some mechanism for ensuring that the relevant agents actually operate in the patients' interests. If when making their purchasing decisions the agents pursue their own agendas and interests, then, unless these coincide with the patients' needs, the latter will not be met, and the quasi market will fail.

In the case of the British NHS, the mechanisms differ between the two kinds of purchasers. In the case of DHAs, the mechanism is primarily one of hierarchical management, ultimately subject to democratic control. More specifically, DHAs are accountable to the NHS Executive; the Executive is accountable to the Secretary of State for Health, who in turn is accountable to Parliament. In theory at least, therefore, if patient interests are not being followed, and if this comes to the attention of the relevant authorities, managerial sanctions can be imposed to ensure that the situation is rectified. Clearly, this broad-brush system of accountability gives a good deal of latitude for decision making to Health Authority members and, more especially, to officers. As a mechanism for ensuring that patients' interests are taken into account, it thus relies heavily on members' and officers' expertise and public spiritedness.

The accountability structure of GP fund holders is vague; but, if current proposals are implemented (NHS Executive 1994), they too will be accountable to the NHS Executive. However, they are also subject to a quite different source of pressure: the ability of patients to choose an alternative fund holder if they are dissatisfied with their own. Although the significance of this in practice should not be overestimated, it is a check on behaviour that does not apply to Health Authorities.

Morality and Market Behaviour

There are two lines of anti-market argument here. One says that the consequences of introducing market-type incentives results in a focus on cost, not on need, and this is intrinsically immoral in the case of health services. The second argues with Titmuss (1970) that markets of any kind (quasi or not) encourage self-serving behaviour and hence drive out other forms of behaviour that are more altruistic and hence morally more desirable.

The first of these involves a misunderstanding of the nature of cost. The true cost of a medical procedure is the other procedures that could have been purchased with the resources concerned. Put another way, the cost of saving a life is the other lives that could have been saved had that cost not been incurred. To focus on cost is not to ignore considerations of need; rather it is to compare the relative importance of one need with another.

With respect to the Titmuss argument, the issue is ultimately an empirical one. Self-serving behaviour by bureaucrats and professionals was not exactly unknown in the command economy that characterised the British welfare state before quasi markets were introduced. Whether that type of behaviour has actually increased, or merely become more explicit, is open to question.

Conclusion

Earlier in this chapter, the question was asked: are quasi markets a partial, or even a complete solution, to the problems of market failure in health care? It should be clear that they are certainly not a complete solution. Problems associated with transactions costs and regulation remain. Also, the relationship problem remains unresolved. We do not know what the long-term effects of the quasi market will be on the relationships between doctors and patients, doctors and managers, and doctors and doctors; and it may be that this will turn out to be one of the more significant problem areas of the British NHS reforms.

However, in other respects the quasi market does seem to do quite well, at least in comparison with pure markets. The difficulties involved in investing in large-scale medical facilities do not necessarily invalidate the use of market mechanisms. The information problem is handled through the use of knowledgeable agents. Admittedly, this creates problems of its own in the relationship between the patient and the agent; but even these may not be insoluble. The use of state finance resolves the external benefit issue, and, if funding is properly applied, it should resolve the equity problem.

Two final points. First, it will be apparent that, of the two forms of purchasing in the British NHS, GP fund-holding emerges as in general rather more suited to the operations of a quasi market than DHA purchasing. This is consistent with some researchers' view that in practice it has indeed operated more effectively (Glennerster et al. 1994); although others are more sceptical (Coulter 1994). This is not very surprising, for, as Robert Maxwell has pointed out (1994),[7] the two come from quite different ideological bases: one, the DHA, from a planning tradition, the other, fund holding, from a market orientation. Fund-holding is therefore much closer to the ideal type of quasi market than DHA purchasing could ever be.

Second, by focusing on market failure, we have not, of course, addressed the parallel issues of state failure (Le Grand 1991) and the ability of the elements of state intervention that are incorporated into quasi markets to deal with these. However, that is for another paper.

Notes

1. As illustrated in a prescient, although sadly unpublished, paper written with Michael O'Higgins more than ten years ago. He has also been a long-standing advocate of pluralism in both welfare values and welfare provision (Klein and O'Higgins 1983).

2. Another term commonly used in this context is the 'internal' market. This is not wholly inappropriate in the case of the NHS where, at the moment, most (although not all) of the purchaser/provider contracting is internal to the system. However, it is not a good description of the similar type of arrangements in other welfare areas, such as community care and hence it does not seem suitable for a chapter part of whose point is to discuss the phenomenon in a wider context than that of simply the British NHS.

3. The others were John Major, then Lawson's number two at the Treasury, the Secretary of State for Health (initially John Moore, then Kenneth Clarke), his number two (Tony Newton, then David Mellor) – and Mrs Thatcher herself.

4. District health authorities (primarily responsible for hospital and community services) are currently being merged with Family Health Service authorities (primarily responsible for general practitioners) to form unified health commissions.

5. There are now three levels of fund-holding: one confined to the purchase of community services, one that purchases community services and some elective surgery procedures and one, 'total fund-holding,' that purchases almost all the services that are currently purchased by the DHA/Health Commission.

6. Blanket state finance of the kind employed in Britain, which enables most medical care to be provided free at the point of use, is clearly something of a blunt instrument in this case. Properly to deal with the problem of external benefits would require identifying precisely the

extent of external benefits for each kind of medical care and then tailoring the subsidy so as to induce only the extra demand that would be necessary to maximise those benefits. However, the information requirements for such a fine-tuned policy would be prohibitive; also anything less than blanket state finance wold create equity problems.

7. Maxwell, R. 1994. Personal communication with Julian LeGrand. October.

References

Barr, N. 1993. *The Economics of the Welfare State,* 2d ed. London: Weidenfeld and Nicolson.

Bartlett, W., J. Le Grand, C. Propper, and D. Wilson, eds. 1994. *Quasi-Markets and the Welfare State.* Bristol: School for Advanced Urban Studies.

———, and J. Le Grand. 1993. The Theory of Quasi-Markets. In *Quasi-Markets and Social Policy*, eds. J. Le Grand and W. Bartlett, 13-34. Basingstoke: Macmillan.

Bowie, C., and R. Spurgeon. 1994. Better Data Needed for Analysis. *British Medical Journal* 309:34.

Challis, L., R. Day, R. Klein, and E. Scrivens. 1994. Managing Quasi-Markets: Institutions and Regulations. In *Quasi-Markets and the Welfare State,* eds. W. Bartlett, J. Le Grand, C. Propper, and D. Wilson, 10-32. Bristol: School for Advanced Urban Studies.

Coulter, A. 1994. Evaluating the British Health Care Reforms. Paper presented to the European Public Health Association, Copenhagen, December 15.

Dixon, J., M. Dinwoodie, D. Hodson, S. Dodd, T. Poltorak, C. Garrett, P. Rice, I. Doncaster, and M. Williams. 1994. Distribution of NHS funds between Fundholding and Nonfundholding Practices. *British Medical Journal* 309: 30-4.

Glennerster, H., M. Matsaganis, and P. Owens. 1994. *Implementing GP Fund-Holding: Wild Card or Winning Hand?* Buckingham: Open University Press.

Klein, R. 1989. *The Politics of the National Health Service, 2d. ed.* London: Longman.

———, and J. Brain. 1994. Parental Choice: Myth or Reality? *Bath Social Policy Paper,* no. 21. Bath: Centre for the Analysis of Social Policy.

———. P. Day, and S. Redmayne. 1993. *Sharing Out Resources: Purchasing and Priority Setting in the NHS.* Birmingham: National Association of Health Authorities.

———, and S. Redmayne. 1992. *Patterns of Priorities.* Birmingham: National Association of Health Authorities.

Lawson, N. 1992. *The View from No.11: Memoirs of a Tory Radical.* London: Bantam Press.

Le Grand, J. 1994. Internal Market Rules OK. *British Medical Journal* 309:1596–7.

———. 1991. The Theory of Government Failure, *British Journal of Political Science* 21:423–42.

——— and W. Bartlett. 1993. *Quasi-Markets and Social Policy.* Basingstoke: Macmillan.

———, C. Propper, and R. Robinson. 1993. *The Economics of Social Problems,* 3d ed. Basingstoke: Macmillan.

Matsaganis, M., and H. Glennerster. 1994. Cream-Skimming and Fund-Holding. In *Quasi-Markets and the Welfare State,* eds. W. Bartlett, J. Le Grand, C. Propper, and D. Wilson, 245-67. Bristol: School for Advanced Urban Studies.

Maxwell, R. 1994. Personal communication with Julian Le Grand. October.

National Health Service Executive. 1994. *An Accountability Framework for GP Fundholding.* London: Department of Health.

O'Higgins, M., and R. Klein. 1983. Concepts, Criteria and Conflicts in Analysing the Mixed Economy of Welfare. Paper presented at the Social Administration Annual Conference, University of Kent at Canterbury, July 13–15.

Paton, C. 1992. *Competition and Planning in the National Health Service: The Dangers of Unplanned Markets.* London: Chapman and Hall.

Propper, C. 1993. Quasi-Markets and Regulation. In *Quasi-Markets and Social Policy,* eds. J. Le Grand and W. Bartlett, 183-201. Basingstoke: Macmillan.

Robinson, R., and J. Le Grand. 1994. *Evaluating the NHS Reforms.* London: King's Fund Institute.

Titmuss, R. 1970. *The Gift Relationship.* London: George Allen and Unwin.

UK Department of Health. 1994. *The Operation of the Internal Market: Local Freedoms, National Responsibilities.* HSG (94)55. London: Her Majesty's Stationery Office.

Whitehead, M. 1994. Is it Fair? Evaluating the Equity Implications of the NHS Reforms. In *Evaluating the NHS Reforms,* eds. R. Robinson and J. Le Grand, 208-42. London: King's Fund Institute.

Williamson, O. 1985. *The Economic Institutions of Capitalism.* New York: The Free Press.

4

A New Institutional Economics of Health Care

James C. Robinson

Economic theory exerts a strong but paradoxical influence on health services research and policy in the United States. The debates over how the system functions and how it can be reformed occur disproportionately on the economist's turf, with great emphasis on the incentive features of payment mechanisms. At the same time, it is widely acknowledged that the health care system violates three major assumptions of conventional microeconomic theory. Textbook economics assumes that buyers and sellers are well informed, but patients, physicians, health plans and purchasers face huge uncertainties as to appropriate price, quantity and quality. Textbook axioms posit that buyers and sellers pursue their self-interest in an honest and law-abiding fashion, but health care is plagued by innumerable forms of opportunism. Textbook equilibrium implies that anonymous, atomistic competition produces the most efficient allocation of social resources, but quality and cost effectiveness in health care require close and stable relationships.

The impact of economics on health policy in the United States has been achieved in spite of rather than because of the ritual allegiance of health services researchers to conventional microeconomic theory. Much mileage has been gained from adherence to commonsensical, empirically verifiable economic precepts (e.g., physician and patient behaviour is influenced by the price of services) that are easily lost in the policy prattle (e.g., health care is different from every other form of human activity). However, this emphasis on empiricism and avoidance of economic theory by health services researchers may be reaching the point of diminishing marginal returns. The long-term contribution of economics to health policy will require solid links to a core theory of how behavioural, technological, and organisational factors interact in complex systems. It will be especially important to integrate organisations and long-term contractual relations into the basic paradigm of how the health economy functions and malfunctions.

In recent years, economic theory has undergone a fundamental transformation that questions much of the conventional wisdom of textbook microeconomics. The new institutional economics has adopted an alternative set of behavioural assumptions and a novel emphasis on the nonreversible nature of many economic decisions. Perusal of leading journals or of an authoritative source such as the *Handbook of Industrial Organisation* (Schmalensee and Willig 1989) quickly reveals the deep influence of principal-agent models, mechanism design, and transactions cost economics on mainstream theory. No comparable influence has been exerted, however, on the academic subspecialty of health economics. More importantly, the insights of the new institutional economics have not reached the health care managers and policy makers, who continue to be informed by the institution-free economics they learned in college. This contrasts with the very strong impact exerted by the new theory on other areas of economic policy in the United States, such as anti-trust law and the regulation of public utilities (Joskow 1991).

The potential applicability of the new institutional economics to other sectors and other nations appears strong. To pick an obvious example, the structure and performance of the British National Health Service (NHS) challenges conventional axioms of market economics, including informed choice by consumers, honest albeit self-interested behaviour by physicians and atomistic competition among organisations (Day and Klein 1991; Klein 1983; 1990). The structure of the NHS embodies a fundamental scepticism concerning the citizenry's understanding of health and medicine, based on responding to patient 'needs' rather than consumer 'demand,' which thereby empowers planners distant from the values and preferences of those in whose name they act. It embodies a faith in the altruistic motivations of the medical profession yet is transforming general practitioners into capitated 'fund-holders' and purchasing agents for their patient clientele. The recent separation of purchasing and providing functions within the NHS has created the thinnest of 'internal markets,' with small numbers of buyers and sellers and the necessity for long-term, relational contracting rather than short-term spot contracting. Yet these violations of textbook axioms can be a spur to creative thinking about information, motivation, and organisational innovation rather than necessitating a reversion to clinical paternalism and bureaucratic rationality (Day and Klein 1989).

This chapter provides an overview of three key elements of the new institutional economics (uncertainty and bounded rationality; opportunism and incentives; long-term contracting and organisational relationships) and contrasts them with the corresponding elements of conventional microeconomic theory. It then offers selected illustrations of how these features could provide important insights into the performance of the health care system. The emphasis is on recent organisational and contractual developments in the United States. Similar principles could further illuminate health system problems and potential solutions in other nations.

The New Institutional Economics

The *homo economicus* of the new institutional microeconomics is not an omniscient maximiser but a more modest figure beset by severe cognitive deficiencies, 'intendedly rational, but only limitedly so' (Simon 1961). The institutional paradigm is critical of market models that presume hyperrationality on the part of managers and consumers but also of planning models that presume hyperrationality on the part of regulators and administrators. Human beings are opportunistic, in this theory, pursuing self-interest with guile. They are neither the altruists of utopian socialism nor the honestly self-interested agents of neo-classical economics who do not buy more than they can pay for, do not embezzle funds, and do not rob banks.

The industrial firms of conventional theory purchase inputs in competitive factor markets and sell outputs in competitive product markets. They are quick to switch suppliers or distributors if price or quality of service changes and they see no special value in stable organisational or contractual ties. In contrast, the industrial firms of the new institutional economics do not enjoy the luxury of combining all-purpose labour and equipment to produce generic output traded in atomistically competitive markets. They must invest in machinery designed to satisfy the specifications of one purchaser, train their employees in skills useful to no other employer, locate their factory adjacent to a particular supplier to conserve on transportation costs and expand their productive capacity to service the needs of a larger distributor. These investments in specialised equipment, skills, locations and productive capacities reduce the narrowly technological costs of transforming inputs into outputs but potentially increase the transactions costs of screening trading partners, negotiating price and quantity and enforcing contracts. They are only partially redeployable to other relationships and thus expose the firm to exceptional losses from unanticipated changes in demand or supply. Organisational structures and contractual agreements therefore are developed to protect the value of these specialised investments.

The importance of these three departures from conventional economics (bounded rationality, opportunism and specialised assets) can only be appreciated when they are considered simultaneously. Any one alone or any two without the third would present no exceptional problems demanding organisational solutions. Uncertainty by itself merely creates a demand for insurance and risk spreading, as in the Arrow-Debreu model of general competitive equilibrium (Arrow and Hahn 1971; Debreu 1959). Opportunism by itself can be controlled through competition, even in concentrated markets; the absence of nonredeployable investments forces monopolists to set prices at competitive levels to forestall new entry, as emphasised in the theory of contestable markets (Baumol, Panzar and Willig 1982). If unaccompanied by uncertainty and opportunism, the problems posed by specialised assets can be controlled by competition for the market rather than competition in the market, as argued by the franchise bidding approach to public utilities (Demsetz 1968; Posner 1972). More generally, uncertainty combined with opportunism but lacking specialised assets creates the world of competition; uncertainty combined with specialised assets but lacking opportunism creates the world of promise; opportunism combined with specialised assets but lacking uncertainty creates the world of planning. All three together create the world of the new institutional economics (Williamson 1985).

Applications for Health Care

Uncertainty and Bounded Rationality

Throughout the twentieth century observers of the medical care system have emphasised the influence of consumer ignorance and cognitive limitations on the structure of social relationships, especially between patients and providers. Evidence of bounded rationality and asymmetric information has been used repeatedly to argue that economic theory cannot explain health care behaviour or, at a minimum, that economic prescriptions should not be allowed to guide health care policy. The new institutional economics abandons the textbook assumption of consumer hyperrationality without embracing the equally extreme assumption that one can fool all the people all the time.

There are at least three approaches by which informational inadequacies can be incorporated into economic theory and policy. The first develops a more complex theory of motivation, interpreting socialisation and constraints on distribution of economic rewards as mechanisms to limit the exploitation of informational advantages (Arrow 1963). Professional ethics among physicians and non-profit ownership structures among hospitals are obvious efforts in this direction. The second approach treats information as an economic good with increasing marginal cost, understanding consumer search and reliance on reputation as rational responses to the costliness of information (Stigler 1961). Policy prescriptions based on informational economics include information disclosure for consumers, 'informed consent' for patients, and a general mandate to interpret popular ignorance as a challenge to be overcome rather than as an invitation for paternalism. The third response to uncertainty highlights the advantage of formal organisation over individuals in information processing ability (Simon 1961). Physician group practice, concentration of specialised procedures in hospitals, and the evolution of integrated delivery systems can be understood partially in these terms.

The important point for institutional economics is that ownership, organisational and contractual forms provide means for limiting the economic losses otherwise to be expected from incomplete and asymmetric information. Boundedly rational individuals tend to select the governance mechanism that provides the best available (which may be far from best imaginable) control on the particular hazards of particular situations (Coase 1937). Farsighted public policy seeks to design political and economic institutions that facilitate rather than impede this discerning alignment of contexts and controls.

Opportunism and Incentive Mechanisms

By itself, uncertainty merely creates a demand for insurance that trades the possibility of a large loss for the certainty of a modest premium. When information is asymmetrically distributed and agents are inclined to exploit any advantage they enjoy, however, the risk-pooling solution to uncertainty is undermined by the two characteristic failures of insurance markets. Moral hazard and adverse selection disrupt markets for formal, explicit insurance but are also found wherever bounded rationality is joined with opportunism (Stiglitz 1987). They are especially important for understanding the structure and performance of reimbursement mechanisms in health care, which differ in striking ways from insurance mechanisms elsewhere in the economy.

Payment mechanisms in the United States have attempted to navigate between the Scylla of moral hazard and the Charybdis of adverse selection. Retrospective payment mechanisms such as fee-for-service and 'reasonable cost' shield physicians and hospitals from the adverse selection risks of treating particularly sick patient populations since the high costs that are incurred lead to the receipt of high revenues. They provide no controls, however, for the moral hazard risks of fee inflation and cost-unconscious treatment styles. Prospective payment mechanisms such as capitation and diagnosis related groups (DRGs) discourage cost-increasing moral hazard by disconnecting revenues from incurred costs.

However, these prospective payment mechanisms expose physicians and hospitals to the adverse selection risks of treating especially sick patients without recourse to extra compensation and create a new moral hazard of undertreatment and quality shading.

The limits of pure retrospective and pure prospective payment mechanisms are prompting payors in the United States to experiment with methods that combine elements of both. Physicians are being paid increasingly on a fee-for-service basis subject to a partial withhold that is returned if annual expenditure targets are attained (a retrospective approach with the discipline of a prospectively determined budget). Alternatively, they are being paid capitation for a subset of the services needed by patients but can refer out to other providers who are paid on a fee-for-service basis (a prospective approach with the safety valve of separate payment for especially high-cost procedures). Hospitals are being paid by Medicare on a prospective basis with outlier payments for especially high-cost patients and by HMOs on a per diem basis with the possibility of splitting the end-of-year surplus in an inpatient risk pool.

Mixed payment modes have much to recommend them and further experimentation is to be encouraged (Ellis and McGuire 1986; Casalino 1992). There are severe limits, however, to what realistically may be expected in a health care system characterised by rapid technological change and extraordinary differences in patient needs. Managed care organisations therefore are seeking to control inappropriate health care services directly, through selective contracting with cost-effective providers, utilisation review and monitoring of process and outcome statistics.

These nonprice mechanisms offer important possibilities but are themselves limited. Their full potential will only be realised when they are combined with incentive-conscious payment methods. Price and nonprice mechanisms cannot be mixed and matched arbitrarily, however, but work best in particular combinations. Different organisational and contractual structures can be interpreted in terms of the different combinations of price and nonprice mechanisms they support. By extension, changing perceptions of the efficacy of particular incentive mechanisms, individually or in combination with others, alters the market shares of particular organisational forms. Together, uncertainty and opportunism potentially provide a behavioural foundation for understanding the population ecology of health care organisations (Robinson 1993).

Specialized Assets and Long-term Relationships

We are witnessing a dramatic restructuring of the US health care system. The boundaries around and between organisations are changing rapidly due to shifts in disease patterns, therapeutic possibilities, cultural attitudes and economic incentives. In seeking to predict the outcome of this restructuring and the future contours of the American health care system, the new institutional economics would emphasise the comparative efficiencies of spot contracting, complex contractual relations and vertical integration. The prevalence of these governance mechanisms in turn would be ascribed to the importance in different contexts of nonredeployable investments in physical assets such as plant and equipment, human assets such as skill and reliability, and site-specific assets such as location immediately adjacent to an important supplier or customer. In general, contexts where the gains from relationship-specific investments are greater will rely more heavily on long-term contracting and vertical integration, whereas contexts permitting use of generalised, non-specific technologies will rely more heavily on arm's length contracting (Williamson 1985).

A salient feature of the health care system, which distinguishes it from other technologically advanced industries, is the generalised rather than organisation-specific nature of the physical equipment, human skills, and geographical sites required. Individual hospitals, for example, do not require unique antibiotics and CT scanners in the same way that automobile manufacturers demand unique transmissions and bumpers. The skills of physicians, nurses and laboratory technicians are typically transferable from one setting to another. The revolution in information systems is rapidly reducing the advantage of grouping disparate medical services into one crowded clinic or campus, allowing medical records rather than patients to do the travelling.

The redeployability of technologies and technicians does not imply that sunk investments and committed relationships do not add substantial value in health care. The type of investments and the manner in which they are specialised to particular contexts is of a different nature. Two features of health care tasks and transactions appear mostly likely to influence 'make-versus-buy' and 'organisation-versus-contract' decisions in the future: reputation for quality and the co-ordination of temporally sequenced procedures.

Consumers evince increasing concern for the quality of care delivered in free-standing diagnostic radiology and ambulatory surgery centres, home health programs, nursing homes and other settings as more complex types of care are being shifted out of the acute hospital setting. This concern creates a demand for organisational mechanisms that monitor and control inadequate care. As argued by the new institutional economics in other contexts, a nonredeployable investment in reputation for quality represents to consumers a commitment by the producer to ensure quality since the value of its investment will be lost if quality problems are not controlled (Klein and Leffler 1981; Williamson 1983). This may provide an edge to hospitals seeking to integrate into non-traditional services where quality problems are of particular concern, such as outpatient surgery and some forms of home care, but a weaker advantage in cases where consumers can more easily evaluate quality, such as routine outpatient care. The hospital's investment for quality of care in acute inpatient care gives it much to lose if quality problems occur in its new subsidiaries, which in turn require it to take steps that would not be required of less visible entrepreneurs with fewer sunk costs (Robinson 1994).

Many forms of health care can be conceptualised as process technologies where a patient is evaluated in one setting, treated for an acute condition in another, helped through a recovery period in a third, and so forth. Costs are minimised at each stage of the production chain if full utilisation of physical capacity and staff resources is maintained. Fully occupied beds and fully extended providers at one stage create a bottleneck for the preceding stage, however, leading to costly inventory problems. Under prospective modes of payment, including DRGs and capitation, the costs of the inability to promptly shift patients to the next appropriate setting must be absorbed by the discharging provider. This dramatically increases the dependency of hospitals on nursing homes, for example. Contractual solutions are conceivable, as when a hospital leases nursing home capacity and pays nursing homes higher rates to admit an unexpectedly complex case mix of patients. Non-linear pricing solutions to inventory control problems have been identified in other process industries (Goldberg and Erickson 1987). Contractual solutions are disadvantaged in health care, however, by the administered pricing systems enforced by Medicare, Medicaid, and other third parties, thereby encouraging organisational solutions through unified ownership by hospitals of nursing homes, home health care agencies, and other postacute services. Internal transfer prices between divisions of vertically integrated health care organisations escape the control of the Health Care Financing Administration (Robinson 1995).

Conclusion

The behavioural assumptions of conventional microeconomic theory depict the rational, self-interested agent. Rational agents are relatively well informed concerning price, quantity and quality and control residual uncertainty through risk pooling and insurance. They are non-altruistic but typically fulfil their commitments. The technological assumptions of conventional theory emphasise discrete, independent decisions and anonymous, atomistic competition. The paradigmatic relationship is the spot contract, where economic partners are chosen based on current price and quality.

The new institutional economics maintains an alternative set of behavioural and technological assumptions. Cognitive limitations prevent individuals from writing comprehensive contracts that anticipate all future developments and even from fully enforcing short-term contracts for complex goods and services. The potential for bad faith prevents trading partners from relying exclusively on promise and trust but necessitates alignment of incentives. The relationship-specific nature of many commitments limits responses to uncertainty and opportunism based on switching partners if dissatisfied. Spot contracting is viewed as the exception rather than the rule. Organisational structures and contractual forms are interpreted as mechanisms of governance. Here lies the foundations for a new institutional economics of health care.

References

Arrow, K. J. 1963. Uncertainty and the Welfare Economics of Medical Care. *American Economic Review* 53:941-73.

——, and F. H. Hahn. 1971. *General Competitive Analysis.* San Francisco: Holden Day.

Baumol, W. J., J. Panzar, and R. Willig. 1982. *Contestable Markets.* New York: Harcourt Brace Jovanovich.

Casalino, L. P. 1992. Balancing Incentives: How Should Physicians Be Paid? *Journal of the American Medical Association* 267:403-5.

Coase, R. 1937. The Nature of the Firm. *Economica* 4:386-405.

Day, P., and R. Klein. 1991. Britain's Health Care Experiment. *Health Affairs* 10 (1):39-59.

——. 1989. The Politics of Modernisation: Britain's National Health Service in the 1980s. *Milbank Quarterly* 67:1-34.

Debreu, G. 1959. *Theory of Value.* New York: Wiley.

Demsetz, H. 1968. Why Regulate Utilities? *Journal of Law and Economics* 11:55-66.

Ellis, R. P., and T. G. McGuire. 1986. Provider Behaviour under Prospective Reimbursement. *Journal of Health Economics* 5:129-51.

Goldberg, V. P., and J. R. Erickson. 1987. Quantity and Price Adjustment in Long-term Contracts: A Case Study of Petroleum Coke. *Journal of Law and Economics* 30:369-98.

Joskow, P. L. 1991. The Role of Transactions Cost Economics in Antitrust and Public Utility Regulation. *Journal of Law, Economics, and Organisation* 7 (special issue):53-83.

Klein, B., and K. B. Leffler. 1981. The Role of Market Forces in Assuring Contractual Relationships. *Journal of Political Economy* 89:615-41.

Klein, R. 1990. The State and the Profession: The Politics of the Double Bed. *British Medical Journal* 301:700-2.

——. 1989. *The Politics of the NHS, 2d. ed.* London: Longman.

Posner, R. A. 1972. The Appropriate Scope of Regulation in the Cable Television Industry. *Bell Journal of Economics and Management Science* 3:98-129.

Robinson, J. C. 1995. Administered Pricing and Vertical Integration in the Hospital Industry. University of California, Berkeley, unpublished manuscript.

——. 1994. The Changing Boundaries of the American Hospital. *Milbank Quarterly* 72:259-75.

———. 1993. Organisational Innovation and the Limits of Health Care Payment Reform. *Inquiry* 3:328-33.

Schmalensee, R., and R. D. Willig. 1989. *Handbook of Industrial Organisation*. Amsterdam: Elsevier Science Publishers.

Simon, H. A. 1961. *Administrative Behaviour,* 2d ed. New York: MacMillan.

Stigler, G. J. 1961. The Economics of Information. *Journal of Political Economy* 69:213-25.

Stiglitz, J. E. 1987. The Causes and Consequences of the Dependence of Quality on Price. *Journal of Economic Literature* 25:1-48.

Williamson, O. E. 1985. *The Economic Institutions of Capitalism.* New York: Free Press.

———. 1983. Credible Commitments: Using Hostages to Support Exchange. *American Economic Review* 73:519-40.

Part II

Institutions, Professions and Policy

5

Can the American State Guarantee Access to Health Care?

Jerry L. Mashaw
Theodore R. Marmor

Asking two American policy analysts to write a chapter on 'the state as guarantor of social welfare' reveals a certain ironic turn of mind somewhere in the collective consciousness of the editors of this volume. We write, in 1995, against the backdrop of the previous year's failure of the Clinton Administration (perhaps temporarily, probably permanently) to persuade the United States Congress to enact comprehensive health insurance reforms (Marmor 1994; Hacker 1995; Health Care Study Group 1994; Hamburger, Marmor and Meacham 1994; Starr 1995). If the nation-state is the guarantor of social welfare and if protection against the economic consequences of ill health is a part of the social welfare package that most citizens of modern states expect, then the United States government seems, in some crucial respects, a failed guarantor.

Of the two assumptions just made, most policy-analytic commentary about the aborted Clinton Administration efforts concentrates on the second 'if.' To put the matter somewhat more accurately, this commentary emphasises the circumstances that led to the political impasse. It concentrates on two questions that generated enormous controversy in the health reform debate: what degree of responsibility should public authorities have for health insurance, and how should that insurance be organised? From this perspective, many have criticised the Clinton Administration for putting forward a plan that was too complex to be understood by the general public. And, adding injury to insult, the plan was to be administered by new and untried governmental entities – a prospect that left the public confused and frightened (Brown and Marmor 1994; Henry J. Kaiser Family Foundation 1994). From a slightly different perspective, many critics have said that reform efforts failed because they attempted to build on existing systems of employer-based private insurance that implicitly treated health insurance as a private rather than a governmental activity (Canham-Clyne, Woolhandler and Himmelstein 1995). Such reforms, it was alleged, were certain to run into problems of both technical complexity and ideological incoherence. Others explained the stalemate largely in class terms. While concern about health care insurance and health care costs are widespread, the great middle class of Americans is sufficiently content, for the moment, with its private employer-based coverage. It cannot be mobilised to support any particular rearrangement that would take the organisation of the health insurance market further out of its hands and into those of the government (Brown 1994).

These circumstantial explanations take on an increasingly particularistic cast in the popular press accounts of what happened in 1994. The Clinton Administration, such accounts claim, wrongly regarded the process of policy development as a technocratic activity rather than a building of political consensus. Republicans are blamed for a political intransigence that has everything to do with prospective electoral gain and little to do with confronting a serious national problem (Meacham 1994). Critics have pilloried the media for reporting who was up and who was down rather than giving sustained attention to feasible alternatives and their likely consequences (Hamburger, Marmor and Meacham 1994).

Analysing the recent failure of health care reform in the United States in these terms focuses attention on solutions that respond to these supposedly circumstantial failures. Appropriate planning, on this view, required a more bipartisan and open process, one far less technocratic and closed than the Clinton task force. The press needed to take on a responsibility to educate, not merely to report, political food fights. What was called for – and will be again – is a simpler and more 'incremental' approach, one that genuinely respects current structures and avoids the fearful prospect of untried and uncertain arrangements (Schneider 1994; DiIulio and Nathan 1994; Morone 1994; Starr 1995; Yankelovich 1995).

There is considerable optimism in this analytic turn of mind. The implicit presumption is that the processes of American policy development can be fixed. It is taken for granted that guaranteed health insurance for all Americans, combined with effective cost constraints, requires only some shifts in the policy options proposed and the political tactics by which they are advanced. There is obviously something to this view. It is particularly comforting to those who believe that universal health insurance at reasonable cost should be an extraordinarily high priority on the national political agenda. That the nation failed in the 103d Congress does not mean it cannot do better next time around – perhaps even in the 104th.

There is, however, a different perspective on these recent events. It is one that views the 1994 American stalemate as rooted in the same structural conditions that defeated universal health insurance in the 1930s, the 1950s, the 1960s, and the 1970s. This is, after all, not the first time that Americans have been around this particular bush. And, if every time we attempt it we get so caught in the brambles that we cannot complete the trip, perhaps there are some deeper causes for our failures than the instances of one particular expedition (Steinmo and Watts 1994).

In short, this essay analyses the contemporary American situation from a more structural vantage point. This is a perch that the honouree of this volume, Rudolf Klein, would obviously find congenial. Indeed, we want to emphasise two of the major structural themes that characterise much of Klein's work and illustrate them in connection with the recent American attempt at health reform.

The first theme is one that borrows from Klein's seminal work on the British National Health Service (NHS) (Klein 1989). For him, the evolution of the NHS is the epitome of a grand social compromise mediated by a state whose powers to act are themselves not at issue. The second theme punctuates much of Klein's later writing concerning mature welfare states. That work emphasises the shrinking scope of welfare state innovation and expansion as greater and greater proportions of state fiscal resources are devoted to existing social welfare programs (Klein and O'Higgins 1985).

Central to both Klein's themes is the question of whether and how the state can be the guarantor of social welfare. For our purposes, the more particular question is whether American government can legitimately function as the guarantor of the population's health security. Klein's early work suggests that the responsibility and authority of the state as a guarantor of social welfare is not problematic. What exactly is to be done and how it is to be accomplished are, to be sure, intensely controversial issues. But, for Klein, it is precisely the task of statecraft to fashion compromise from the available opportunities. Klein's later work, however, emphasises the problematic character of significant expansion or radical change in the structure of mature welfare states. The limiting constraint here is not so much one of political legitimacy but of the realities of fiscal capacity.

The United States of the late twentieth century, in our view, is in the unhappy position of facing both problems. It must deal with the strained fiscal capacities of a relatively mature welfare state and with the uncertain political legitimacy that has always attended governmental activity in the United States (Marmor, Mashaw and Harvey 1992). Taking our cue from Klein, therefore, we argue that the United States faces structural problems, both institutional and fiscal, that limit its capacity to be the guarantor of social welfare in any new domain. From this perspective, America's recent failure to enact universal health insurance was a relatively expected outcome of these structural realities. So understood, one would have been surprised by success in the most recent American effort rather than surprised by its failure.

The Problem of the Problematic State

This is hardly the place for an extended discussion of the structure of American governance. Nevertheless, a 'structural' argument must begin with the fundamental features of America's political system. We will concentrate on those features of American politics that make deeply problematic any vision of government as the guarantor of citizens' health security or welfare. As Lawrence Jacobs (1993) puts it, 'Research on public opinion has consistently found that Americans' enduring unease regarding state interference awkwardly coexists with an acceptance of state involvement in specific social welfare programs.'

To many readers, this view of the modern American state may seem peculiar. They believe that public provision of social welfare benefits – or federal regulation of private activity for social welfare aims – was decided decisively in favour of the public responsibility during and immediately following the New Deal. But this, in our view, is a partial (and misleading) account of New Deal realignments, particularly in connection with the financing of health insurance and the delivery of medical care.

Much of the constitutional realignment associated with the New Deal had, after all, validated the regulatory role of government. It legitimised the use of the 'police powers' of individual states, freeing the due process clause of the Fourteenth Amendment from its laissez-faire interpretation. Much if not most social welfare experimentation in the United States, both before and after the New Deal, has taken place in the individual states, not at the federal level. What was most decidedly validated in the 1930s was the authority of states, not that of the national government. The states are, indeed, the inheritors of the powers of colonial land grant communities in which the authority of the collective was seldom questioned. That these communities had ample strength to protect the 'health, welfare and morals' of their citizens is part of a constitutional common law antedating the American federation. That legacy was reaffirmed in the face of late nineteenth-century attempts to shrink the scope of legitimate state action (Tribe 1988).

It is true that the New Deal confirmed broader authority for the federal government as well. Taxing and spending for the general 'welfare' was indeed recognised as a separate basis for the legitimate exercise of federal power. Yet the use of that authority to reorganise medical care or health insurance has remained highly contested on ideological grounds (Jacobs 1993). If the Social Security Act is the document that confirmed the legitimacy of federal guarantees of American social welfare benefits, it must be read for what was left out as well as for what it put in. The act's promoters omitted from their reforms health and disability insurance because of the intransigent claim that medical care was not within the legitimate province of the federal government. This under-standing, combined with the parallel presumption that the regula-tion of insurance is pre-eminently a preserve of American states, influences current thought. It continues to make federal interven-tion in medical markets highly controversial (Piper and Chisman 1985).

Meanwhile, state involvement in health and health insurance is well entrenched. States certify all medical care professionals. They regulate health insurance markets, provide public health services, establish charity hospitals for care of the indigent and license the construction of hospitals and other medical facilities. Indeed, state provision and regulation of medical activities is so commonplace that the federal Social Security Disability Insurance program, when added to the Social Security Act in the late 1950s, was left to be administered through state vocational rehabilitation agencies. Likewise, when the federal government made a major commit-ment to finance medical care for the poor through Medicaid, it did so through the financial support of state programs meeting certain federal conditions.

Only for special populations – veterans Indians, and the aged – has the federal government either directly provided or directly financed health care in the United States.[1] Federal regulation and the financing of American medicine has instead been indirect: the deductibility and nontaxability of employer–based health insur-ance benefits and the regulation (largely an exemption from state regulation) of voluntarily established employer health and welfare plans under the Employee Retirement Income Security Act (ERISA).

We recount this history of state and federal medical activity because it bears directly on the structural impediments that cur-rently bedevil the politics of American health reform. Put epigram-matically: the level of government with the political legitimacy to assure universal health insurance – states – lacks the fiscal and legal authority to accomplish it. The level of government with the fiscal and legal muscle to provide universal health insurance – the federal government – lacks the political legitimacy to enact a com-prehensive program. Let us unpack these arguments.

First, it might well appear from the foregoing that the individual states are the logical authorities to provide comprehensive health benefits. After all, they have the general police power. They are already heavily engaged in many of the activities that would be necessary (certification, public health programs, insurance regulation, and so on) for a comprehensive health insurance program that both rationalised the use of medical resources and constrained its costs. Indeed, the case for state-led reform is almost overwhelming if one adds to these considerations the following: the undoubted heterogeneity of the health, medical and insurance circumstances of the American population; regional differences in patterns of medical practice and the expectations of patients; differences in the priority that local political cultures accord medical spending. Yet contemporary debates have defined comprehensive health care reform in the United States almost exclusively as a 'national' problem. Why should this be the case?

The answer lies in the piecemeal but cumulatively significant incursions that the federal government has made into health insurance and medical provision. The employer-based nature of health insurance in the United States is itself largely an accidental by-product of federal regulatory authority exercised during World War II. The wage and price controls imposed during that period did not cover fringe benefits. As a result, employers and employees could agree to wage increases so long as they were in the form of fringe benefits rather than cash. Federal tax policy rewarded the provision of health insurance as a fringe benefit in two ways: by the decision not to tax such benefits as income to employees and by allowing the continued deductibility of those expenses by employers. Employers and employees could, and can, divide up public subsidies to health insurance. They do so in massive amounts. By the mid-1990s, such health insurance subsidies will be the single largest 'tax expenditure' within the federal tax expenditure budget (Bipartisan Commission on Entitlement and Tax Reform 1994).

This huge infusion of federal dollars into the health insurance market is available only so long as health insurance remains employment-based. As a result, states are severely limited in their options for reconstructing health insurance to provide universal coverage. But the situation is worse than that. The federal government's regulation of health and welfare plans through the ERISA strikes a Faustian bargain with employers who are 'self-insured' for health benefits. (Virtually all employers with more than 100 employees are self-insured if they provide health insurance).

Employers accepted federal regulation of their plans' financial security (along with provisions on 'non-discrimination' between different levels of employees) in partial return for federal protection from virtually all forms of state regulation of self-insured, employer-provided health insurance.

States cannot, for example, mandate certain levels of coverage for all employees in the self-insured employers' plans. They cannot regulate the costs of those plans, and they cannot require standardisation in health insurance options. Indeed, it may be the case that states cannot force self-insured employers – either by direct taxes or by redistribution of the hospital charges – to pay for the care of the uninsured or low-wage population. Moreover, large national employers appear as committed to retaining this freedom from state regulation of their health insurance plans as the National Rifle Association is to preserving every American's right to own a handgun.

Finally, the federal government's major program in health insurance, Medicare for the aged and disabled, has created powerful constituencies for maintaining a national effort. States may be able to obtain 'waivers' from the federal government to manage the Medicare program on the guarantee that it will cost no more than if the federal government were managing it. But they are quite unlikely to obtain permission to alter the care currently available to Medicare's beneficiaries as a part of a comprehensive reform of a state's medical care arrangements.

In short, fiscal realities dominate the formulation and scope of proposals for state health reform. Given the structure of federal income taxation, states cannot tap into federal tax subsidies for health insurance to finance reform unless they maintain employment-based funding. This constraint applies even when state reformers regard employment-based coverage as an anachronistic and flawed form of organising health insurance. Political realities, meanwhile, keep Medicare untouchable by the states and simultaneously prevent them from effectively regulating the huge, self-insured, employer-based insurance market.

To be sure, one might interpret these constraints as merely 'technical' difficulties. After all, it is possible to 'cash out' the federal government's contribution to health insurance through the tax code. Congress 'could' eliminate the ERISA pre-emption and allow states to fold Medicare into a more comprehensive state program of health insurance. But we encounter here not only the usual difficulties of legislating but some special ones as well.

The usual difficulties were obvious in the stalemate over health reform in the first two years of the Clinton Administration, 1993-4. The American Constitution makes national legislation enormously difficult. The designers of our Constitution were more than usually successful in this effort. Popular presidents with substantial mandates and significant congressional majorities can, it is true, overcome these hurdles to enact new social legislation. But these episodes are rare. The Social Security Act of 1935 is one example. Otherwise, only in the mid-1960s, during the heyday of Johnson Administration activism, was the federal government able to enact a limited program of health insurance for the elderly along with financial support for state-administered medical insurance for the indigent. It should not have surprised observers that President Bill Clinton, with a minority of a popular vote and a slim majority in the Senate, was unable to completely reorient historic arrangements concerning federal governmental responsibility for health insurance (and, under the Clinton Plan, the organisation of medical care) (Marmor 1994).

An attempt to launch a national program designed only to unfetter the states to become laboratories for comprehensive health insurance may appear less politically ambitious (DiIulio and Nathan 1994). But lack of ambition may make such a strategy even less likely. A national crusade to give the states authority over health reform misconceives one of the bases of political support for national health insurance. That support is strongest amongst those who regard health insurance as a basic human right available to all on the basis of medical need not class, race, employment, location or financial circumstances. Liberating states to experiment with their own versions of universal health insurance would obviously produce variable results across the United States. And that is not popular with the constituencies that have traditionally supported national health insurance. State experimentation and programmatic diversity do not match ideologically with the political sentiment that health insurance is, or should be, an entitlement of national citizenship.

It is hardly an accident that the United States has not enacted comprehensive health insurance – either nationally or of different types in different states. This is in large measure a result of the structure of American governance and how our institutional arrangements have evolved over some 200 years. Situational factors – the quality of leadership, economic circumstances, political demands, and so on – all count as partial explanations for the failure of various movements for comprehensive health insurance in the United States. Nevertheless, it is our view that a large part of the story of American exceptionalism arises from an inhospitable combination of institutional structures and political culture (Morone 1990). These include underlying presuppositions about the state – particularly presuppositions about the authority of federal and state governments. The grand compromise that Rudolf Klein so brilliantly described in *The Politics of the National Health Service* is much less available in a polity organised like the United States of America. One may wonder whether it is available at all.

The Problem of the Mature Welfare State

Rudolf Klein has persuasively argued that substantial policy changes, particularly expansionary ones, are exceedingly difficult in mature welfare states. The cause of this difficulty is quite apparent – or so it seemed once Klein pointed it out (Klein and O'Higgins 1985). When public social welfare programs account for a major proportion of the national budget, small percentage increases in these expenditures crowd out larger and larger proportions of discretionary spending elsewhere. As a result, competitors for public resources constrain the expansion of the welfare state, whether in the form of new programs or additional funding for existing ones.

This would not be true, of course, should the citizens of mature welfare states decide that greater and greater proportions of gross domestic product (GDP) should be run through the public sector itself. However, in the short run the amount of GDP that passes through national budgets is relatively stable (Mashaw 1993-4). Only in extraordinary periods – a movement from state capitalism to state socialism, or back again, for example – is dramatic expansion (or contraction) a real option. As welfare states mature, their capacity for cost–increasing innovation declines.

This is surely the case in the United States in the late twentieth century. Indeed, Americans are increasingly worried that their national government will shortly have no 'discretionary' public spending at all. All federal spending will be devoted either to the payment of 'entitlements' – mostly welfare state entitlements – or interest on the national debt. The Clinton Administration's appointed Entitlements Commission issued a preliminary report suggesting that, if current trends continue, all discretionary spending will come to a halt in about 2012 without massive increases in either taxation or the public deficit. (We are critics of this doomsday futurology, as is evident in our book. But we understand the widespread fixation amongst policy analysts among long range fiscal projections. [Marmor, Mashaw and Harvey 1992].)

Once again there are multiple solutions to this problem. For one, Americans might decide to tax themselves more. Yet, if one looks at the way tax revenues have related to gross domestic product (GDP) over a number of decades, one finds a remarkably constant relationship. While the taxes are rearranged, along with their incidence, Americans seem to be willing to tax themselves only at about 20 per cent of GDP. In addition, some believe that taxing themselves more to fund further entitlements, particularly welfare state programs, will have a deleterious effect on GDP. (This view, of course, mirrors what fiscal conservatives repeatedly tell the public.) Rather than seeing themselves as taxing themselves too little to fund an appropriate welfare state, many Americans see the mature welfare state as already demanding too much taxation. Other OECD nations have higher rates of taxation in relation to GDP but similar regularities in the historic proportions of GDP devoted to public purposes or at least run through public treasuries.

In principle, funding new programs could also be accomplished by reducing old ones. But here the entrenched nature of welfare state entitlements rears both its beautiful and ugly heads. The beauty lies in the political stability of arrangements that are designed, after all, to provide social security. The ugliness, of course, is that the same rigidities hamper needed rearrangements to deal with demographic or technological shifts (Marmor and Mashaw 1992).[2] Given fiscal realities, major rearrangements of the shape or size of mature welfare states are enormously difficult – even in the absence of severe ideological conflict.

The United States, strangely enough, seems to have an opportunity unavailable to most mature welfare states, but one the nation

Table I   Federal Outlays As a Percentage of Gross Domestic Product

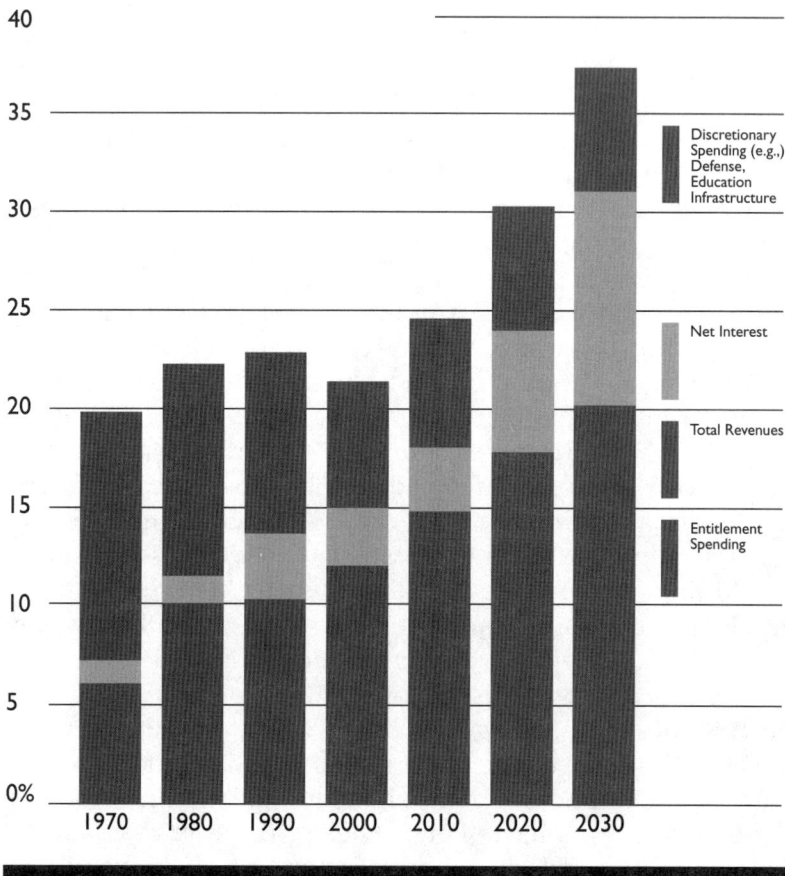

Source: Bipartisan Commission on Entitlement and Tax Reform, 'Finding Number I: Interim
  Report to the President.' Washington, DC : Government Printing Office. August 1994.

is currently unwilling or unable to take. Because American medical
arrangements are administratively inefficient and subject to
demonstrably ineffective market or government restraints, a movement from private to public provision of health insurance might
well reduce the total share of GDP devoted to the health care
sector. In short, Americans are in the lucky situation where an
expansion of entitlements might actually save money. Yet
strangely, perhaps perversely, Americans refuse to grasp these savings – savings that could be in the range of hundreds of billions of
dollars per year (Canham-Clyne, Woolhandler and Himmelstein
1995).

This perversity, or idiosyncrasy, flows from the very same structural situation we discussed at length above. On the one hand, Americans do not view the question of whether monies flow through private pocketbooks or state treasuries as politically neutral. Our ideology of limited government, particularly limited federal government, strongly predisposes us to favour private over public expenditure.

But this is not the full explanation. The problem is also that US health expenditures show up in a multitude of different budgets – those of the federal government, state governments, employers and households. Rearranging how health insurance is provided might not only shift money flows from private to public hands. It would also rearrange who actually pays for the medical care provided. That aggregate costs for the 'public household' should fall may do little to reassure those parties whose expenditures could go up. And, given the multiple levers that American governance provides to those who wish to block action, those who fear paying more under various options for reforming health insurance can wield plenty of political muscle to block change.

Conclusion

While this chapter may appear to forecast nothing but gloom and doom, that is not its intention. Our message is not that nothing can be done – or that nothing should be done. Our attempt instead has been to look realistically at the structural impediments to change in the United States that make it difficult for the state – whether understood as the federal government or the individual states – to shoulder the burden of guaranteeing health care insurance. Americans have a polity that, for this issue, is organised in a particularly problematic fashion. We have managed to structure our political system in such a way that state governments cannot, and the federal government will not, act. Movement away from the status quo, therefore, requires us to think in the ways that Rudolf Klein has so assiduously developed over his distinguished career. We have to see the impediments to action not just as current political circumstances, faulty leadership or the inanities of public debate but rather as a larger question of structural political arrangements. Once we do that, the problems of orchestrating changes in the state's role appear no less difficult. On the other hand, a structural perspective may lead to improved strategic thinking. That, we contend, is the necessary but not sufficient condition for producing change in policy rather than a stalemate that mocks both state power and state responsibility.[3]

Notes

---

1. This is not, of course, strictly true. For special populations with a peculiarly national status – not only veterans, but Native Americans, seamen and federal employees – there are special programs of provision and finance. In addition, the federal government has extensively subsidised medical research, the education and training of medical professionals, and the construction of medical facilities. These programs faced neither the bitter ideological disputes nor the daunting institutional hurdles that confront national health insurance. Nonetheless, no account of American health politics would be complete without attention to them.

2. These quite general constraints are magnified in the United States by the relative weakness of consensus-generating institutions and the rather hysterical tone of public discussion of how social change and technological innovation affect long-term programs in social insurance. Absent authoritative fact finding and a widespread faith in the integrity of the public service, changes in the future easily become what we call 'future dread.' One USA Today poll in 1994 reported that only 7 per cent of young working Americans believe they will receive Social Security payments when they retire. It should also be noted that 47 per cent of this same sample believe that UFOs were piloted by extraterrestrial beings. The obvious irony here is that commentators simultaneously report such fears and claim that Social Security is sacrosanct, 'the third rail of American politics,' according to one constant refrain, that 'electrocutes all who touch it.' Social Security is understood as simultaneously unstable and untouchable, and the debate about it defies rational description.

3. The scope of our essay may require reiteration. One of the volume's editors noted that we do not emphasise that the 'US is the only developed country in the world where a sizable minority of the population has no right of access to health care...[and that we] seem to imply the problems of uninsured and underinsured Americans... are simply an interesting illustration of constitutional inertia.' Our aim here, however, was not to explore the normative basis for reform (or opposition to it.) Rather, it was to supply an explanation for why it is so hard in American politics to change the rules of a major industry even when there are massive and acknowledged problems.

The editor raised two other questions, both of which are interesting but outside the scope of this effort. One was how American federalism compared with that of the similar, but not identical federal systems of Australia and Canada. The fragmentation of American political authority – and the absence of parliamentary institutions – makes American federalism somewhat different. That, along with the relatively weaker labour movement and different party system, is part of a broader account of the distinctive politics of the American welfare state.

Finally, some have wondered why we have not concentrated on the particular strategic difficulties that faced the Clinton Administration's reform effort, particularly that apparent dilemma of how to extend coverage and to control costs. It is true that most expansions of government insurance have taken place at times of relative national prosperity. But here again the focus of our argument was on the structural features of American politics and society that make this kind of policy change difficult, not on the particulars of the Clinton effort. There will be many books and article on the latter; it is the former that is given too little attention. Framed as a syllogism, because it is always difficult in American politics to enact major reform, it would have taken exceptional timing, skill and luck for the Clintons to have been successful. All, it turned out, were for them in short supply.

References

Bipartisan Commission on Entitlement and Tax Reform. 1994. *Interim Report to the President.* J. R. Kerrey, chairman. Washington, D.C.: Superintendent of Documents.

Brown, L. D. 1994. Who Shall Pay? Politics, Money, and Health Care Reform. *Health Affairs* (spring [II]): 175–84.

——, and T. R. Marmor. 1994. The Clinton Reform Plan's Administrative Structure: The Reach and the Grasp. *Journal of Health Politics, Policy and Law* 19(1): 193–200.

Canham-Clyne, J., S. Woolhandler, and D. Himmelstein. 1995. *The Rational Option for a National Health Program.* Stony Creek, CT: Pamphleteer's Press.

DiIulio, J. J., Jr., and R. P. Nathan, eds. 1994. *Making Health Reform Work: The View from the States,* Washington, D.C.: Brookings Institution.

Hacker, J. 1995. *Setting the Health Reform Agenda: The Ascendance of Managed Competition,* Princeton: Princeton University Press.

Hamburger, T., T. R. Marmor, and J. Meacham. 1994. What the Death of Health Reform Teaches Us about the Media. *The Washington Monthly* 26: 35–41.

Health Care Study Group. 1994. Understanding the Choices in Health Care Reform. *Journal of Health Politics, Policy and Law* 19(3): 499-541; *Domestic Affairs* (winter 1993-4):1-23.

Henry J. Kaiser Family Foundation. 1994. National Election Night Survey (news release, November 15). Menlo Park, CA.

Jacobs, L. R. 1993. *The Health of Nations: Public Opinion and the Making of American and British Health Policy.* Ithaca, NY: Cornell University Press.

Klein, R. 1989. *The Politics of the National Health Service,* 2d ed. London: Longman.

——, and M. O'Higgins. 1985. *The Future of Welfare.* Oxford: Basil Blackwell.

Marmor, T. R. 1994. *Understanding Health Care Reform.* New Haven: Yale University Press.

——, J. L. Mashaw, and P. L. Harvey. 1992. *America's Misunderstood Welfare State: Persistent Myths, Enduring Realities.* New York: Basic Books.

——, and J. L. Mashaw, eds. 1988. *Social Security: Beyond the Rhetoric of Crisis.* Princeton: Princeton University Press.

Mashaw, J. 1993-4. The Case for State-led Reform. *Domestic Affairs* (winter): 1-23.

Meacham, J. 1994. The GOP's Master Strategist. *The Washington Monthly* 26(9): 32-9.

Morone, J. A. 1994. The Administration of Health Care Reform. *The Journal of Health Politics, Policy and Law* 19: 233-8.

——. 1990. *The Democratic Wish.* New York: Basic Books.

Piper, A., and F. Chisman, eds. 1985. *The Fiftieth Anniversary Edition of the Report of the Committee on Economic Security of 1935 and Other Basic Documents Relating to the Social Security Act.* Washington D.C.: National Conference on Social Welfare.

Schneider, W. 1994. Why Health-Care Reform May Be Beyond Saving. *Los Angeles Times* (August 14): M1.

Starr, P. 1995. What Happened to Health Care Reform? *The American Prospect* 20 (winter): 20-31.

Steinmo, S., and J. Watts. 1994. It's the Institution, Stupid: Why Comprehensive Health Reform Fails in America. Paper presented at the Annual Conference of the American Political Science Association, New York, September.

Tribe, L. H. 1988. *American Constitutional Law.* 2d ed. Mineola, NY: Foundation Press.

Yankelovich, D. 1995. The Debate That Wasn't: The Public and the Clinton Health Care Plan. Paper presented at the Brookings Institution, Washington, D.C., January 23-24.

6

The Limits of Simple Fixes

Robert J. Maxwell

This paper is about the successive reorganisations of the National Health Service since 1974. While there was a rationale for each of these, and each has made some enduring contribution, there is a high price to be paid for organisational upheaval.

Restructuring is not unique to the United Kingdom. It has been common in other national systems in recent years, since governments find themselves faced by a complex set of problems in relation to the financing and delivery of health care and there is a temptation to believe that these can be resolved by organisational change.

The lessons to be drawn from this case study suggest grounds for caution in relation to further restructuring because (a) there is probably no perfect or ideologically neutral organisation for health services (b) the real problems within health care – e.g. rationing – will never be solved by organisational change (c) you simply cannot go on restructuring again and again without affecting staff morale and public confidence and (d) organisational change absorbs an enormous amount of management and political attention which would often be better spent in other ways.

Author's Note: The case study in this chapter concerns the National Health Service (NHS), but (I will argue) it also has relevance for countries other than the United Kingdom.

I wrote this chapter for Rudolf because the topic is one that interests me and which I hope would interest him. He may well not agree with what I have written, but he will certainly have views about the events that we have both lived through. He is quite simply the best commentator on health-related issues of his and my generation – accurate, creative and stylish, tough, without the least hint of arrogance. I hope that he enjoys the chapter and I look forward to discussing it with him.

When the NHS was set up under the NHS Act of 1946, the organisational form that was chosen for it was in some ways radical and in others perpetuated the arrangements of the past. The radical bit was the nationalisation of the voluntary hospitals. The cautious part (reflected in Figure 1) was to have four separate organisational strands, representing public health and community health services (which remained under local government control), family practitioner services (under executive councils, stemming ultimately from the insurance committees set up under the National Health Insurance Act of 1911), the nonteaching hospitals (under hospital management committees of the new regional hospital boards) and the teaching hospitals (with their own boards of governors, answering directly to the minister).

There was little merit in this organisation, which meant that nobody short of ministers and their most senior advisers dealt with all aspects of the NHS, even in a single locality. But it survived intact until 1974 – in other words, for a quarter of a century or more than half the history of the NHS from its beginnings until the present. In 1968, however, when Kenneth Robinson was Minister of Health, he published a green paper (UK Ministry of Health 1968) proposing the integration of all these strands under area boards, which would correspond geographically to local government boundaries. In 1968 Richard Crossman, as Secretary of State for Social Services, proposed a variant to these arrangements in a second green paper (UK Department of Health and Social Security 1970). The Labour government then fell and the task of deciding on a new organisation for the NHS passed to Sir Keith Joseph, the incoming Conservative Secretary of State.

Case Study: Round 1

Sir Keith, in his Thatcherite mode, was later to become extremely penitent about the cumbersome, ornate management arrangements that he was responsible for inflicting on the NHS via what came to be called the Grey Book (UK Department of Health and Social Security 1972). This report was overseen by a large steering committee comprising people from the NHS and from the Department of Health and Social Security, chaired by the then civil servant head of the department, Sir Philip Rogers. Under the steering committee was a study group, assisted by a team from the Health Services Organisation Research Unit at Brunel University and from McKinsey and Company, management consultants.[1]

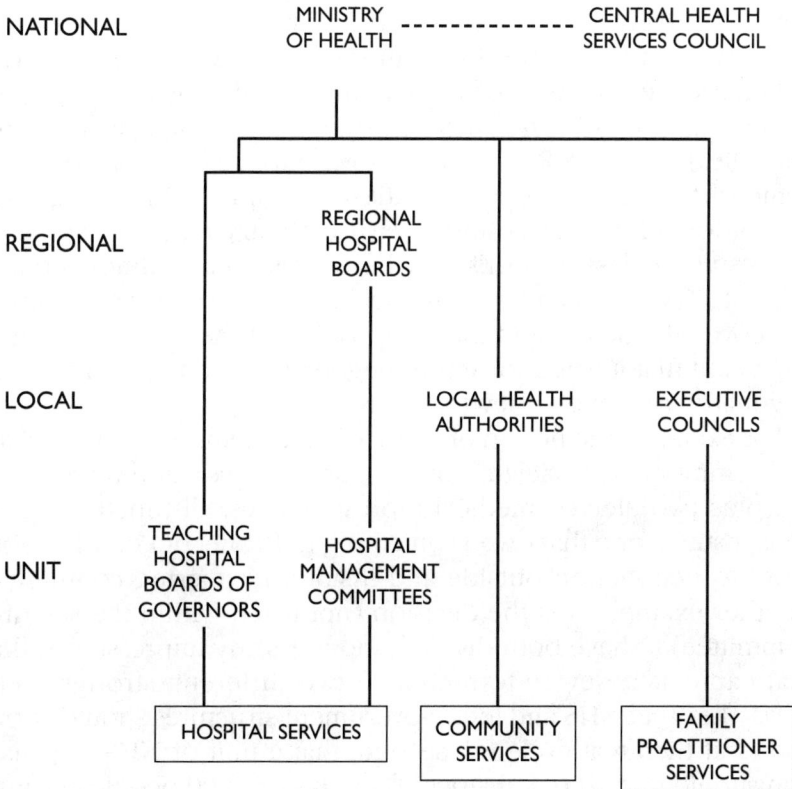

Figure 1   The National Health Service, 1948-74

Source: R. Levitt and A. Wall, The Reorganised National Health Service, 4th ed. London: Chapman and Hall, 1992.

The Grey Book is the most detailed management blueprint ever published for the NHS. It defines its organisation and the nature of the relationships between the levels (Figure 2), the functions and organisation at each level, all the main job specifications in the structure, and the management processes (planning, monitoring and control, and personnel management) that were to be used. While the status of the Grey Book was a report to the Secretary of State, which he would accept or reject, it in fact became the management bible of the 1974 reorganisation, in standard form throughout the NHS in England, and substantially in Wales. There was more variation in Scotland and in Northern Ireland.

In later years, the Grey Book has come to be seen as a high-water mark of the discredited structural approach to management that had already had its heyday in British business a decade earlier. But it was actually a good deal more complicated than that. The detailed differentiation of roles and relationships owed a lot to Brunel's research in the NHS, led by Professor Eliot Jacques and his colleague Ralph Rowbottom (Rowbottom 1973) and reflected some of the particular complexities of hospitals, including their professional hierarchies and interdisciplinary tensions. Some of the resulting classifications may be overelaborate, almost botanical, but they are peculiar to the health field, not imported into it. Moreover, the nature and the composition of the steering committee meant that it was a forum for negotiation and that some of the negotiations went on elsewhere.

For example, the notion of a district management team comprising community physician, nurse, finance officer, and administrator, plus two elected medical representatives, all functioning by consensus, is one that owed something to Brunel but considerably more to negotiation outside and inside the steering committee. Another example was the decision (not taken within the steering committee) to have both districts and areas. My impression is that that came as a device to reconcile two different, strongly held ideas: first, that NHS and local government structures should correspond at the area level and, second, that a unit of NHS organisation should consist of a district of roughly 250,000 people because that was the natural catchment area for a district general hospital (DGH) and hence was the first level at which all local NHS services could be integrated managerially. In rather more than a third of NHS areas in England and Wales the two ideas came together, because the local authority's population was small enough to correspond to a hospital district in what came to be called the single-district areas. But in roughly two thirds of areas (comprising 80 per cent of districts) this was not the case: hence, there were to be management teams at both district and area levels. There was also strong advocacy for the continuation of regions in England on the grounds that they formed a sensible unit for planning tertiary services and that there were in any case too many areas to be dealt with directly by national government.

The implementation date for the Grey Book reorganisation was 1 April 1974. Ironically, Edward Heath's Conservative government fell in February, so the task of presiding over the reorganisation switched back to a Labour government, with Barbara Castle as Secretary of State. The new government considered whether to review the whole matter, but in the event let the reorganisation go ahead, introducing only relatively minor modifications in the name of strengthening local accountability (UK Department of Health and Social Security 1974). Community Health Councils (CHCs) were given certain limited statutory powers, the new Health Authorities were to meet in public, and a proportion of their members were to be nominated by the local authorities from among their own elected members.

In the event the new organisation took about two years to settle down. It turned out to have both strengths and weaknesses. Among the strengths was – as had been hoped – the concept of an integrated district, with the opportunity and the incentive to allocate money across traditional service boundaries. Not that the opportunities were always taken, partly because the integration of family practitioner services under Area Health Authorities was more theoretical than real: they retained their own separate administration and were separately funded from the national level with allocations that were open-ended and outside the main NHS budgets. Nevertheless, the existence of defined NHS districts did prompt attempts to define needs and the impact of services on the basis of population studies rather than assumptions. Clinicians and managers who wanted to work across the traditional separation between hospital and community-based services were encouraged to do so.

On the other hand, the new organisation proved in some ways cumbersome. Decision-making processes could be slow because

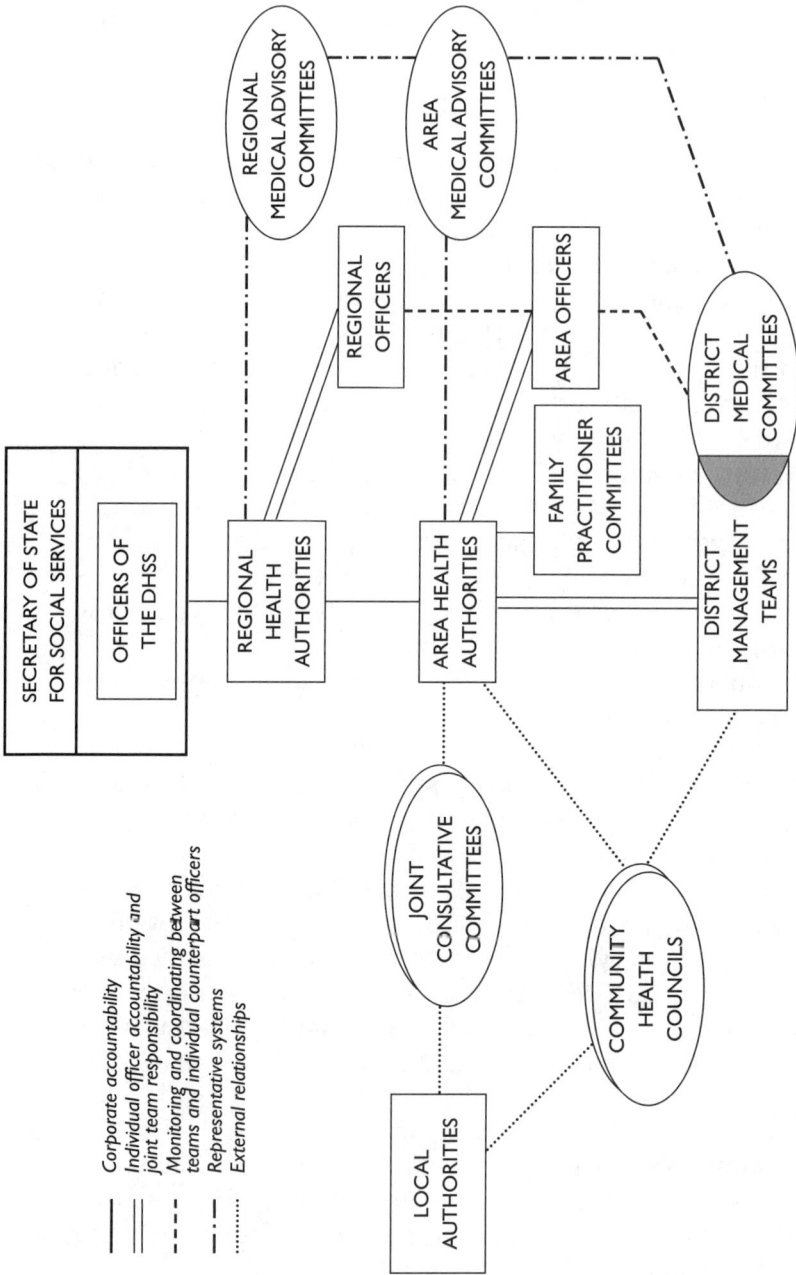

Figure 2   The NHS Reorganisation of 1974

Source: Department of Health and Social Services, Management Arrangements for the Reorganised National Health Service, London: Her Majesty's Stationery Office, 1972.

of the elaboration of the structure and the heavy emphasis on consultation and consensus. The strength of management at the hospital level tended to be eroded as administrators saw the new jobs at district as their path to the top. Probably the most widely voiced criticism was (as one might have foreseen) that there was one tier too many in the new structure. On the whole, the single-district areas seemed to work better than the multidistrict areas where there could be substantial tensions between the two levels.

This dissatisfaction with some aspects of the 1974 reorganisation was a factor (though certainly not the only one) in prompting Harold Wilson in 1976 to nominate a Royal Commission on the National Health Service to examine the best use of its financial and manpower resources. Wilson was a past master at the use of royal commissions as a diversionary device, so the fact that the commission reported after the general election of 1979 was no accident. Granted the profound seismic shift away from consensus politics represented by the arrival of Mrs Margaret Thatcher at No. 10 Downing Street, it was inevitable that the Royal Commission's report (UK Royal Commission on the National Health Service 1979) would have limited relevance to anything she would decide to do. For what it is worth, however, the Royal Commission did in fact conclude that the organisation of the NHS was overelaborate and that one tier should be removed in most places. The commission also wished to abolish family practitioner committees.

Case Study: Round 2

Mrs Thatcher became prime minister in May 1979. In December, a slim consultation paper, *Patients First* (UK Department of Health and Social Security and Welsh Office 1979), on the structure and management of the NHS in England and Wales was published by the new government, chiefly, it seems, as a response to the royal commission report. It proposed the abolition of the area tier and the establishment of Health Authorities at district level. In effect, this meant that the single-district areas of 1974 would survive in most cases, while the multidistrict areas would be split up. Hence, the number of health authorities would increase sharply, and coterminosity on a one-to-one basis between health and local government would generally be lost.

The consultation paper considered, but rejected, a number of ideas for more radical change discussed by the royal commission.

These included the idea that regional Health Authorities might become directly accountable to parliament; the abolition of family practitioner committees; transferring responsibility for the NHS to local government, or for social services to the Health Authorities; and the replacement of management teams by individual chief executives. Apart from the abolition of areas and the establishment of health authorities at the district level, professional advisory machinery was to be simplified as was the planning system. There should be maximum delegation of management responsibility to the local level – a familiar slogan of every NHS reorganisation.

The reorganisation based on *Patients First* was implemented following legislation, from 1 April 1982, with consequential changes spread over the next 18 months. The intention was to avoid the turbulence of the 1974 reorganisation, but in practice the management turbulence was great as virtually every senior job was affected. It was like a game of musical chairs, in which people feared to find themselves without a post when the music stopped.

Case Study: Round 3

Almost before this game had ended, another management inquiry had been set up. Norman Fowler, as secretary of state, had asked Roy Griffiths, managing director of Sainsbury's, to advise on 'the effective use and management of manpower and related resources' in the NHS. What lay behind this request was an increasing restiveness on the part of the cabinet generally and Mrs Thatcher in particular at the capacity of the NHS to absorb real increases in funding and then come back to ask for more. NormalnFowler had an unusually long period as secretary of state for Social Services, from 1981 to 1987. He was adept at negotiation with the Treasury and at astute manoeuvering to avoid confrontation within the Social Services. The remit to Roy Griffiths was a way (following the government's re-election in 1983) to expose the inner managerial workings of the NHS to the scrutiny of a group of businessmen, who would not be easily fobbed off with bureaucratic or wimpish social welfare excuses. The prime minister herself had confidence in him. She was not seeking a public confrontation on the NHS, which was not then at the top of her hit list for the radical reform of Britain, but equally she thought it needed a good hard external look at its efficiency.

The inquiry was completed in approximately six months. The resulting brief report (UK NHS Management Inquiry 1983) criticised the diffusion of management responsibility in the NHS ('if Florence Nightingale were carrying her lamp through the corridors of the NHS today she would almost certainly be searching for the people in charge') and the lack of a clearly defined focus and drive for the planning, implementation, and control of performance ('the NHS is so structured as to resemble a "mobile": designed to move with any breath of air, but which in fact never changes its position and gives no clear indication of direction'). Griffiths recommended the creation of a single general management line to run from the secretary of state at the centre to individuals in charge at the operational (e.g., hospital) level. The secretary of state would chair a Health Services Supervisory Board, below which there would be a management board charged with heading the general management process in the NHS. Its chairman would be an experienced executive, probably drawn from outside central government and the NHS – in short, someone like Roy Griffiths himself. From the management board outwards there would be a single general manager at each level – region, district, unit. While no attempt was made to remove the regional and district health authorities, they were urged to clarify what decisions they would reserve to themselves and what should be done on their behalf by the general manager and chief officers. In essence, the task at the centre was to set the direction for the NHS, not simply in intellectual terms but in terms of energy and leadership. The task at unit level was to achieve change and maximise performance, in partnership with the clinicians. In between centre and unit were the link mechanisms, to convey direction, protect and support local managerial autonomy, and hold to account.

The Griffiths report met a hostile response, particularly from the professions.[2] Despite this opposition, the report was quickly accepted by the secretary of state, with a view to immediate implementation.

Once again, as with the 1982 reorganisation, the game of musical chairs followed as, at all levels, people competed for general manager jobs. A few went to the professions and some to candidates from business, local government and the armed forces. Most, however, went to what had previously been called NHS administrators, who found themselves in more powerful positions than ever before but positions that were also more politically exposed. Nursing was in disarray, as a result of the virtual annihilation of nursing management. The medical profession did not know quite what to make of it all.

Case Study: Round 4

The Griffiths recommendations, with their accent on building a general management process and culture, were designed for the long term. Their impact continues ten years later, and their force is still by no means spent. But they did not provide any immediate resolution to the problems of financing the NHS. Once again, in the run-up to the 1987 general election, the Conservative manifesto did not major on the National Health Service. 'The NHS is safe in our hands,' countered Mrs Thatcher to allegations by the Labour Party that her government could not be trusted on this issue.

The Conservatives were re-elected, winning for the third time in succession, but within months the government was subject to an unprecedented public attack by the presidents of the three premier royal colleges who claimed that the NHS was falling apart for lack of money. Mrs Thatcher countered with the argument that year-by-year expenditure on the NHS had increased in real terms. Although this was true (at least on one set of assumptions) it did not feel like the truth to many of those working in the NHS nor to the general public. Among the reasons was the fact that increases in salary and wage costs were determined nationally and were funded only on the assumption of efficiency savings that had to be achieved by the Health Authorities. Moreover, the position was much worse in places like London, which were at the same time losing money under resource redistribution policies, designed to achieve greater fairness between north and south.

The statement by the college presidents in early December 1987 struck a chord of public response. Day by day and week by week the funding of the NHS was headline news: as so often before, individual cases were used (with incomplete facts) to illustrate the impact of rationing. The opposition called for an independent inquiry or royal commission. Mrs Thatcher, forced on the defensive, ultimately yielded a governmental review, to be led by herself. She was – and remained – angry at being wrong footed, and resentful at the influence exerted by the profession in the persons of the royal college presidents.

Her review took place in the calendar year 1988, behind closed doors. For some time, even the composition of her review team was unknown, and it was never formally announced. (It included besides herself the chancellor of the Exchequer, the secretary of state for Social Services, and their next-in-line ministers). No public evidence was taken.[3] A certain amount of information leaked out about the topics considered and the stage reached – for example, that a switch from general taxation to insurance-based funding was considered and rejected. Late in the day, John Moore, the secretary of state for Social Services, who had not been a great success in the post, was replaced by Kenneth Clarke (previously minister of state), who appeared to have a particularly strong influence on the ultimate conclusions. These were published in January 1989, under the title *Working for Patients* (UK Department of Health 1989).

Working for Patients is a very uneven document. It contains what it describes as 'seven key changes,' but these range from the modestly incremental (one half of one extra hospital consultant post per district) and the barely controversial (medical audit) to the truly radical (self-governing status for hospitals and some form of competition among providers). Two of the most important ideas – the NHS district as the key unit for purchasing and general practitioner fund holders as purchasers – had different intellectual parentages and seemed bound to be mutually incompatible in the long term. Thus, the NHS reforms, as they were called by their progenitors, were something of an intellectual hotchpotch. Nevertheless, it would be wrong to view them as a cynical attempt to undermine the NHS.

The implementation of changes began in April 1990. From a political viewpoint the timing was bad. With a general election likely in 1991, what people would remember at election time would be the controversy and disturbance associated with the changes. A period of about 12 months would be too short to demonstrate benefits. Hence, the strong directive from the NHS Management Executive (as Sir Roy Griffiths's management board had become) down through the NHS, was that managers should hasten slowly.

In the event, the government was reelected for a fourth term. Had the opposition won, the Thatcher NHS reforms, reflected in the present NHS structure shown in Figure 3, would have been reversed. As it is, the process of implementation is continuing. To date, the jury is still out on the net impact of the changes. The most comprehensive assessment yet published (Robinson and Le Grand 1994) is by no means conclusive, partly because of the complexity of the research task and partly because it is still in the early days. Some observations, however, can be made. For example, transactions costs have risen, as a result of the new management structures and the additional information required by the new system. On the other hand, cost information has improved sharply.

In terms of service quality, the patients of general practitioner fund holders, in particular, have benefited from shorter waiting times and better feedback of information to their general practitioners but at the expense of equity, since gaps have opened between them and other patients. The maxim that, in the new system, money would follow the patient may be true for the patients of general practitioner fund holders. For others, it seems more true that patients have to go where the contracts say they should. Extracontractual referrals (i.e., referrals outside the main contracts) can create substantial tensions and are much less straightforward than cross boundary referrals used to be under the old system.

In the main, it is simply too soon to give a balanced verdict. Hospital and community trusts have greater autonomy on paper than their predecessors. Will this autonomy be eroded over the years? Will it prove beneficial? How real will competition among providers prove to be, and will it deliver benefits? Will the initial weaknesses in purchasing be overcome? What modus vivendi will be achieved between districts as purchasers and general practitioner fund holders?

What does seem likely is that, if there is a change of the party in power at the next election, something will survive. It probably will not be general practitioner fundholding. It may be a degree of managerial autonomy for providers, though the composition of their boards will change. It is quite likely to be, in some form, a continued differentiation between the commissioning of services and their provision. There seems now to be a general acceptance that government's task is more about ensuring the provision of services then it is about providing them and that direct responsibility for provision can at times weight the scales too much towards the perpetuation of existing services and institutions.

Reflections on the Case

Perhaps the best starting point for reflection (in true Kleinian spirit) is a paradox. Each of the changes described in the four rounds of the case study had some justification, and each has left some benefits, but overall it is highly questionable whether they have been worthwhile. Let us explore the paradox further and then ask what advice, based on the case study, one would give governments for the future.

1. Organisation is important, but not all-important, and there is probably no such thing as organisational perfection. In *Patients First* the apparently reasonable proposition is put forward that 'It

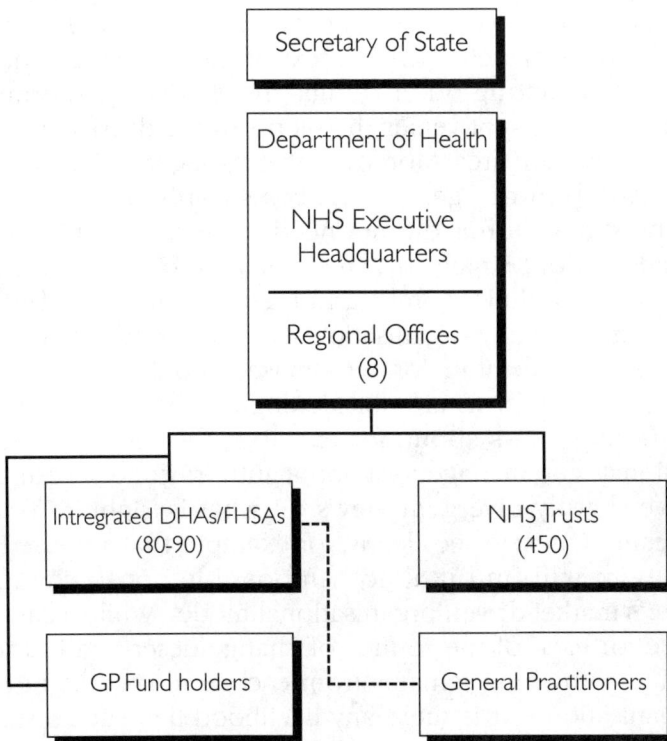

Figure 3   New Structure of the NHS

Source: Department of Health, Managing the New NHS, London: DoH, 1993.

is fundamental to making a national health service work well in response to patients' needs that the structure and management of the service should be right' (UK Department of Health and Social Security and Welsh Office 1979). But what does 'right' in this context mean? There is no doubt that organisations can get in the way of human action: for example, working across organisational boundaries is always difficult, whether the boundaries are those between government departments or between health and social services. Nevertheless, organisations are simply frameworks that are more or less well-tailored to the work to be done within them at the time. How well they function is an empirical question rather than a theoretical one, so anybody whose field is organisational design would be wise to test the design in action.

It is highly unlikely that there is any such thing as a perfect organisation for several reasons. For example, there are often trade-offs to be made: in the context of the case study, the trade-offs between, among other things, the merits of coterminosity with local government versus the merits of the district as a natural hospital catchment area. Moreover, the management agenda faced by an institution or agency changes sharply over time, and it would be strange if this did not need to be reflected in organisational adaptation. Finally, organisations are only as good as the people in them, their morale, and their commitment. Ultimately people can make any organisation work, while no organisational framework can substitute for demoralised people.

Organisational forms are not ideologically neutral. People who hold differing views about, for example, the respective roles of professionals and managers, or about authority and accountability, will have sharply divergent views on what is 'right' in organisational teams. One can see clearly, for example, that a future Labour government will find it almost impossible not to change Mrs Thatcher's market-driven organisational model. While a case could be made for each of the rounds of change described in this case study, and something remains from each, none resulted in a perfect organisation nor is there any likelihood that such a state will ever be reached.

2. Governments work to short time horizons, and they like quick fixes. In the United Kingdom, the maximum lifetime of a government is five years. More typically it is four, so that the party in power can pick its moment to go to the polls. The average period for any politician in any one office, such as secretary of

state for Health, is more likely two and a half years. These political realities affect the thinking and the behaviour of virtually every minister and every government. Faced with a complex, chronic problem, they are seldom attracted to complex, long-term solutions. What they must have is an action that can be taken relatively fast and preferably one that will show a political return before the next election. Organisational change has too often seemed to meet these requirements. But whatever the real problems of the NHS are (and we will come to that in a moment) they are not of a kind that are resolved by a quick fix.

3. Whatever the merits of large-scale organisational change, it carries a high price tag in terms of its impact on people, particularly if it is done repeatedly. The initial organisation of the NHS – imperfect as it was – lasted from 1948 to 1974. Since then the service has been subject to repeated reorganisations, at shorter and shorter intervals. It seems as though the NHS is always contemplating reorganisation, or undergoing it, or recovering.

When I first came across Petronius' classic comment on this subject in the *Satyricon,* I was amused by its aptness. I am no longer so amused. The words describe only too clearly the state of mind of those who have been continually reorganised.[4]

4. One effect of constant NHS reorganisations has been to occupy the attention of senior managers and politicians and distract them from what the NHS is actually about. There is a real danger that the institutional leadership of the NHS is busy with an agenda that neither most of those working in it nor the public understand. In the period from, say, the publication of *Working for Patients* in January 1989 until now, what proportion of the time and energy of health ministers and NHS senior managers has gone into the actual problems of delivering services to patients, as compared with (in its broadest sense) structural change and its implications? It is almost as though senior management and the politicians were detached from the reality of what they are there to lead and contribute virtually nothing to the service from day to day.

5. So what is the real problem to which organisational change has been the symptomatic response rather than the solution? The heart of the matter is about finding and allocating the resources for health care in a situation where the gap continually widens between expectations and what is available. It can be variously expressed as achieving excellence within tight constraints or

obtaining value for money or balancing aims that pull in different directions. It is a wicked rather than a tame problem in the sense that it has no neat or permanent solution.

Government has to be a participant (not only in the United Kingdom but everywhere) because of the importance of health and the scale of public resources committed to it. But there is no way in which government can itself handle the detailed, day-to-day issues nor fix them in a way that stays fixed. As an OECD publication, *The Reform of Health Care* (Organisation for Economic Co-operation and Development 1992) suggests, based on a comparative analysis of seven OECD countries, it may be useful to differentiate between on the one hand setting the framework for tackling these issues and on the other tackling them in a micro or operational sense. Government can do the first; it cannot do the second and is unwise to try.

In conclusion, the advice to governments based on this case study might be, first, to be as specific as possible about the problems they are trying to solve rather than reaching too quickly for solutions. Second, to try to resist the temptation to make repeated massive systems changes, whether these are organisational or process, and to recognise the price of repeated change in terms of morale. Third, to take a more evolutionary approach, with a greater respect for evidence, than is shown in this case study. All the indications are that no intervention on the scale of any of the rounds in this case produces precisely what is intended. Whether or not one accepts the argument for piloting change, one should in a broader sense see change as a learning process where it is in everyone's interests to assess effects before anyone intervenes again. Gardening is quite a good analogy for management: continually digging up the plants to re-examine their roots and move them around is not a good way to establish a flourishing NHS.

Notes

1. At this point I first became personally involved in the story as I was working for McKinsey and Company at the time and was their health specialist, having among other things worked on health service reorganisation in New York and the Republic of Ireland. I was not a member of the NHS study team because I was working on a separate reorganisation of the Department of Health, but I was sufficiently close to the NHS work to have a fair knowledge of it.

2. I was asked by Cliff Graham, chief of staff to the inquiry, to host a dinner to discuss the conclusions at the draft stage. It was quickly clear that this was more a selling than a consultation exercise. At that time, I felt that Sir Roy (as he later became) had underestimated the strength of the case for interdisciplinary management teams in the NHS and I wanted the approach to change to be more experimental, less mandatory. Not for the last time in the context of this case study, I lost that argument. Once the secretary of state had accepted the Griffiths report, I sought, in conjunction with my colleague, the late Tom Evans, to persuade all those involved in the NHS to grasp the opportunity presented by Griffiths's recommendations and show what the NHS could do with them. In particular, we stressed the possibility of combining central strategic direction with a truly decentralised operational management of health services (Evans and Maxwell 1984).

3. There appeared to be two routes by which ideas could be fed into the review. One was from the right-wing policy think tanks, the other the Department of Health. Perhaps the Treasury was a third. In my experience (using the Department of Health route) one did not hear what the reaction had been. Along, no doubt, with many others, I sought to persuade the protagonists of the merits of pilot projects. The idea did not appeal nor later did the suggestion that the changes that resulted from the review should be systematically evaluated as hostile critics alleged. My own view was, and is, that they comprised an assortment of right-wing radical ideas, intended to reconcile the virtues of a collective NHS with the encouragement of enterprise through the workings of a managed market. These ideas may or may not prove beneficial. That is an empirical not an ideological question. But I see no reason to impugn the integrity of those who promulgated them.

4. 'We trained hard – but it seemed that every time we were beginning to form up into teams we would be reorganised. I was to learn later in life that we tend to meet any new situation by reorganising, and a wonderful method it can be for creating the illusion of progress while producing confusion, inefficiency and demoralisation.' From Petronius, The Satyricon, c. 65 AD

References

Evans, T., and R. Maxwell. 1984. *Griffiths: Challenge and Response*. London: King's Fund Institute.

Organisation for Economic Co-operation and Development. 1992. *The Reform of Health Care: A Comparative Analysis of Seven OECD Countries. Health Policy Studies No. 2.* Paris: Organisation for Economic Co-operation and Development.

Robinson, R., and J. Le Grand. 1994. *Evaluating the NHS Reforms*. London: King's Fund Institute.

Rowbottom, R. 1973. *Hospital Organisation: A Progress Report on the Brunel Health Services Organisation Project*. London: Heinemann.

UK Secretaries of State for Health. 1989. Cmnd. 555. *Working for Patients*. London: Her Majesty's Stationery Office.

UK Department of Health and Social Security. 1974. *Democracy in the National Health Service*. London: Her Majesty's Stationery Office.

——. 1972. *Management Arrangements for the Reorganised National Health Service*. London: Her Majesty's Stationery Office.

——. 1970. The Future Structure of the National Health Service. London: Her Majesty's Stationery Office.

UK Department of Health and Social Security and Welsh Office. 1979. *Patients First*. London: Her Majesty's Stationery Office.

UK Ministry of Health. 1968. *The Administrative Structure of Medical and Related Services in England and Wales*. London: Her Majesty's Stationery Office.

UK NHS Management Inquiry. 1983. Report. London: Department of Health and Social Security.

UK Royal Commission on the National Health Service. 1979. Cmnd. 7615. Report. London: Department of Health and Social Security.

7

Negotiating Health Policy

Daniel M. Fox

For some years I have used two idiosyncratic criteria to evaluate explanations for events in health policy. The first was that an explanation should make sense to people who run for public office and those who make strategic decisions for public and private organisations. The second idiosyncratic criterion was that Rudolf Klein should not dismiss an explanation. Would he even describe it as 'rubbish,' a word I once enjoyed hearing him use to a critic of a paper that Patricia Day, Rudolf and I had written (Fox, Day and Klein 1988)? This chapter begins by describing Rudolf's contribution to my education. Then it ventures an explanation of recent health politics in the United States.

Making Policy

People who make health policy are guided by ideas, interests and illness (Fox 1986; 1995). Because most decision makers care about ideas, they are principled, analytical and compassionate, although hardly ever in ways that satisfy advocates for particular causes. Advocates always want more of whatever it is they are righteous about. Decision makers, in contrast, worry about how to divide limited resources among an ever larger number of people who

insist that their wants are needs. Most academics who study politics design universes whose inhabitants ask different questions
about policy than decision makers ask. A recent example of such a
question is whether students of politics ought to be 'bringing the
state back in' as an 'independent actor' (Evans, Rueschemeyer and
Skocpol 1993). A recurring example is whether social class is more
determining of events than race or culture. The answers to such
questions may be fascinating, but most decision makers do not
regard them as helping to solve practical problems.

Because decision makers are sensitive to interests, most of them
value loyalty to friends, respect their most effective enemies, and
work to recruit allies. Most advocates and academics, in contrast,
value loyalty to convictions over loyalty to friends. They frequently
present demands, even to potential allies, as if bargaining about
them would be immoral. And they often relish rather than regret
their roster of enemies.

Because decision makers in health affairs are sensitive to illness,
they measure the political salience of diseases, how voters feel
about them, and their incidence and prevalence. The politics of
AIDS, cancer and Alzheimer's disease are very different from those
of, for instance, diabetes, heart disease and arthritis. In the last two
decades, to take an example, the political salience of chronic disease has caught up to its prevalence. As a result, decision makers
have begun to change how they allocate resources for treatment
among professional groups and institutions.

Health policy is a result of negotiations among people who continually assess ideas, interests and illness. Negotiations are usually
about particular proposals for legislation or regulation. What is
written for and said during negotiations is mainly about ideas
(notably about the role of government and the power of medical
science), interests (who wants what and who supports them
among voters and political contributors) and illness (what afflicts
individuals, distresses families, and burdens populations).

Consensus

In the mid-1970s, most people who studied health affairs believed
that interests were more important than ideas and illness.
Colleagues in both the United Kingdom and the United States

explained most events in health policy by referring to evidence about the behaviour of parties and pressure groups. According to the standard interpretation, for example, the National Health Service (NHS) was created by the Labour Party, defying the British Medical Association (BMA), in order to serve the interests of its core constituents. The United States, in contrast, had not achieved national health insurance because opponents among medical associations and private employers had been more effective than the proponents of reform in labour unions and organisations that advocated for the poor and minority groups.

In 1980-1, I sought Rudolf's help when I began work for a book explaining why the influence of interest groups on health policy had been so different in the two countries. I had just completed nine years of intense political work. The idea that created my job was that establishing a public academic health centre (a new teaching hospital and degree programs in 16 health professions) would lead to more accessible and appropriate health services and eventually to better health status for two and a half million people living on eastern Long Island in New York State.

Many interest groups negotiated over the creation of the new health centre. These groups included academic and community doctors; officials in the federal government; officials of New York State and two of its counties; the real estate, banking and construction industries; labour unions representing the building trades and public employees; retail businesses; and people who aspired to jobs at what would become the second-largest employer (behind the defence industry) in our region. Moreover, my colleagues routinely assessed data about the incidence and prevalence of disease in our metropolitan statistical area, noting especially the increase of chronic disorders in an ageing population.

When I discussed my research with Rudolf in the fall of 1980, I was not taking this experience seriously enough. Political behaviour still seemed mainly the result of economic competition among interest groups. The political salience of ideas and the burden of illness appeared to be too obvious to require analysis. Everyone who mattered in health politics in every industrial country agreed that biomedical science was advancing inexorably and was applied most effectively by professionals who were arrayed in hierarchies of technical sophistication. These hierarchies had laboratories and teaching hospitals at the top and community medical and public health practices at the bottom. Differences among countries in policy for financing health services was a result of differences in interests that were grounded in ideology and political culture.

Similarly, everyone who mattered in politics agreed that the burden of the diseases that were the leading causes of death could and should be reduced. The major targets of policy were heart disease, cancer and stroke. Bargaining among interest groups was determining what resources were allocated to whom in order to prevent and treat these diseases. Rudolf lent me a large envelope of photocopied documents about the formation of the NHS that he had selected at the National Record Office. Because of the rule prohibiting access to official documents for 30 years, the records of the run-up to the NHS in the Ministry of Health and the cabinet had only recently become available. Rudolf had gathered these documents as sources for the early chapters of what became the first edition of *The Politics of the National Health Service* (Klein 1983).

In Rudolf's reading of these documents, two ideas – equity and administrative rationality – had been of greatest importance to the people who planned the NHS during World War II and enacted it in 1946. Consensus about these ideas made the NHS feasible and set the terms on which it would be organised and financed. Equity, translated into policy by negotiations among ministers, civil servants and leaders of the BMA and the royal colleges, meant that the NHS would be accessible to everyone in the country. As a result, the principle that patients would not be charged at the time they received service was not controversial.

Administrative rationality was Rudolf's phrase for the desire of managers to impose efficient schemes of organisation on hospital care and medical practice. Such rationality prevailed in the creation of the hospital service and arrangements for consultants' practices but could only be negotiated to an unstable compromise for general practitioners.

In the Public Record Office, I found additional evidence about the centrality of ideas about equity and administrative rationality in the early politics of the NHS. These documents revealed that the planners of the NHS assumed that medical scientists knew how to discover the causes and cures of disease; how to transform these discoveries into effective methods of treatment; and then how to disseminate knowledge about proper treatment down hierarchies from laboratories to teaching hospitals, to district hospitals and consulting practices, and then to general practitioners and workers in public health agencies.

After pursuing this finding backward in time to the beginning of the twentieth century in documents from both the United Kingdom and the United States, I called it hierarchical regionalism and elaborated it in talks, articles and books (Fox 1986; 1987). Rudolf, as usual, made a better phrase. He called my thesis a 'technological imperative' and placed it slightly below equity and administrative rationality in his explanation of the ideas that mattered in the origins of the NHS.

The fundamental health policies of industrial countries, their decisions about priorities in expenditure, resembled each other because this technological imperative easily crossed national boundaries. From the 1890s to the 1950s, health policy in Europe and North America had been driven by the assumption that progress in understanding and treating infections and injuries would be continuous and would soon lead to better knowledge about how to control degenerative diseases. Decision makers in most industrial countries gave priority in spending for health to building, equipping and staffing acute care hospitals and training medical specialists. Many countries made subsidy for biomedical research a related priority.

Obviously, policies differed in important ways among countries. Each country had a different history, demography and political culture. Nevertheless, ideas that seemed to be self-evidently correct became the basis of different national policies.

Negotiating

Negotiations are the process by which ideas, interests and perceptions of illness become policy. Official records almost always understate what occurred in negotiations. These records rarely record the analysis and private conversations that precede and follow formal negotiating sessions. Moreover, because many people who study health policy and politics have little experience and hardly any appreciation of what people in public life do all day, they rarely try to imagine why participants in particular instances of negotiation behaved as they did. Those who do write about negotiations invite reviewers to condemn their 'long dreary stretches of prose.'

Most of the work of negotiation is anticipatory. People who make policy agonise about what positions will be acceptable to whom. They craft, debate and revise arguments. They script and rehearse the public events of negotiations: meetings, hearings, telephone calls, committee votes. Anyone who has experienced both a day of doing research and a day of negotiating can compare the physical and emotional differences between these two kinds of work.

By the early 1980s there was considerable evidence of erosion in the consensus about ideas that had sustained policy in the United Kingdom and the United States. Since the 1970s, a growing number of influential critics had been complaining that advances in biomedical science did not produce more effective measures of prevention and treatment, especially for chronic degenerative diseases. Then AIDS raised new questions about the effectiveness of measures against infection. Much was said and written about the limits of medicine, the necessity of rationing and alternatives to expensive care in hospitals.

By the late 1980s advocates for reforming health policy had influenced some decision makers in both the United Kingdom and the United States. The conditions that irritated these reformers had existed for decades. In both countries, for example, there was a long history of complaints about the need to contain the costs of acute services in order to increase spending for primary and long-term care. In both, purchasers of services and an increasing number of consumers resented the power, often arbitrary and self-serving, deployed by doctors. In both, some people were offended while others were pleased because the health sector did not behave like most other industries in a market economy.

These irritations became compelling justifications for reform when people who held powerful positions ceased to regard them as problems that were acceptable within a consensus about ideas. Major innovations in policy became a possibility when decision makers began to doubt that better health was a result of the application of medical science down a well-ordered hierarchy of institutions that were properly dominated by professionals who usually acted in the best interests of their patients.

Negotiating Policy in the United States, 1993-4

Shortly after he was inaugurated, President Clinton appointed his wife to lead a task force of cabinet members and senior White House staff to devise reform in health policy. The task force then recruited about 500 experts, mainly from universities and the middle grades of the federal civil service, to assess alternatives and recommend reform. For the next several months, most journalists on the health beat and people who study health policy focused their attention on the work of the task force and its staff.

Meanwhile, the people who had been negotiating about health policy until February 1993 waited and fumed (or pretended to fume in order to dramatise their frustration). These people included senior members of Congress, both Republicans and Democrats and their staffs; executives of the dozen largest insurance companies; the managers who purchase health care for employees of multistage corporations; members of the governing boards of the largest associations of doctors; executives of companies; a few non-profit organisations that sell managed health services, hospital care and prescription drugs; and governors and legislative leaders from states with expensive and relatively generous Medicaid programs.

The only organisation of consumers that had been prominent in negotiations during the 1980s and early 1990s was the American Association of Retired Persons (AARP), which has more than 30 million members. The AARP's major issue in 1993 and 1994 was defensive: preventing reductions in social insurance for the elderly. Nevertheless, the AARP's leaders also waited and fumed.

The people who had been negotiating about health policy before the Clinton Administration had different priorities than the members of the task force and their staff of experts. Leaders of business, politics and medical care assumed that most voters wanted no noticeable changes in the four funding streams that financed health care: social insurance (for the elderly and disabled), tax expenditures (mainly tax receipts foregone as a result of health insurance purchased by employers), direct taxes (federal, state and local support for Medicaid and care for the indigent) and direct ('out of pocket') consumer spending.

Along with stable costs, most voters wanted the security that they could purchase, transfer and maintain their health insurance.

Employers wanted workers to have such security, but they also wanted to be reasonably certain that every dollar they removed from their health care budgets by efficient management would go directly to the bottom lines of their balance sheets. Thus, they wanted to avoid cross-subsidising the health care costs of both people without jobs and workers whose employers did not offer insurance plans.

The states and providers also had high stakes in seeing that the four funding streams were preserved. Officials of state government wanted protection against budget, and therefore tax, increases as a result of new mandates from Washington. They were dismayed by the increasing and unpredictable costs of emergency care for recent immigrants and other persons who, for a variety of reasons, lacked public or private health insurance. Providers of care wanted higher or at worst stable income and profits at the expense of their less adaptable competitors or, failing that, of employers, government, and consumers.

The negotiations between these interest groups were about ideas and illness, though these words are rarely used in political work. Purchasers of care had some years earlier ceased to assume that health services were self-evidently effective technologies that were properly applied under the direction of the medical profession. The largest purchasers and institutional providers of care understood, for example, that if patients and their families felt secure about choosing their doctors and retaining their insurance, they could reduce many costs without doing serious damage to anybody's health. Increasingly, they agreed – and many health professionals shared their views – that the major task of health services was the prevention and management of chronic disease. Moreover, most purchasers and large providers agreed that managing care by fixed, capitated payments was a more effective way to prevent, postpone, and treat chronic illness than negotiating fees for units of service.

The most important ideas in the politics of health reform in 1993 and 1994 concerned the living American constitution. Most of the leaders of interest groups in business and health abhorred government that they could not control. In practice, this abhorrence became opposition to the federal government taxing health insurance premiums, setting standards for coverage and the quality of care, monitoring health care budgets in states or regions and, worst of all, setting prices for goods and services.

For most of the twentieth century, leaders of business, health care organisations and the professions had preferred state to federal policy. Influencing governors and state legislators was cheaper and had more certain results than lobbying the United States Congress and the federal executive. In health affairs, this situation was reversed during the 1980s. Multistate business corporations and providers of health services, labour unions and medical associations now focused on frustrating health reform in the states as well as on making or preventing national policy.

This reversal occurred because of changes in state politics. Health care became a major expenditure of state government in the 1980s, interfering with allocations for economic development, roads and bridges, prisons and corrections, and education. The formal constitutions of all but one of the states require balanced annual budgets, which in practice means that deficit spending is achievable only by borrowing for capital projects, making hopeful assumptions about the earnings of public employees' pension funds, and rolling expenses from one fiscal year to the next.

By the early 1990s, it had become good politics in about half the states for legislators and governors to advocate a variety of policies that acquired the label 'health reform.' By 1993, eight states required large corporations and labour unions to join property and sales taxpayers in subsidising care for the poor and had adopted techniques to limit the overall costs of health care (Fox and Iglehart 1994). More than a dozen other states were improving consumers' security in the coverage, continuity and portability of their health insurance (Nelson 1994).

Leaders of business, labour and provider organisations complained about a centralised, overbearing federal government while simultaneously using their influence in Washington to thwart health reform in the states. Congress, the executive branch and the federal courts tried to prevent or limit state reform at the urging of interest groups whose spokespersons claimed to be implacable enemies of centralised government.

The Clinton Administration and its major allies, who were mainly to the left of the political centre, misread the politics of the living constitution. The Administration proposed reforms that lobbyists for interests groups opposing them could easily disparage as complicated, centralised and expensive. Although the Administration insisted that these attacks served special interests, it was also principled. Many people who spoke for employer and provider groups passionately dislike and distrust government. That is why, as practical people, they seek to control it.

Many voters share this principled distrust of government, as the results of the congressional and state elections of 1994 demonstrated. In contrast, many intellectuals like to say that the problems for which health reform is the solution create unnecessary costs. They describe their favourite solutions to the problems of access, coverage and costs as technical rather than ideological fixes, solutions that, they claim, are compatible with a variety of partisan views. But the public and the people who are surviving in electoral politics know better. The day after the 1994 elections, the incoming chairman of the Committee on Ways and Means of the House of Representatives told the *Wall Street Journal* that universal coverage for health care was a euphemism for socialised medicine. Representative Archer understood the hidden message in the liberals' insistence that universal coverage is a technical fix that offers security at a price that can be spread equitably among consumers and their employers. According to this message, an American version of the welfare state is desirable because government is potentially benign.

This optimism about a benign state, not the concept of universal coverage for health care, offended the majority of voters and their representatives. Americans accept a great deal of state authority in domestic affairs. For example, they have repeatedly endorsed universal elementary and secondary education and mandatory automobile insurance. Most Americans have a more limited view of the role of the state than do people in Canada or Europe. But very few of them regard the state as merely another interest group. And even fewer have so far agreed with the libertarians of the right that the state is a 'criminal band.'

Because the rules of politics change slowly when they change at all, Americans who seek reform in the way health services are distributed, organised and financed must participate in ceaseless negotiations. Spectators may debate the merits of incrementalism; players know that maintaining or making modest changes in the status quo are the only alternatives to it.

Health reform has been occurring for some years in ways that are politically acceptable. Almost half the insured population of working age is now covered by managed care plans. Most of the states are reorganising their Medicaid programs using capitated managed care in the private sector as their model. Consolidation and elimination ('downswing') has been accelerating in the hospital industry.

Policy intellectuals and advocates for more thoroughgoing reform frequently describe many problems that these changes in policy cannot solve. But these changes are the results of intense negotiations that have powerful effects on a seventh of the American economy and about a tenth of its workforce. The persons who are negotiating know the limits of what they can achieve. They also know that they are working at the only health politics America has.

An essayist who seeks to honour Rudolf Klein must be extraordinarily sensitive to the limits of an argument. The foregoing analysis may be an example of what Rudolf recently called 'ethnocentric overexplanation' (Klein 1993). That is, it may unjustifiably generalise from events in a single country. The analysis certainly reifies the concept of negotiations, doing with it what I have previously criticised in scholarship about policy that emphasises the state, society, and class rather than issues of central concern to decision makers.

Bagehot, the columnist for *The Economist*, recently recalled an aphorism attributed to Aneurin Bevan: 'Why gaze at the crystal ball when you can read the book?' (Bagehot 1994). There are, however, very few books in which people who make decisions about health policy can recognise themselves. The best informed analysts of policy and politics talk or write in unpublished prose. Moreover, the conventions of the negotiators' craft require them to write for publication as if they are gazing at the crystal ball. We need more published writing that, like Rudolf Klein's, aspires to the critical acceptance by people for whom politics is a vocation.

References

Bagehot (pseudonym). 1994. From Villain to Martyr. *The Economist* 333 (November 5): 60.

Evans, P. B., D. Rueschemeyer, and T. Skocpol. 1993. *Bringing the State Back In*. New York: Cambridge University Press.

Fox, D. M. [1993] 1995. *Power and Illness: The Failure and Future of American Health Policy*. Berkeley: University of California Press.

————. [1986] 1989. The National Health Service and the Second World War: The Elaboration of Consensus. In *War and Social Change: British Society in the Second World War,* ed. H. Smith, 32-57. Manchester: Manchester University Press.

————. 1986. *Health Policies, Health Politics: The British and American Experience, 1911–1965.* Princeton: Princeton University Press.

————, P. Day, and R. E. Klein. 1988. The Power of Professionalism: Policies for AIDS in Britain, Sweden and the United States. *Daedalus* 118: 93-112.

———— and J. Iglehart, eds. 1994. *Five States That Could Not Wait.* Cambridge, MA: Blackwell Publishers.

Klein, R. E. [1983, 1989] 1995. *The Politics of the National Health Service.* London: Longman.

————. 1993. National Variations on International Trends. In *The Changing Medical Profession: An International Perspective,* eds. F. W. Hafferty and J. B. McKinlay, 202-9. New York: Oxford University Press.

Nelson, H. 1994. *Federalism in Health Reform: Views from the States That Could Not Wait.* New York: Milbank Memorial Fund.

8

The Accretion of History: What Is the British Prime Minister For?

Peter Hennessy

In 1990s Britain we live in the age of management. Management means targets. Targets mean performance indicators. Each level of activity has to agree with the action plans of the tier above. Salary and status depend upon it as do, in the scholarly business, the financial resources required to lubricate the life of the mind. Neither the public nor the private sectors are immune from the new managerialism and the acronymia that accompanies such new-born life like so much nappy rash. The first question to be asked about this latest form of displacement activity by those in positions of responsibility – who have not the faintest idea what to do about the really fundamental factors affecting our relative national economic decline – is not 'when will it end?' but 'where does it end?' The answer, conveniently enough, brings me to the little patch of British turf in London SW1 that is the subject of this chapter: No. 10 Downing Street, home to both the prime minister (PM) and the Cabinet Room.

Shortly after he won the 1992 general election, John Major received a suggestion from his Policy Unit, one of the power-houses behind the Citizens' Charter where PIs (performance indi-

Author's Note: This chapter is based upon the IHR lecture delivered to the Friends of the IHR at the Institute of Historical Research, University of London, on 7 July 1994.

cators to you and me) are all. How about performance-related pay for the cabinet? This was an idea that did not fly. 'The suggestion was meant to be a joke,' a managerially-minded cabinet minister told me later (Anonymous 1993). It struck me as quite the reverse when a well-placed senior civil servant first divulged the idea to me at a private occasion (Anonymous 1994).

So, now we know. The new public management is stopped, like any unwelcome intruder, by the policeman outside the front door of No. 10. Both the Cabinet Room and the prime minister's study (though this one, unlike his immediate predecessor, prefers to work beneath Walpole's portrait in the Cabinet Room rather than upstairs) are PI-free zones. We should not be surprised. 'Institutionalised hypocrisy' is a good description of high politics. It ranks with David Marquand's 'the mobilisation of prejudice' (Marquand 1994) as the job description of the politician competing for power.

'Job description.' Now there's a phrase we must linger upon. If a proper defence had been mounted of the PM's decision to ignore his Policy Unit's proposal about cabinet remuneration (and I have no indication that such an operation took place), it's to here that the case for the defence could turn for assistance. Because you cannot have PIs in the absence of a proper job description. And the British head of government, like the British head of state across St James's Park, is palpably lacking in this department. The little boy's question to his father about Queen Victoria – 'Daddy, what is that lady for?'[1] – is as applicable to Her Majesty the Queen as it is to her First Minister, and always has been.

I am something of a follower of Walter Bagehot. For the purposes of this chapter, like Walter, I shall take the line that we must not let in too much 'daylight upon magic.' So I'll confine my attentions to the Whitehall end of the park and the figure of John Major, himself something of a stranger to matters magical it has to be said.

Yet any scholarly attempt to replicate Private Eye's wicked little series on 'The 101 Uses for a John Major' (ironing board, poopa-scoopa, that sort of thing) (*Private Eye* 1994) does involve elements of a magical mystery tour because it requires an expedition into that strange unmapped terrain known, with enduring imprecision, as 'the British constitution.' And, as this particular province of that mist-laden land is almost entirely free of statutory signposting, we need the theodolites that only the passion and of the historical profession can provide. Of all our post-war premiers, Harold Wilson understood this best (or at least articulated it most plainly) when in the months after he left No. 10 for the last time he described his recently relinquished job as 'a calling that must be one of the most exciting and certainly one of the best organised – organised by history – in the democratic world' (Wilson 1976). Professor Anthony King put it another way. 'The person,' he said, 'who walks for the first time through the door of No. 10 as prime minister does not create or re-create the prime ministership: the job, to a considerable extent, already exists' (King 1991).

What I would like to do in this chapter is to trace the various job descriptions of the British premiership from the mid-nineteenth century through to the late twentieth century, finishing up with my own version just in case a personable 41-year-old with a constituency in County Durham should find himself in need of it in the next couple of years or so and as an offering to Mr Major in case, belatedly, he should wish to bring himself within the scope of the Citizens' Charter (UK Parliament 1991) and present himself for that most highly prized of baubles, the 'Chartermark.'

The place to begin is with the creator of the modern premiership, the man on whom Mr Gladstone based his notions of how the job should be done – Sir Robert Peel. (Gladstone described Peel's ministry of 1841-46 as a 'perfectly organised administration' [1879]). Peel, like his protégé, a glutton for work, gave Gladstone a breakdown of the job just before vacating it in 1846:

> There is the whole correspondence with the Queen, several times a day, and all requiring to be in my own hand, and to be carefully done; the whole correspondence with peers and members of parliament, in my own hand, as well as other persons of consequence; the sitting seven or eight hours a day to listen to the House of Commons. Then I must, of course, have my mind in the principal subjects connected with the various departments. . .and all the reading connected with them. . . .
> Then there is the difficulty that you have in conducting such questions on account of your colleague whom they concern. (Morley 1903)

Mr Gladstone knew that 'learning from Nellie,' to use a vulgarism from a later age, was hugely important for a post that not only was bereft of a job description but remained without mention on an official piece of paper until 1878 when Disraeli signed the treaty emerging from the Congress of Berlin as 'First Lord of Her Majesty's Treasury, Prime Minister of England' (Low 1904) or, if you will only accept a wholly British document, until December 1905 when a royal proclamation awarded 'the Prime Minister' a place in the order of precedence on state occasions one behind the Archbishop of York (Wilson 1976). So, depending upon one's degree of pedantry, either Disraeli or Sir Henry Campbell-Bannerman wins the palm as the first officially recognised British prime minister. Not until 1917 with the Chequers Estates Act did the office find itself noticed by statute (Wilson 1976).

Gladstone, writing around the time Disraeli presumed to flaunt the title in the service of his country abroad, declared that 'Nowhere in the wide world does so great a substance cost so small a shadow; nowhere is there a man who has so much power with so little to show for it in the way of formal title or prerogative' (Gladstone 1879). Peel, in fact, had elaborated a little on the functions of the prime minister four years after briefing Gladstone on its intricacies. In 1850 he told a House of Commons Select Committee on Official Salaries:

> You must presume that he [the PM] reads every important despatch from every Foreign Court. He cannot consult with the Secretary of State for Foreign Affairs and exercise the influence which he ought to have with respect to foreign affairs, unless he be master of everything of importance passing in that department. It is the same with respect to other departments; India, for instance; how can the Prime Minister be able to judge of the course of policy with regard to India, unless he be cognisant of all the current important correspondence? In the case of Ireland and the Home Department it is the same. Then the Prime Minister has the patronage of the Crown to exercise. . .he has to make inquiries into the qualifications of persons who are candidates; he has to conduct the whole of the communications with the Sovereign; he has to write probably with his own hand, the letters in reply to all persons of station who address themselves to him; he has to receive deputations on public business; during the sitting of parliament he is expected to attend six or seven hours a day. . .for five or six days a week; at least he is blamed if he is absent. (UK Parliament 1850)

Bagehot, as astute as ever, culled from Peel's testimony some important lessons about the condition of the mid-Victorian premiership. 'The necessary effect of all this labour,' Bagehot wrote in 1856 in his celebrated essay on 'The Character of Sir Robert Peel,'

> is that those subject to it have no opinions. It requires a great deal of time to have opinions. . . .That leisure which the poets say is necessary to be good, or to be wise, is needful for the humbler task of allowing respectable maxims to take root respectably. . . .Our system, indeed, seems expressly provided to make it unlikely. The most benumbing thing to the intellect is routine. You see this in the description just given which is not exhaustive. Sir Robert Peel once asked to have a number of questions carefully written down which they asked him one day in succession in the House of Commons. They seemed a list of everything that could occur in the British Empire, or to the brain of a member of Parliament. A premier's whole life is a series of such transitions. It is rather wonderful that our public men have any minds left. (Bagehot 1856)

Bagehot was describing what political scientists more than a century later depicted as 'overload.' Peel himself had had a good stab at this when he said in 1845, 'I defy the minister of this country to perform properly the duties of his office. . . .The worst of it is that the really important duties to the country – those out of the House of Commons – are apt to be neglected' (King 1975; Low 1904). Bagehot for his part was strong on both the causes and the consequences of tired minds trying to do too much. In another essay on 'The Premiership' in 1875, two years before he died, he attempted to capture the further increase in workload over the quarter of a century since Peel had outlined the problem before the Commons Select Committee and had urged them to 'ascertain the progressive increase of business in each department' caused in part by the advent of 'the penny post' (UK Parliament 1850).

In doing so, Bagehot also drew up a useful job description for the premiership that led him to doubt 'how long Mr Disraeli's frame can stand such fatigues as these' (Bagehot 1875). For Bagehot detected

> a process which has gone on augmenting from 1850 till now, till it must make the miscellaneous work of a Prime Minister most teasing and vexing. And independently of that, and considering only the principal points, if we consider what it must be to lead the House of Commons to consult with, and often control, colleagues; to be chairman of the Cabinet; to compose the quarrels

of the Cabinet; to write to the Queen [this is the era before Cabinet minutes were taken] in the careful, delicate way neces- sary in dealing with a superior; to dispense the most critical patronage; to form some kind of idea of the legislative plans proposed and contemplated – we shall wonder how any man can be equal to so much. (Bagehot 1875)

That, by my calculation, is seven chief functions of the premier circa 1875. But Bagehot, in that uncanny way of his, goes on to pre- echo the findings of both the Haldane Report of 1918 (UK Ministry of Reconstruction 1918) and Ted Heath's 1970 white paper on *The Reorganisation of Central Government* (UK Parliament 1970) by pointing out the need for a strategic analytical capacity over and above the numbing routine. Even this list, he declares,

is scarcely all, for the Prime Minister is at the head of our busi- ness, and, like every head of business, he ought to have *mind in reserve* [my emphasis]. He must be able to take a fresh view of new contingencies, and keep an animated curiosity as to coming events. If he suffer himself to be involved in minutiae, some great change in the world, some Franco-German war may break out, like a thief in the night, and if he has no *elastic thought* and no *spare energy* [my emphasis again], he may make the worst errors. (Bagehot 1875)

'Mind in reserve,' 'elastic thought,' 'spare energy' – they have a certain salience inside the late twentieth-century 'cabinet circle,' to borrow a phrase of Churchill's (UK Public Records Office 1951), do they not? Bagehot rounded off this prescient passage with one of his most famous bon mots: 'A great Premier must add the vivac- ity of an idle man to the assiduity of a very laborious one' (Bagehot 1875). Not a bad aspiration for an academic, too, come to think of it.

Three years after Bagehot committed these vibrant one-liners to the pages of *The Economist,* Gladstone displayed his thoughts on the nature of premiership in the pages of the *North American Review* as part of a comparison of the British and American ways of government entitled, interestingly enough, 'Kin Beyond Sea' (Gladstone [1878] 1879). Gladstone was a great dissembler on this theme; no advocate he of any prototypical argument about prime ministerial government. For him, it had to be a 'Government of Departments' (Hennessy 1995), and, like several of his successors, he tended to stress how puny were the powers of the monarch's First Minister.

In his Anglo-American comparison he said: 'The head of the British Government is not a Grand Vizier. He has no powers, properly so called over his colleagues: on the rare occasions, when a Cabinet determines its course by the votes of its members, his vote counts as only one of theirs' (Gladstone [1878] 1879).

Immediately, however, he contradicts himself by homing in on the PM's power to hire and fire, a power Enoch Powell a century later likened to those of Henry VIII ('conversation in the Cabinet is a conversation influenced by the knowledge that we all have to hang together. . . . [But] it's like having a debate with Henry VIII in the chair . . . I was conscious that he [Harold Macmillan, PM 1957-63] had the axe down by his chair' [Hennessy and Anstey 1991]). Ministers, Mr Gladstone said plainly, 'are appointed and dismissed by the Sovereign on his advice' (Gladstone 1879). And, if knowledge is the currency of power, Gladstone had the measure of the prime minister's share of that particular treasury too: 'In a perfectly organised administration, such for example as was that of Sir Robert Peel in 1841-6, nothing of great importance is matured, or would even be projected, in any department, without his personal cognisance; and any weighty business would commonly go to him before being submitted to the Cabinet. He reports to the Sovereign its proceedings, and he also has many audiences of the august occupant of the Throne' (Gladstone 1879).

Gladstone takes note, too, of what in today's jargon we would call the premier's 'self-destruct button' but which I, and I suspect he, would prefer be seen as the Sampson-in-the-Temple prerogative: 'As a rule,' he wrote, 'the resignation of the First Minister, as if removing the bond of cohesion in the Cabinet, has the effect of dissolving it' (Gladstone 1879). Neither his contemporaries nor his colleagues were deceived by this Gladstonian camouflage. Morley in his famous 1889 life of Walpole was widely regarded as describing cabinet life under Gladstone rather than the commonly accepted first holder of the office of prime minister. Indeed, he admitted as much to Asquith (Blake 1975; Low 1904; Oxford and Asquith 1926). Morley depicted the prime minister as 'the keystone of the Cabinet arch' and went on to deploy a Latin phrase that has rung down the years ever since: 'Although in Cabinet all its members stand on an equal footing, speak with equal voice, and, on the rare occasions when a division is taken, are counted on the fraternal principle of one man, one vote, yet the head of the Cabinet is primus inter pares, and occupies a position which, so long as it lasts, is one of exceptional and peculiar authority' (Morley 1889). Indeed, Morley continued, 'The flexibility of the Cabinet system allows the Prime Minister in an emergency to take upon himself a power not inferior to that of a dictator, provided always that the House of Commons will stand by him' (Morley 1889).

Add to the late nineteenth-century reality of Cabinet Room life as sketched out by Morley the fact that in 1870 Gladstone ended the practice whereby cabinet members other than the PM could call meetings of what Sidney Low was later to call 'the most power- ful committee in the world' (Low 1904) and you have what I think amounts to the first modern premiership. Peel was the model (Rosebery was right to describe him as 'in name and deed that functionary, so abhorred and repudiated by the Statesmen of the eighteenth century – a Prime Minister' [Rosebery 1899]). But Gladstone turned precedent into procedure, adding an important prerogative to the armoury of premiership – the power to summon or not to summon a meeting of the cabinet. 'Agenda set- ting,' we would call it today (Mackintosh 1968).

A premier's inheritance is most certainly 'organised by history', but as a history maker himself or herself, a new prime minister can add to this particular piece of the national heritage, which grows like coral, or in a possibly apter metaphor, like a stately home that acquires additions and alterations with each succeeding genera- tion as if it were a kind of Hatfield House.

On the subject of Hatfield, we know what the Marquess of Salisbury thought a premier should be thanks to his rather catty remarks about other holders of the office to his nephew A. J. Balfour, himself a future prime minister. Salisbury did not care much for the top job. His heart lay always in the Foreign Office where the cabinet would meet, symbolically enough, when Lord S. held both posts simultaneously. As Balfour put it: 'He knew his capacity as Foreign Secretary; he knew that the country had need of his services, and he gladly gave them. But as Prime Minister he was required also to do other work equally important, but much less congenial; and though he did it, he did not always do it gladly' (Balfour 1930).

It was in a discussion about Disraeli at Hatfield in May 1880 that the Marquess ventured his notions of what premiership should be by using Disraeli as an exemplar of what its holder should not be. 'As a politician,' Lord S. said,

> he was exceedingly short-sighted, though very clear-sighted. He neither could, nor would, look far ahead, or attempt to balance remote possibilities. . . .As the head of a Cabinet his fault was want of firmness. The chiefs of Departments got their own way too much. The Cabinet as a whole got it too little, and this necessarily followed from having at the head of affairs a statesman whose only final political principle was that the Party must on no account be broken up, and who shrank therefore from exercising coercion on any of his subordinates. (Balfour 1930)

Interestingly enough, it was the apparently languid Balfour who not only sharpened up the machinery of government as PM by creating the Committee of Imperial Defence and by putting himself in its chair but also ended the uncertainty about a prime minister's absolute power to hire and fire ministers (Young 1963; Blake 1975). Though it was not until Lloyd George's time that it was finally established that only a PM can ask the sovereign for a dissolution of Parliament (Marshall 1984).

Have you noticed that most of the first-hand sources on what a PM is for have come from holders of the office musing on their predecessors? There is a kind of free masonry or trade unionism about this. Harold Wilson begins his account with the famous quote from Asquith's memoirs that 'The office of the Prime Minister is what its holder chooses and is able to make of it' (Wilson 1976). Asquith in his turn looked at Rosebery (Wilson 1976) and Rosebery looked at Peel (Rosebery 1899). In more recent times, James Callaghan has told me that experience as a junior minister, with occasional cabinet attendance, under Attlee, and full cabinet service under Wilson, helped shape his own Downing Street craft (Hennessy 1989). Of all of them it is Rosebery, though PM only for a very short span a century ago, who set himself most directly to answer the question 'What is a Prime Minister?' (Rosebery 1899).

His answer is worth savouring at length not least for the strange pre-echo of relatively recent events with which he concluded. The title of prime minister, Rosebery declared, 'expresses much to the British mind. To the ordinary apprehension it implies a dictator, the duration of whose power finds its only limit in the House of Commons. So long as he can weather that stormful and deceptive ocean he is elsewhere supreme' (Rosebery 1899). Shades of Morley there (Morley 1889). But, Rosebery continues,

> the reality is very different. The Prime Minister. . .is technically and practically the Chairman of an Executive Committee of the Privy Council, or rather perhaps, of Privy Councillors, the influential foreman of an executive jury. His power is mainly personal, the power of individual influence. That influence, whatever it may be, he has to exert in many directions before he can have his way. He has to deal with the Sovereign, with the Cabinet, with Parliament and with public opinion, all of them potent factors in their various kinds and degrees. (Rosebery 1899)

But Rosebery knew well even in the 1890s where the locus of real constraint lay: 'A machinery liable to so many grains of sand requires obviously all the skill and vigilance of the best conceivable engineer. And yet without the external support of his Cabinet he is disarmed. The resignation of a colleague, however relatively insignificant, is a storm signal' (Rosebery 1899). That is the strange pre-echo of events in Whitehall and Westminster in November 1990, the dramatic change in the weather pattern brought about by Sir Geoffrey Howe's resignation and the political storm that blew Margaret Thatcher out of Downing Street. The crucial moment of that storm was the evening of November 21 when a majority of the cabinet told her she could not go on – the night she unforgettably described as 'treachery with a smile on its face' (British Broadcasting Corporation 1993). In a rather rambling way, she caught this perfectly in a television interview eight months later. 'It was just very strange,' she said. 'Have you seen a situation slip away from you? I'm a politician . . . I can sense it. And when some people whom I expected to be absolutely staunch had very different views, said, 'Look, I will support you, but I don't think that it is a foregone conclusion,' then. . . . No general can fight without a really good army behind' (Bevins 1991).

Eavesdropping on former prime ministers is fascinating and adds to the stock of knowledge. But, in the end, it is infuriatingly imprecise and goes only so far towards the piecing together of that elusive job description for the British premiership. I have something of a taste for the sweet and the sour in scholarly life –

political science plus archive – allowing as accurate a sense of the past as possible to inform the here and now. Cabinet and premiership is an area that cries out for this as the debate, now on its zimmerframe, between the prime ministerial school and the continuing detectors of genuine cabinet government all too often collapses into competitive anecdote at what Anthony King has called 'the level of a bar-room brawl' (King 1975).

My preferred approach not just to this but to British constitutional matters generally has been to raid the files at the Public Record Office to see what the keepers or the guardians of that constitution, in the Cabinet Office, No. 10, and Buckingham Palace thought it was at any given moment as they, the members of the so-called golden triangle are the ones who advise PMs and monarchs what 'it' is when they, the head of government or head of state, are requested to act upon 'it' (Hennessy and Coates 1991; Hennessy 1995). For such research raids, the richest pickings lie in the Cabinet Office's dustbin file (where all the awkward bits are deposited – what to do if the Queen dies [UK Public Record Office 1956-8], how to piece together a cabinet for World War III [UK Public Record Office 1949-51], that kind of thing). It's known as the CAB 21 series.

In CAB 21 we find a paper compiled in the Cabinet Office and the Treasury between 1947 and 1949 that attempts to answer Rosebery's and my question 'What is the British Prime Minister for?' (UK Public Record Office 1947-9). In Mr Attlee's time, according to the collective wisdom of Whitehall and the palace in the era of Edward Bridges, Norman Brook, and 'Tommy' Lascelles, it was something like this (this is my summary not the precise wording of the document):

1. Managing the relationship between the monarch and the government and whole.
2. Hiring and firing ministers.
3. Chairing the cabinet and its most important committees.
4. Arranging other 'cabinet business,' that is, the chairmanships of other committees and their membership and agendas.
5. Overall control of the Civil Service as First Lord of the Treasury.
6. The allocation of functions between departments and their creation and abolition.

7. Relationships with other heads of governments.
8. An especially close involvement in foreign policy and defence matters.
9. Top civil service appointments.
10. Top appointments to many institutions of 'a national character.'
11. 'Certain scholastical and ecclesiastical appointments.'
12. The handling of 'precedent and procedure.'

To those dozen late 1940s junctions I would have added – had I, though less than three months old when the file began to do the rounds in Whitehall in 1947, been invited to help – the following:

1. Special responsibility for the secret services.
2. The making of nuclear weapons policy.
3. Management of relations with opposition leaders.
4. Preparation of the 'War Book.'
5. Responsibility for the overall load on government and Whitehall efficiency generally.
6. Management of the 'special relationship' with the United States as part of that heads-of-government section.
7. Management of changes in the United Kingdom's constitutional relationship with the Empire and/or its former members.

To the best of my knowledge, no modern equivalent of that 1949 document exists in the cabinet secretary's cupboard. If one did, what would it look like? I have had a stab at creating a mock-up. Between Attlee and Major those functions have increased in a fashion that would leave Peel, Gladstone, Lord S., A.J.B., and Asquith (and even L.G.) breathless. Let me put them into bundles.

Constitutional and Procedural

1. Managing the relationship between government and monarch.
2. Managing the relationship between the government and the opposition on a Privy Counsellor basis.
3. Establishing the order of precedence in cabinet.
4. Interpreting and providing content of procedural guidelines both for ministers and civil servants (including the final say on whether or not they should appear before parliamentary committees).

5. Changing civil service recruitment practices.
6. Establishing classification levels and secrecy procedures for official information.
7. Requesting that the sovereign grant a dissolution of Parliament.

Appointments

Note: By 'appointment' I mean the recommendation of an appointment to Her Majesty the Queen in whose name all these things are done.

1. Appointment and dismissal of ministers (final approval of their Parliamentary private secretaries and special advisers).
2. Top appointments to the headships of the intelligence and security services.
3. Top appointments to the Home Civil Service and, in collaboration (with the Foreign Secretary), to the Diplomatic Service as well as (with the Defence Secretary) the Armed Forces.
4. Top ecclesiastical appointments plus a handful of regius professorships and the mastership of Trinity College Cambridge.
5. Top public sector appointments and top appointments to royal commissions and committees of inquiry.
6. The awarding of peerages and honours (except for those in the gift of the sovereign).

Conduct of Cabinet and Parliamentary Business

1. Calling meetings of cabinet and its committees. Fixing their agendas.
2. The calling of 'political cabinets' with no officials present.
3. Deciding issues where cabinet or cabinet committees are unable to agree.
4. Granting ministers permission to miss cabinet meetings or to leave the country.
5. Ultimate responsibility (with the leaders of the houses) for the government's legislative programme and the use of government time in the chambers.

6. Answering questions twice a week (when the House of Commons is sitting) on nearly the whole range of government activities.

Organisational and Efficiency Questions

1. Organisation and staffing of No. 10 and the Cabinet Office.
2. Size of cabinet, workload on ministers, civil service and the overall efficiency of government.
3. The overall efficiency of the secret services, their operations and their oversight.
4. The creation, abolition and merger of government departments and executive agencies.
5. Preparation of the 'War Book.'
6. Contingency planning of the civil side (with the Home Secretary), for example, for industrial action that threatens essential services or for counterterrorism.
7. Overall efficiency of the government's media strategy.

Special Foreign and Defence Functions

1. Relationships with heads of government (e.g., the nuclear and intelligence aspects of the United States/United Kingdom 'special relationship').
2. Representing the United Kingdom at 'summits' of all kinds.
3. With the Defence Secretary, the use of the royal prerogative to deploy Her Majesty's forces in action.
4. With the Foreign Secretary, the use of the royal prerogative to sign or annul treaties, recognise or de-recognise countries.
5. The launching of a UK nuclear strike.

There you have it. The last act a British Prime Minister would take is not a matter for the Cabinet but just for the PM (Hennessy 1989).The Polaris or Trident missile would whoosh out of the Atlantic thanks to a prime ministerial decision made by the PM under the royal prerogative in the name of the Queen. Not a bad list of powers for a politician whose job is mentioned, almost in passing, in but a handful of statutes and who did not exist officially until 1905. Morley was right. Those powers are not inferior, in an emergency, to those of a dictator provided (the nuclear strike apart) that the cabinet first, Parliament second and the electorate (a long way third) can be carried. Modern commentators have echoed Morley on this. Anthony King concluded in 1991 that the British PM 'is probably able to be more powerful inside his or her own government than any head of government anywhere else in the democratic world' (King 1991), while 12 years earlier Tony Benn had declared, 'Britain was now subject to our "Absolute Premiership"' (Benn 1979). Whether this power is sufficiently constrained is a subject for another essay. But one conclusion can be drawn. Placing a set of PIs on those activities and responsibilities truly is beyond the reach of any management consultant. Let's forget about performance-related pay and leave it to the crude accountabilities of party, parliament, and the voters.

And, in the wider scheme of things, there is a need to fill in the black hole at the centre of British government with as much precision and detail as possible if any serious attempt is to be made to understand the methods and the mechanics of policy making at the very top – the apex where politics and administration meet.

In the meantime, I shall send the list to Mr Major and Mr Blair. I'm only here to help, after all.

Notes

1. Possibly apocryphal. But it has acquired the status of legend.

References

Anonymous. 1994. Personal communication to Peter Hennessy. April.
——. 1993. Personal communication to Peter Hennessy. April.
Bagehot, W. [1875] 1974. The Premiership. In *The Collected Works of Walter Bagehot,* vol. 6, ed. Norman St John Stevas, 65-8. London: The Economist.
——. [1856] 1968. The Character of Sir Robert Peel. In *The Collected Works of Walter Bagehot,* vol. 3, ed. Norman St John-Stevas, 256-6. London: The Economist.
Balfour, A. J. 1930. *Chapters of Autobiography.* London: Cassell.

Benn, T. 1979. *The Case for a Constitutional Premiership, Institute for Workers' Control Pamphlet No. 67.* London: Institute for Workers' Control.

Bevins, A. 1991. Decision to Quit Followed Loss of Faith among Friends. *The Independent,* June 29.

Blake, R. 1975. *The Office of Prime Minister.* London and Oxford: British Academy/Oxford University Press.

British Broadcasting Corporation. 1993. The Thatcher Years, Programme I. London.

Gladstone, W. E. 1879. *Gleanings of Past Years,* vol. 1. London: John Murray.

—— 1878. Kin beyond Sea. *North American Review.* September. Reprinted in his *Gleanings of Past Years,* vol. 1 (1879), 203–48. London: John Murray.

Hennessy, P. 1995. *The Hidden Wiring: Unearthing the British Constitution.* London: Cassell.

——. 1994. Searching for the 'Great Ghost': The Palace, the Premiership, the Cabinet and the Constitution in the Post-war Period. Inaugural Lecture as Professor of Contemporary History at Queen Mary and Westfield College, London, February 1. Published in *The Journal of Contemporary History,* summer 1995.

——. 1989. Premiership: 3. Lord Callaghan. London: British Broadcasting Corporation, 1989.

——, and C. Anstey. 1991. Diminished Responsibility: The Essence of Cabinet Government. *Strathclyde Analysis Papers* 2: 1–28.

——, and S. Coates. 1991. The Back of the Envelope: Hung Parliaments, the Queen and the Constitution. *Strathclyde Analysis Papers* 5:18.

King, A. 1991. The British Prime Ministership in the Age of the Career Politician. In *West European Prime Ministers,* ed. G. W. Jones, 25-47. London: Frank Cass.

——, 1975a. Overload: Problems of Governing in the 1970s. *Political Studies* 22(2–3): 164.

——. 1975b. In *The British Prime Minister,* ed. Anthony King, 230-40. London: Macmillan.

Low, S. [1904] 1914. *The Governance of England.* London: Fisher Unwin.

Mackintosh, J. P. 1968. *The British Cabinet.* London: University Paperback.

Marquand, D. 1994. Personal communication to Peter Hennessy. 17 June.

Marshall, G. 1984. *Constitutional Conventions: The Rules and Forms of Political Accountability.* London: Clarendon.

Morley, J. 1903. *The Life of William Ewart Gladstone,* vol. 1. London: Macmillan.

——. 1889. *Walpole.* London: Macmillan.

Oxford and Asquith, Earl of (H. H. Asquith). 1926. *Fifty Years in Parliament,* vol. 2. London: Cassell.

Private Eye. 1994. The 101 Uses for a John Major. May 20.

Rosebery, Lord (A. P. Primrose). 1899. *Sir Robert Peel.* London: Cassell.

UK Ministry of Reconstruction. 1918. Cmnd. 9230. *Report of the Machinery of Government Committee.* London: His Majesty's Stationery Office.

UK Parliament. 1991. Cmnd. 1599. *The Citizen's Charter.* London: Her Majesty's Stationery Office.

———. 1970. Cmnd 4506. *The Reorganisation of Central Government.* London: Her Majesty's Stationery Office.

———. 1850. *Report of the House of Commons Select Committee on Official Salaries.* London: Her Majesty's Stationery Office.

UK Public Record Office. 1956-8. CAB 21/3728, Demise of the Crown. London: Her Majesty's Stationery Office.

———. 1949-51. CAB 21/1647, *Structure of the War Cabinet.* London: His Majesty's Stationery Office.

———. 1947-9. CAB 21/1638, *Function of the Prime Minister and his Staff.* London: His Majesty's Stationery Office.

Wilson, H. 1976. *The Governance of Britain.* London: Weidenfeld and Michael Joseph.

Young, K. 1963. *Arthur James Balfour.* London: Bell.

9

Doctors and Health Policy: The Long Slide from Influence

Richard Smith

I want to begin with the present confusion among doctors in Britain and then try to understand how we came to be here and where we are going. One morning in December 1994 I was on national radio, supporting arguments made in the *British Medical Journal* (BMJ) that secrecy in the National Health Service (NHS) is increasing (Craft, Sheard and Smith 1994). We even talked in the journal of 'Stalinism.' Doctors, managers and other health workers, I argued, fear to say what they really believe both within their trusts and commissioning agencies and in broader public debate. The chief executive of the NHS disagreed, and his main thought was surely that this was doctors fighting a rearguard action and resenting their loss of influence within the NHS. Perhaps he was right: it's so hard to have clear insights into what drives us.

Two days ago, the British Medical Association (BMA) council debated consultants taking sanctions if the NHS executive made moves to introduce locally negotiated pay (Beecham 1994). The consultants' leader argued that this would be the end of the NHS: it would no longer be national but would be reduced to a multitude of small health services, all offering different services and standards. The council supported unanimously the idea of sanctions, but a member of the council with close parliamentary connections warned the doctors that they would be bitterly attacked if they ever invoked the sanctions: they would be accused of acting against the NHS reforms only when their pockets were under threat.

Last week a survey of young British doctors found deep demoralisation: two thirds had contemplated giving up medicine (Allen 1994). In the same week, *The Economist* (1994) said: 'The future of doctors looks bleak. To improve efficiency, health care managers are interfering more in decisions, such as the choice of operations or drugs, that were once the preserve of the medical profession. Much diagnosis and even some surgical procedures are being automated. Although doctors still control these things they may not do so for much longer if cheaper alternatives can be found. And although demand for health care is growing relentlessly, especially in rich countries with ageing populations, a few doctors are beginning to ask themselves whether they will have much of a role in the next century.'

The Economist was writing not just about British doctors but about doctors everywhere. But I hope by gaining an understanding of what has happened to British doctors to throw some light on what has happened to doctors everywhere. The same social, economic and technological forces have led doctors world-wide to feel (probably correctly) that they have less influence on health and health policy than they once had and less control over their own destinies.

The Beginnings of the British Story

An historian of the twenty-second century will no doubt take a different view, but from our vantage point a crucial turning point in the history of the influence of British doctors seems to be the publication of the report of the *NHS Management Inquiry* (Griffiths 1983), chaired by Roy Griffiths, the deputy chairman of Sainsburys, a large grocery chain. But before describing that report I want briefly to take a longer view.

In 1948 doctors supported the principle of the NHS. Indeed, in the 1930s the BMA had proposed a national scheme. Even so, doctors resisted some of the Labour government's proposals for its implementation – essentially those affecting the profession's independence and pay (Webster 1988). But once the NHS arrived, many doctors found themselves in a world that was agreeable to them. Aneurin Bevan, the politician who founded the NHS, may have argued that the NHS was 'pure socialism,' but, says Maurice Shock, it was closer to impure liberalism with its beliefs in minimal government and professional self-regulation (Shock 1994). General practitioners no longer had to take money from their wealthier patients and yet through their independent contractor status had considerable freedom. Consultants may have been salaried, but they had merit awards, access to private practice, and considerable clout within their hospitals.

'Britain's NHS,' writes Rudolf Klein, 'is the child of a marriage of convenience between social engineers and social idealists, between the values of efficiency and equity' (Klein 1984). Medicine was taken out of the market to promote equity, but in the NHS Bevan was also interested in promoting efficiency. Doctors were placed at the heart of the system: it was they who would define need and who got what. Bevan said that the NHS gave 'a greater degree of professional representation than any other scheme I have seen' (*Hansard* 1946). The result, writes Klein, was 'an instrument for the deployment of paternalistic expertise, rather than a system of health care responsive to consumer demands . . . which makes the NHS unique in the Western world' (Klein 1984).

For the first 10 years of its life, the NHS hardly featured in national politics, although as early as 1953 the minister of health set up a committee to inquire into the rising costs of the service (UK Ministry of Health 1956). The report diagnosed some deficiencies – the tripartite structure being one – but suggested no structural changes. Periodic disputes about pay occurred, leading in 1960 to an independent review body for doctors but not for other staff.

The mid-1960s saw a major confrontation between general practitioners and the then Labour government about the deteriorating family doctor service. This became a major political battle and eventually led to radical restructuring of the organisation of practice and a big pay rise that salvaged general practice. In the 1960s and 1970s, a series of disputes affected the health services, mostly over staff conditions and pay but also – in the mid-1970s – over private practice in the NHS. A major structural reorganisation in 1974 intended to close the gaps in the tripartite service worsened rather than improved the bureaucratic tangles. Decision making became slower than ever. This outcome and increasing discontent among nurses and other health service staff prompted Harold Wilson, Labour's prime minister, to set up a royal commission. The commission reported in 1979 just after the Labour government had fallen in part because of protracted pay disputes in the public services, in which health workers were prominent. Meanwhile, the consultants had been having an acrimonious confrontation with the government about private work in the NHS. During this confrontation the rank and file threw out a proposed new contract. Junior doctors were adding to the uproar in the NHS with demands for cuts in their long hours.

Margaret Thatcher's incoming Tory government found a rebellious health service. It also had a royal commission report with a multitude of recommendations that seemed unlikely to cure either the NHS's structural faults or its perceived underfunding although 'it was management of the NHS which emerged as the crucial issue' (Levitt and Wall 1992). The new government's response, in December 1979, was a slim document, *Patients First*, which concentrated on structural change.

Until this point, 30 years after its foundation, the NHS remained 'cocooned' within a political consensus, surprisingly perhaps given its troubles. As Klein aptly put it, the health service 'was a monument to Britain's national public philosophy' (Klein 1984). Up to this point, the doctors had retained substantial clout within the service, especially in the hospitals. Furthermore, successive governments had traditionally consulted closely with them about changes in the service – even if such consultations sometimes became acrimonious.

That was soon to change. Preoccupied perhaps with navel gazing within the NHS, doctors had failed to notice the world changing fundamentally about them and so were quite unprepared for the 'blitzkreig from the right' that eventually hit them at the end of the 1980s (Shock 1994). During the last 20 years, argues Shock, the rights of man have given way to the rights of the consumer, the social contract has given way to the sales contract, and, above all, the electorate has been fed with political promises about rising standards of living and levels of public service (Shock 1994). The appearance of the consumer society, medical advances on an unprecedented scale, and the dramatic increase in the number of the elderly has meant that 'the doctor is different, the patient is different and the medicine is different' (Shock 1994).

The Griffiths Report

Between 1954 and 1972, there were nine reports on management within the NHS (Kember and Macpherson 1994), but they all stayed with the idea that management was a team activity based on the kind of consensus management that meant proceeding with the lowest common denominator – what all the parties could accept. As late as 1979 a consultative paper on the structure and management of the NHS said: 'The government has rejected the proposition that each authority (health district) should appoint a chief executive responsible for all the authority's staff. It believes that such an appointment would not be compatible with the professional independence required by the wide range of staff employed in the service. Instead, each authority should appoint a team to co-ordinate all the health service activities of the district' (UK Department of Health and Social Security 1979). As Day and Klein put it in 1983, 'the NHS is rather like a feudal society in which independent authority is exercised by a number of groups, notably by the medical profession, in a fragmentary system' (Day and Klein 1983).

Doctors did well in this system. 'One of the greatest difficulties in making consensus work was in persuading the doctors on the management team (consultants and general practitioners) to co-operate' (Kember 1994). They were uneasy about speaking for their fiercely independent colleagues and the medical advisory machinery was slow and cumbersome. Doctors preferred to 'pick off' the 'administrators' within individual wards and departments, and often they had little difficulty doing so. They had prestige and clout, whereas many NHS administrators had little training and little respect. High flying managers did not choose to work in the NHS.

Consequently, management in the NHS was poor. Decisions were slow, leadership was lacking, staff motivation was low and patients' services suffered. Anxieties about management within the NHS combined with increasing political unrest about the financing of the service led Prime Minister Margaret Thatcher to ask her private adviser Roy Griffiths to look at the possibility of introducing business principles into the NHS to make it more managerially effective. In a taste of things to come, Griffiths undertook his review with a small team of two businessmen and a former chairman of a regional health authority with a union background. The team included no doctors or NHS managers. In six months – rather longer than was expected – they produced their report.

Their diagnosis was that the NHS was insufficiently customer oriented and focused on process rather than outcome. The service was suffering from 'institutionalised stagnation'; health authorities were 'swamped with directives without being given direction'; and the NHS was an organisation in which it was very difficult to achieve change. The treatment proposed by Griffiths was simple. Every region, district and unit would have a general manager, and they would have a chain of command stretching up to a supervisory board within the Department of Health and Social Security. Some managers were to be brought in from outside the NHS but many would come from within the service. Griffiths was particularly keen that some doctors and nurses would become managers. He later regretted that this had not happened more and that so many managers, with different cultural values, had come in from outside (Griffiths 1991). The managers would have objectives, and their pay would be linked to their performance in meeting those objectives.

The government accepted Griffiths's ideas, and implementation began in 1984. As 'administrators' turned into 'managers' many felt liberated. They could begin to make decisions and act. As they became more confident they were willing to say no to consultants. The intention was not to lead to confrontation between doctors and managers, but inevitably as managers' power increased and consultants' ability to have their own way declined conflicts emerged. Indeed, one of the ideas implicit in general management was to move away from the slow, ineffective consensus management style.

The substantial reforms that came later were probably only possible because of the changes that Griffiths had introduced. Furthermore, the Griffiths changes perhaps led inevitably to the changes that came later. Day and Klein wrote prophetically in

1983: 'In short, if the Griffiths proposals are to succeed in their aims there would have to be more radical changes than implied in the report: the NHS would have to move towards being a system of producer co-operatives, each of which is accountable to management not for the individual clinical encounter between doctors and patient but for their overall performance in terms of producing value for money and services to patients' (Day and Klein 1983).

The changes introduced by Griffiths reflect changes in thinking that were happening around the world and not only in the sphere of health. In particular, politicians were beginning to value increasingly the abilities of managers. They could implement what the politicians wanted, increase value for money, and respond to the needs of customers/clients/patients/voters. Doctors and other professionals could not be relied on to achieve any of these ends: they are less concerned with the objectives of politicians, less easily controlled, have their own agendas and ideas on what constitutes value for money, and still tend to have an old-fashioned paternalistic attitude to customers/clients/patients/voters. The second major world-wide change was the increasing sophistication of patients. The traditional NHS patients' attitude of unquestioning gratitude has changed. Health pressure groups have multiplied, and health and health care have become prominent subjects in the media. Doctors, however, have been slow to adapt.

Build up to the Blitzkreig

The implementation of the Griffiths proposals was one important element that set the scene for the political blitzkreig that followed. A second element was that Thatcher's government won a third term of office and was ready to take on the major professions of medicine and law after taming the unions, local government and groups like the universities and the teachers. The third element was increasing political unrest, driven by the increasing gap between demand for health care and resources to pay for it. This, I believe, is the central question of health care policy. John Kitzhaber, the political force behind the Oregon rationing scheme and now governor of the state, has written: 'The question of what is covered [by health care] is the most difficult, the most controversial, and yet perhaps the most important of the three [fundamental questions of health care reform]. It is the sine qua non of lasting health care reform' (Kitzhaber 1993). Until the question is tackled, which it still has not been in Britain, all reforms are unstable.

The NHS had seen steady real growth during the 1960s, but in the late 1970s the rate of growth began to slow. By the 1980s the government expected growth through efficiency savings. Yet the demands on the health service – driven by increasing patient expectations, technological advances and an ageing population – continued to grow. Hospitals came under enormous pressure, waiting lists lengthened and the media were full of lurid stories of the failures of the NHS. Doctors, their lives made much less comfortable than in the early days of the NHS by increasing managerial power and relatively reduced resources, made a move. The BMA had for years complained about underfunding, but the blitzkreig was launched in response to the presidents of the medical royal colleges, the patrician groups concerned with standards and education rather than politics, saying publicly that the NHS was facing ruin. This, combined with stories of children dying in Birmingham Children's Hospital because of inadequate resources led Mrs Thatcher in 1988 to announce on the television programme *Panorama* a government review of the health service.

The Blitzkreig Begins

Mrs Thatcher's review followed the pattern set by the Griffiths review. It seems to have been announced to the surprise of Mrs Thatcher's ministers and the Department of Health, and it included a handful of people – none of whom knew much about the day-to-day workings of the NHS but all of whom were politically 'one of us.' In particular, there were no doctors, no senior NHS managers and no civil servants from the Department of Health. The work went on in secret for a year, and staff from the Department of Health were asked to comment only occasionally.

The review team considered moving to an insurance-based system like those in Germany and France but quickly abandoned the idea because it would not solve the problem of containing expenditure. The team drew heavily on the ideas of an American health economist, Alain Enthoven. He had visited Britain in 1985 and written a highly influential essay on the NHS (Enthoven 1985). He observed gridlock, perverse incentives whereby those who performed well were penalised by exceeding their budget, too much uniformity, a lack of experimentation, poor medical leadership and ignorance about costs in the NHS. He advocated an 'internal market' whereby district health authorities would be given a weighted sum of money for each resident and then be free to buy services from each other and perhaps from the private sector. This should lead to more thought on what needed to be purchased and greater efficiency as providers competed with each other.

Professor Enthoven's ideas proved to be the heart of the white paper *Working for Patients*, which appeared in 1989 (UK Secretaries of State for Health 1989). Mrs Thatcher wrote in the foreword to the paper: 'We aim to extend patients' choice, to delegate responsibility to where the services are provided and to secure the best value for money . . . the patients needs will always be paramount.' The white paper said that there would be self-governing hospitals (NHS trusts), budgets for some general practitioners to cover activities like purchasing non-urgent hospital services, and that money would follow patients. District health authorities would concentrate on ensuring that the health needs of the population for which they are responsible were met, that there were effective services for the prevention and control of diseases and the promotion of health, that their population had access to a comprehensive range of high-quality, value-for-money services. Each authority had 'to buy the best services it can from its own hospitals, from other authorities' hospitals, from self-governing hospitals and from the private sector.'

These enormous changes were to be introduced in April 1991, and the Department of Health had a huge amount of work to do to put flesh on the bones it had simply delivered. While the civil servants worked on the flesh the politicians began promoting the bones. They used videos and other public relations material and a cascade system through the NHS. Managers were soon attracted by the ideas and the freedom and opportunities they offered. Some doctors also liked the proposals, but most did not. In particular, the BMA decided that it was very much against the changes proposed.

The BMA objected on many grounds. First, it didn't like the way that the proposals had been thrown together by a small highly political group that didn't include any doctor or, indeed, anybody with prolonged experience of working in the NHS. Second, the BMA didn't like the rapid implementation without consultation: this felt like imposition of the changes (true BMA people never talk about the reforms). Third, the proposals didn't address at all what the BMA saw as the fundamental problem – underfunding. Fourth, doctors were worried that Mrs Thatcher's true aim was privatisation of the NHS, and these proposals were just a devious means to that end. Fifth, resources would be wasted in administrative costs that could be better put to patient care. Sixth, the proposals smelled of markets, commerce, written contracts and competition, all of them inimical to doctors but familiar to managers. Seventh, patient choice, the BMA believed, would be limited rather than increased – patients would have to go to wherever contracts were negotiated; referral anywhere would not be possible. Eighth, the proposals would lead to a two-tier service with some patients – probably those in wealthy areas – receiving much better services than others. Ninth, a market meant losers and winners, which eventually would lead to some local hospitals closing and patients (and doctors) being displaced.

In addition, the association had many questions: What would happen to expensive, superspecialist services? What would happen to research and education? Who would guarantee quality? Wouldn't cost cutting rather than the pursuit of quality become the order of the day? Wouldn't 'profitable' services drive out less profitable ones, meaning that commercial considerations would override clinical ones? Wouldn't the continuity of services – so important for patients with chronic conditions – be destroyed? Would doctors who were 'purchasers' be set against doctors who were 'providers'?

The more that the BMA thought about the reforms the more it decided that it didn't like them, and increasing pressure came from members to stop them. The chances of the association influencing the government behind closed doors in the time-honoured fashion seemed minimal because Mrs Thatcher's government had a large majority and a radical antiprofessional mission. Consequently, the association thought that it would have to convince the government of the error of its ways by convincing the public first. An expensive campaign against the reforms was mounted. It enjoyed great success in achieving a high profile and irritating ministers but failed to stop the reforms because the government's large majority ensured the health bill's steady passage through Parliament. As Day and Klein have put it, through 'its billboard advertising campaign, the profession had simply advertised its own impotence: its failure to block, or even significantly dent, government policies' (Day and Klein 1991).

Blitzkreig: The Second Front

General practice is in many ways the strongest part of Britain's NHS. Its strength allows the NHS to spend a much smaller proportion of its gross domestic product per head on health care and yet achieve results comparable with countries that spend more. Care in general practice is cost effective and good for patients, who in the best practices get true, whole patient care. But pressure for reform of general practice began to build up during the 1980s, driven by four main factors (Day and Klein 1991): the government wanting to encourage general practitioners to undertake more preventive work; the Treasury wanting to move away from demand-driven spending that was not cash limited; some leaders of the profession, particularly within the Royal College of General Practitioners, wanting to do something about the poor quality of many general practices, especially within the inner cities; and the government wanting to have greater managerial control over general practitioners.

Negotiations over a new government-initiated contract began in the 1980s, with ministers wanting to increase the proportion of the general practitioners' income that came from the capitation fee (the amount paid for having a patient on the list), to introduce an award for good practices, and to give incentive payments for achieving high levels of immunisation and other preventive activities like cervical screening and screening of the elderly. Prolonged negotiations were proceeding (and not going well) when *Working for Patients* was published and relations between the profession and the government began to turn even more sour. A package was agreed upon between the government and the leaders of general practice but then thrown out by the rank and file. The government simply went ahead – and for the first time in the history of the NHS – imposed the new contract.

Life after the Blitzkreig

'A blitzkreig can certainly achieve conquest but it cannot ensure effective occupation,' Maurice Shock told British doctors at a summit meeting of the leaders of the profession held in 1994 (Shock 1994). The government needs the co-operation of doctors and other health professionals. Once the NHS changes were made law and implemented, British doctors found themselves divided. Some, particularly fund-holding general practitioners, saw great opportunities and seized them; others wanted to do what they could to sabotage the changes; and the majority decided that they must go along with the law of the land. John Marks, the BMA leader who had led the fight against the blitzkreig, was followed by Jeremy Lee-Potter, who proposed a more moderate line – working with the government and being constructively critical.

Despite this initial stance, doctors have slowly but surely become more hostile to the reforms, insisting that the criticisms that they made at the beginning are coming true. They especially dislike what they see as a two-tier service where patients are treated not by clinical need but according to whether their fund holding general practitioner has a contract and money left. The doctors dislike managers giving priority to people who have been on the waiting list for a long time (for political reasons) when many of those who have not been on the list so long have more severe conditions. The doctors also resent what they see as continuing underfunding and the wastage of resources on administrators/managers, a group who have grown fast since the reforms were implemented. Relationships between doctors and managers, although good in some places, do not seem to be improving and may well be becoming worse.

The moderate Dr Lee-Potter was ousted, and his place has been taken by Dr Sandy Macara, who was presented by the press as a 'hard man.' Dr Macara is by instinct a moderate, but his troops, particularly the hospital troops, are growing steadily more restless. The announcement of the intention to take sanctions if locally negotiated pay is imposed, which is where I began this chapter, may presage severe confrontation.

Doctors Try to Take Charge of the Future

Doctors realise that they have been reacting to the agenda of others rather than setting the agenda, and at least two attempts have been made to 'get out in front.' Dr Lee-Potter led the first and set up a group to consider health and health care in the next century. The first step was to consider what the key issues were likely to be and to attempt to frame the right questions. The result was a document, *Leading for Health,* that was generally well received (British Medical Association 1991). Klein praised the document and said that its great merit was 'that it not only sets out a comprehensive agenda but offers a warning against the dangers of precipitate oversimplification' (Klein 1991). Unfortunately, the questions raised by the document were not followed through.

The second attempt to set the agenda was prompted by the chief medical officer, who attended the council of the BMA (where he received a polite but sceptical reception) and suggested that doctors should try and define the core values of medicine (Beecham 1994). What is it that doctors offer that nobody else can offer? (The question might be cynically posed as 'What is it doctors do that others can't do that justifies them being paid more?'). Dr Calman wanted the profession to have a clear idea of the future and offer leadership. He also wanted the various institutions of doctors to come together, recognising from inside government that their divisions led to weakness.

The summit meeting of doctors, the first in 30 years, was held a couple of weeks ago and was described very much as a beginning (Smith 1994). Some have scoffed at mostly elderly doctors wasting their time reflecting on the distant future when the NHS is under such pressure (O'Donnell 1994), but there are signs that the broader profession is ready for such a debate.

Organisation of British Doctors

Before ending, I want to look at how the medical profession organises itself – and so perhaps partly explain its declining influence. The organisation of the British medical profession is similar in principle to the organisation in the United States, Canada, Australia and many other English-speaking countries. The largest organisation of British doctors is the British Medical Association, which is really a trade union for doctors with professional activities (like publishing the BMJ and running a large medical library) bolted on. About three quarters of Britain's doctors belong, from all parts of the profession. The reforms have been good for the BMA in the sense that scared doctors have joined up in large numbers. It is a highly democratic organisation, which is a strength in that it potentially has a good sense of what the scattered profession thinks and a weakness in that its strategic ability is curtailed. The supreme body of the association is the representative body, which meets once a year and brings together doctors from all parts of the country and the profession. Unfortunately, it is not as representative as it might be because many doctors would never contemplate giving up four days of their lives to take part in an often dull debate.

The main foci of activity of the association are in its 'craft' committees, representing general practitioners, senior hospital doctors, junior hospital doctors, public and community health doctors and medical academics. The allegiance of many active members of the association is first to the craft committee and only secondarily to the broader association. It is the job of the council and its chairman to keep the broader association together and stop it flying apart into its federal factions. Sometimes this can be difficult – the chairman has been compared to a prime minister without whips – but mostly the association manages to stay together, not least because doctors see what has happened to other professional groups, like teachers, who have split into different unions: the government has walked over them.

The strengths of the BMA are its high membership, considerable wealth, skilled staff, and regional structure as well as its professional contribution to national debates on sociomedical issues and its public relations skills. Its weaknesses have been in its limited strategic ability and low reputation among academics, who are in one sense the leaders of the profession. The BMA has always been against the NHS reforms but has varied in the strength of its opposition. Also, some parts of the association, the hospital consultants, have been more strongly against than others, the general practitioners.

The royal colleges are the natural haunt of the academically inclined doctors, and the older colleges have a long history and a high reputation. They are concerned with standards, research and education of graduate doctors but customarily avoid medicopolitics. They provide medical advice to the community – on, for instance, smoking or deprivation and health – and they whisper in the ear of government. Their high reputations and their cleverness are their main assets, and their main weakness is that they keep splitting into smaller and smaller colleges: the Royal College of Physicians, for example, begat the Royal College of Pathologists and the Faculty of Public Health Medicine and eventually the Royal College of Paediatricians. The colleges have linked themselves together in the conference of medical colleges, but this is as yet a talking shop. Other weaknesses of the colleges are their elitism, lack of a strong democratic structure, metropolitan domination, and political naivety.

The 14 colleges and faculties are not of course all the same, but I think that my generalisations have enough validity to be useful. Linked with the colleges are a host of specialist associations, which might be viewed as embryonic colleges: they share many of the same characteristics as the colleges.

The royal colleges have tried to stay on the sidelines in the debate over NHS reform – constitutionally they cannot act as medicopolitical organisations like the BMA – apart from expressing their legitimate concern over the possible effects on standards, education, and research. But many senior members of the colleges are horrified by the reforms, and the colleges are often tempted to express their unhappiness.

The General Medical Council (GMC) is invested by the power of the Medical Act with keeping the register of fully qualified medical practitioners. All doctors who want to practice in Britain must register with the council. The council must assure the adequacy of the training and examinations that lead to doctors being added to the register. It must also have mechanisms for removing those who are wicked, sick, or incompetent. Unfortunately, although dating from the last century, the council does not yet have efficient mechanisms for removing incompetent doctors from the register: it soon should have. The GMC has been much criticised from within and without the profession, and the survival of self-regulation – the contract with society – may well be in the balance. In these circumstances, the GMC has to be very careful about upsetting the government and expressing worries about NHS reforms.

Another important faction of doctors are the chief medical officers and their medically qualified staff – the doctor civil servants. They are the doctors inside government who advise not only the ministers in the departments of health but also all other ministers. Potentially, they could be powerful within government and leaders of doctors. In fact, they live in an uncomfortable hinterland. Doctors regard them as creatures of government and see them very much as 'them' rather than as 'us.' Within government they are 'on tap rather than on top,' and their influence seems to have declined just as the influence of all doctors has. Sir George Godber, who retired in 1973, is regarded as the last chief medical officer in England to have any strong influence. Life is especially difficult for the doctor civil servants when, as now, the profession and the government are disagreeing.

British medicine is thus not short of institutions, but none of them can truly speak for the whole profession. The BMA comes the closest in that it has the highest membership (from all parts of the profession) and the most democratic structure, but its territory is limited, and if the government or others don't like what they hears from the BMA then they can turn to the colleges. The colleges should not really stray onto political territory, but, as in 1988, they sometimes do – often with poor results. All practising doctors must be registered with the GMC, but it is not an effective voice for the profession as, again, its territory is limited and its ultimate loyalty must be to the public not the profession.

When he addressed the first summit meeting of the medical profession in 30 years in 1994, Maurice Shock informed it that doctors' institutions were inadequate for the modern age (Shock 1994). In the 1970s and early 1980s, he told the meeting that something of a vacuum had been left in directing the NHS. 'In the main, doctors had failed to seize, or even to recognise, the opportunity.

That charge of sluggishness must be extended also to include the snail's pace at which the profession was willing to change itself. For many of its members, an appropriate motto might have been, 'The status quo is the way forward.'"

It was recognition within the profession that it had no coherent voice and no effective way to plan strategically that led to the profession calling the summit meeting. There has been talk for many years of the need for an institute or academy of medicine (British Medical Association 1979), but nobody has ever been quite clear how the new organisation would look or how it would be created. The political will to set it up has never been there, and the mutual suspicion among the existing organisations has always been too great. It is perhaps a measure of the profession's anxiety about its future that such an organisation is probably more likely to appear in the next couple of years than at any previous time.

Sir Maurice gave doctors some idea how the organisation might look and how it might be achieved: 'It almost goes without saying that to achieve action on such a scale will require the leading professional bodies to surrender some of their independence to a new representative body which in its turn would be guided by a cabinet, serviced by a small but first rate administration. The remit of this top body should be clearly defined within a federal structure and largely confined to strategic and high political matters. Most of the functions that I shall be mentioning would naturally fall to the constituent parts of the federal framework, but without the top body the profession will be unable to punch its weight.'

Doctors and Leadership

Recently, I lunched with a Cambridge mathematics don turned businessman who had lately had an opportunity to observe the medical profession at close quarters, and he had made some interesting observations: 'Doctors are so keen to be kings that they don't mind how small their kingdom, and they are also inclined to think that they are experts on everything – from architecture to foreign policy.' The fact that doctors world-wide seem to be losing influence is undoubtedly due to external factors like the rise of consumerism and the questioning of professional values, but it is probably also a result of internal factors like those described by the ex-don. In particular, doctors set very high store on individual autonomy and have great difficulty with leadership, strategic thinking, teamwork, and understanding organisational behaviour (Smith 1993). Doctors are suspicious of those who set themselves up as leaders and are inclined to vote in compromise candidates and to create institutions where leaders are very constrained in what they can do. Doctors are also shy about putting themselves forward as leaders. 'Leading doctors is like herding cats,' said Warren Bennis, one of the world's foremost authorities on leadership (Smith 1992).

The Future

Anybody who looks to the future risks being dramatically wrong, but I recently made an attempt – together with Ian Morrison, the president of the Institute for the Future, to envisage the future of medicine (Morrison and Smith 1994). We saw five key driving forces: the power of big ugly buyers; the rise of sophisticated consumers; new technology, particularly molecular biology and information technology; shifts in the boundaries of health and medicine; and questions about the ethics of controlling human biology.

Doctors, we concluded, will be at the centre of the new health system but not as autocrats. Their dominance as caregivers will be eroded by new tools, technology and systems of care. But the profession will have to play a central leadership role in policy making, in planning, and in management as well as in its role as a member of the care teams and integrated delivery systems of the future. If doctors do not take up the challenge of leadership in health care and instead retreat into a selfish artisans' union, they will be letting down the patients and the society they swore to serve.

All I want to add in this more analytical and less exhortatory article is that I hope that doctors can change and achieve these ends – but I'm by no means sure that they can. The history of their influence within the NHS does seem to show that it has fallen steadily, but not all lines that have gone down for 46 years continue to go down.

References

Allen, I. 1994. *Doctors and Their Careers: A New Generation.* London: Policy Studies Institute.

Beecham, L. 1994. Consultants Consider Sanctions over Local Pay. *British Medical Journal* 309: 1600-1.

British Medical Association. 1991. Leading for Health: a BMA Agenda for Health. London.

British Medical Journal. 1979. Does Britain Need an Academy of Medicine? 2:1611.

Craft, N., S. Sheard, and R. Smith. 1994. The Rise of Stalinism in the NHS. *British Medical Journal* 309: 1640-5.

Day, P., and R. Klein. 1983. Two Views on the Griffiths Report. The Mobilisation of Consent versus the Management of Conflict: Decoding the Griffiths Report. *British Medical Journal* 287: 1813-16.

———. 1991. Britain's Health Care Experiment. *Health Affairs* (fall): 39-59.

Economist. 1994. Why Doctors? December 10.

Enthoven, A. C. 1985. Reflections on the Management of the National Health Service. London: Nuffield Provincial Hospitals Trust.

Griffiths, R. 1983. Report of the NHS Management Inquiry. London: Department of Health and Social Security.

———. 1991. Seven Years of Progress - General Management in the NHS. *Lecture to the Audit Commission,* London, June 12.

Hansard (House of Commons) 1946. 30 April, cols 43-63.

Kember, T. 1994. General Management - The Management Inquiry and the Griffiths Report. In *The NHS - a Kaleidoscope of Care - Conflicts of Service and Business Values* by T. Kember and G. Macpherson, 26. London: Nuffield Provincial Hospital Trust.

——— and G. Macpherson. 1994. *The NHS - a Kaleidoscope of Care - Conflicts of Service and Business Values.* London: Nuffield Provincial Hospital Trust.

Kitzhaber, J. 1993. Prioritising Health Services in an Era of Limits: The Oregon Experience. In *Rationing in Action,* 35-48. London: BMJ Publishing Group.

Klein, R. 1984. The Politics of Ideology versus the Reality of Politics: The Case of Britain's National Health Service in the 1980s. *Health and Society* 62: 82-109.

———, 1991. Society, Health, and the NHS. *British Medical Journal* 303: 867-8.

Levitt, W. A. 1992. *The Reorganised National Health Service.* London: Chapman and Hall.

Merrison, H. W. 1979. *Royal Commission on the National Health Service: Report.* London: Her Majesty's Stationery Office.

Morrison, I., and R. Smith. 1994. The Future of Medicine. *British Medical Journal* 309: 1099–1100.

O'Donnell, M. 1994. Doctors' Leaders out of Touch. *Monitor Weekly.* November 30: 40.

Shock, M. 1994. Medicine at the Centre of the Nation's Affairs. *British Medical Journal* 309: 1730–3.

Smith, J. 1994. A Rebuke from the Chief Medical Officer. *British Medical Journal* 308: 1322.

Smith, R. 1992. Leadership and Doctors. *British Medical Journal* 305:137–8.

———. 1993. Doctors and Leadership: Oil and Water? In *Transactions and Report* 1992–3. Liverpool: Liverpool Medical Institution.

———. 1994. Medicine's Core Values. *British Medical Journal* 309: 1247–8.

UK Department of Health and Social Security, Welsh Office. 1979. *Patients First; Consultative Paper on the Structure and Management of the National Health Service in England and Wales.* London: Her Majesty's Stationery Office.

UK Ministry of Health 1956. Cmnd. 663. *Report of the Committee of Enquiry into the Cost of the National Health Service [Guillebaud Report].* London: Her Majesty's Stationery Office.

UK Secretaries of State for Health 1989. *Working for Patients.* London: Her Majesty's Stationery Office.

Webster, C. 1988. *The Health Services since the War.* Volume 1. *Problems of Health Care. The National Health Service before 1957.* London: Her Majesty's Stationery Office.

10

Reconciling the Demand and Provision of Health Services

David Mechanic

Changes in patterns of disease and mortality, increased knowledge and technological innovation, and growing population expectations make inevitable tensions between demands for medical care and the capacity of nations to satisfy them. Although many people continue to view rationing of health care as abhorrent, rationing is in fact now more openly discussed in most nations and policy-makers are struggling with various rationing alternatives. Here I review some of these developments and explain why implicit rationing is likely to remain a dominant approach despite growing interest in more explicit methods.

Many Americans look with envy at the capacity of the national health insurance systems of some Western industrialised countries to guarantee universal entitlement while policy makers in these countries are increasingly intrigued by such American concepts as competitive markets, health maintenance organisations (HMOs),and utilisation management. Although the United States spends far more than any country in the world on health care, whether measured in actual dollars or as a proportion of domestic product, medical care costs in all systems are rising at comparable rates, reflecting advances in medical science and technology, growing population expectations and the extension of life (Newhouse 1994). Thus, all systems are struggling with alternatives for constraining the growth in costs, allocating care fairly and efficiently, and respond to increasingly sophisticated population demands. All systems seek an accommodation between what is technologically possible and what the economy and political process is willing to pay. None have found sufficiently successful solutions to be complacent.

The Imperatives of Science and Technology and Outcome Research

Advances in biomedical science and technology make possible new health services that potentially reduce discomfort, increase function and extend life. Many of these interventions, however, are incredibly expensive and will result increasingly in tensions between what is technically possible and what is demanded by the population through their willingness to pay. Better educated and more sophisticated patients are aware of and demand these interventions often before their physicians are fully knowledgeable about them. Expectations are inflated by the extraordinary attention the mass media give to new advances in medicine. Major newspapers and television networks monitor major medical journals closely, often bringing to the public's attention new possibilities in their earliest stages. Advocacy groups for persons with cancer, AIDS, mental disorders and many other conditions have increasingly sophisticated capacities available to them for monitoring new trends and possibilities as well as for promoting them more widely to their membership. There is a growing gap between expectations and financial realities.

In very recent years, there has been an extraordinary range of new, expensive technologies introduced, including computerised tomography (CT); nuclear magnetic resonance (NMR); lithotripters; angioplasty; implantation of intraocular lenses; total hip replacement; liver, heart and bone marrow transplantation; and many more. One estimate suggests that three recently introduced innovations–automated implantable cardiac defibrillators, erythropoietin for treating the anaemia of kidney failure, and non-ionic contrast media for safer radiology–could alone add $5 billion to US health costs (Schwartz and Mendelson 1992). Advances in genetics, immunology and molecular biology promise an enormous range of new, expensive products for treating major diseases that will be irresistible to consumers. New biotechnology products such as TPA for the treatment of heart attacks, far more expensive than its alternative Streptokinase, is preferred by many doctors despite its uncertain superiority. Should such products prove advantageous, there will be relentless pressures to adopt them. A recent description of emerging health care technologies includes a wide range of procedures and technologies including skin replacement, new uses for lasers, blood substitutes, disc transplantation, cancer susceptibility testing and so on (Health Care Technology Institute 1994).

These technologies, once introduced, diffuse widely, and medical industrial firms have strong incentives to promote them to the public as well as to health providers as a way of getting these technologies recognised and accepted. Even technologies that fail to equal more traditional approaches, such as fetal heart rate monitoring, are widely diffused and seem impervious to repeated randomised trials that not only show no advantages but some additional risks (Shy et al. 1990).

Despite concern about the cost issue, few politicians or policy makers advocate that we risk slowing new technological developments or possibilities, and the public strongly endorses this view. Thus, the emphasis is increasingly on technology assessment, outcomes research, and practice guidelines. These are all useful and important tools, but their promise is being vastly oversold. Producers, physicians and patients greatly resist withholding possibly efficacious technologies from immediate use. By the time definitive studies are completed, new technologies typically have become well entrenched. Often these technologies have already gone through several iterations or been put to different uses so that advocates can challenge the meaningfulness of negative evaluations of earlier less developed versions.

Outcomes research, unlike clinical studies, focuses on a broad range of possible end-points beyond mortality, including disability, cost effectiveness, satisfaction, quality of life and well-being. In increasing the range of outcomes under consideration, the possibilities of disagreement about relevant criteria increase. The more complex the outcomes included in studies, the more likely the results will be ambiguous and disputable. Most doctors use interventions because they believe them to have value. With disagreement and uncertainty, findings have less influence on professional judgements and are more difficult to use in making explicit rationing decisions. It remains unclear how definitive outcomes research must be if it is to be helpful as a basis for overruling individual professional judgement. Much health services research will present a mixed picture.

Guidelines offer similar difficulties. They are only as good as the quality of research that underlies them, but in most areas of medicine much uncertainty remains and expert groups will often disagree. Thus, it is not surprising that guidelines are commonly perceived as arbitrary and are often ignored by physicians. Guidelines have to be readily modifiable as new knowledge and experience emerge, but the process of developing guidelines is sufficiently lengthy and complex to raise issues about the timeliness of revision. Guidelines also have to be relatively simple and appropriate for generic cases. Since real life possibilities are more diverse, physicians may find that their experience conflicts with guidelines or that characteristics of particular patients do not fit generic models.

Expert groups focused on the latest scientific knowledge probably are in better positions to distil existing research and experience than the busy individual practitioner. But the individual practitioner tends to be suspicious of theoretical or statistical knowledge and is much more influenced by immediate clinical experiences and those of peers. Patients used in sophisticated clinical work are selected to be diagnostically specific, but the typical patient is more likely to have complex comorbidities that can readily raise issues of comparability. Nevertheless, it is reasonable to devote considerable effort to developing sophisticated guidelines for highly prevalent conditions that are costly to treat. As on-line computers become a more common facet of every physician's practice, carefully developed guidelines with interactive possibilities can be an enormously valuable educational tool. The danger is that administrators, alarmed at health care costs, will take a good educational opportunity and in prematurely using it as a regulatory tool will undermine its acceptability.

Even if outcomes research and developing practice guidelines were easier tasks, they would not significantly resolve resource constraint issues. There is a tendency to assume that lower levels of utilisation within the range of practice variations will be more suitable as appropriate standards than higher levels. Thus, attention is usually focused on encouraging high utilisers to move closer to the mean. However, large numbers of people receive care that departs from guidelines because their physicians do considerably less than recommended. The literature is replete with studies documenting significant failures to perform expected diagnostic procedures and treatments in a wide range of situations. While there is waste to be eliminated and economies to be achieved, too heavy a focus on practice variations may mislead us about possible resource savings.

Tensions between Equity and Quality

Despite the dazzling quality of medical science and technology, the practice of medicine in its most basic sense is a transaction between clinicians and patients that fundamentally depends on integrity and trust. Medical care can be described in terms of specific technical procedures, but its core activity is an iterative relationship between doctor and patient in which the doctor seeks to ascertain the underlying difficulty contributing to the patient's complaints and to agree with the patient on a management strategy that is acceptable. What the patient is willing to reveal in the diagnostic and treatment process, the willingness to cooperate in treatment, and even the likelihood of returning for further care is dependent on confidence and trust that the doctor acts in the patient's interest.

As the technologies and possibilities for medical care have advanced and economic stakes have risen, many have come to think of medical care as a commodity distributed across markets in a way not substantially different from other products and services. Thus, they increasingly focus on legal arrangements, regulations, financing schemes, and economic incentives. Medicine in all advanced countries is increasingly organised and bureaucratised with growing centralisation of decision making and the transfer of many responsibilities from clinicians to managers and regulators. Confusion is now common between functions and responsibilities associated with organising, maintaining, and financing health services as well as the responsibilities of individual clinicians caring for individual patients. A core issue for all health systems is how to carry out the organisational, financial and managerial tasks necessary while intruding as lightly as possible on trust relationships. Intrinsic to this task is discovering an appropriate, and publicly accepted, balance between equity considerations and responding to the particular needs and tastes of individual patients.

One obvious solution is to let the marketplace decide, a position strongly preferred by conservative economists. Given the departures of medical care from a true market and the inevitability of insurance systems, most settle on advocating significant cost sharing as a means of making patients' relative preferences applicable to allocation decisions. As the respected RAND Health Insurance Experiment demonstrated, cost sharing reduces demand for care (Newhouse and the Insurance Experiment Group 1993). Although economic theory would have us believe that cost sharing helps differentiate between appropriate and trivial care, in fact it operates more like a general barrier, comparably affecting the use of efficacious and unnecessary care (Newhouse and the Insurance Experiment Group 1993). Significant cost sharing, of course, also places disproportionate burdens on the poor. This is correctable by linking cost sharing to income, but the political will to do so is often absent and implementation is administratively difficult and cumbersome.

Recognising the limits of marketplace mechanisms at the point of service delivery, the marketplace discussion has centrally focused on 'managed competition' and various ideas articulated by Alain Enthoven (1993) and others on how patients can be made more conscious of costs. Basically, Enthoven advocates eliminating tax subsidies that encourage 'over insurance' and establishing incentives for people to choose lower cost policies among a menu of health care plans. The theory is that once cost consciousness occurs and patients become selective, health care plans will have to compete, requiring them to become more efficient. The competition, however, must be managed to prevent the plans from competing in nonconstructive ways, for example, selecting only healthy patients or excluding patients with known risks.

The assumption underlying managed competition – that enrollees can be induced to make more thoughtful decisions about health coverage and would respond to price – has been confirmed to some degree in multichoice plans. How competitively health plans actually respond, the efficiencies that result and the ultimate effects on price and quality of care remain more theoretical and conjectural. A great deal hinges on how well competition is managed and the ability to deter skillful health plan managers from finding new approaches to identify and select low risks, or from encouraging high-risk persons to seek their care elsewhere. Risk-adjusted payment is, of course, one option, but efforts to develop workable risk adjustments have not been particularly successful.

A major agenda behind managed competition is to induce individuals to join HMOs that generally offer more comprehensive coverage at lower cost. HMOs, however, are a mixed bag offering varying levels of access, quality and amenities. Many consumers reject HMOs because they value the broader choice available in traditional insurance policies, but the market has responded with a wide range of alternatives that provide flexibility within a managed care framework. Preferred providers allow individuals to avoid copayments when they use these providers, and one variation, the point-of-service plan, gives patients the option whenever they seek care. Managed care (MC) is increasingly seen as the solution to the dilemmas of resource allocation.

Is Managed Care the Answer?

Although the effectiveness of MC remains uncertain and disputed, common visions of the future of health care place management of care in a central position. Even in such areas as mental health, where practice uncertainties exceed those commonly present in general medicine, there is much faith that MC can resolve the imbalance between demand and appropriate allocation of resources. Exemplary of this view was the Clinton plan, which stated, without qualification, that 'a comprehensive array of services, along with the flexibility to provide such services based on individual medical and psychological necessity through effective management techniques, produces better outcomes and better cost controls than traditional benefits' (Bureau of National Affairs 1993).

The basic idea of MC appears irresistible, and it is not difficult to understand why it captures the imagination of policy makers. There is now broad recognition of variabilities in practice, of inappropriate and uncertain use of expensive technologies and of waste and abuse. If only we could have a thoughtful and competent umpire to determine 'medical and psychological necessity' then when particular interventions are - or are not – required we could appropriately meet people's needs at reduced cost. If it were that easy to assess necessity and quality, however, and if a reasonable consensus on these matters prevailed, we would have little need to worry about developing new approaches. Waste and even fraud could be reduced. But the real, and more difficult, issue is how much can be pruned without also reducing the quality of care. Or, more metaphorically, is MC more of a rifle – or a shotgun?

Types of Managed Care

MC comes in many varieties, and the term without specification reveals little about the logic or administrative mechanisms involved (Mechanic, Schlesinger and McAlpine 1995). Different systems of MC have varying structures, incentives and umpires. For convenience, we can distinguish MC by approaches that are more or less explicit. On the implicit side are MC programs built around primary care physicians who work within prospective budgets, providing basic services and controlling entry to more specialised and expensive services – a mode of care with long historical precedents. At the other extreme are newly developing administrative systems that use algorithms developed by knowledgeable clinicians and experts that are then applied to individual cases by other personnel, typically nurses. Each of these approaches comes with a wide range of variations.

Although we can distinguish types of MC approaches by how explicit they are, all health care systems, in fact, ration health care through mixed approaches, putting either more or less emphasis on cost sharing, prospective budgets, controls on the availability and location of facilities and technologies and explicit decisions to include or limit care for particular conditions, procedures, types of practitioners and service locations. But whatever the constraints on overall facilities and personnel, various decisions must be made at the point of service to either use or not use particular diagnostic technologies, to initiate expensive but uncertain courses of treatment or to admit patients to hospitals or other expensive facilities. Resource constraints on technology and beds set limits on the decisions that can be made, but much still depends on triage decisions made by professionals who control access to these resources.

Initially, it was much simpler to differentiate between implicit systems of decision making. In a prepaid group practice, for example, plans had to expend resources within a budget established by capitation in contrast to more explicit utilisation management approaches that certified the appropriateness of inpatient admission, monitored the inpatient length of stay, and intensively managed high-cost cases. In recent years, however, procedures within each of these approaches have become more elaborate and complex, and the approaches themselves have been joined in many different ways. Thus, increasingly, physicians working on capitation are additionally affected in their decisions by reimbursement incentives pushing them toward specified cost containment targets and by utilisation review of their decisions. The scope of doctor autonomy has been constrained to a narrower range with managers of insurance plans exercising greater control over many expensive decisions.

Much emphasis has been put on the development of HMOs. The initial model, based on prepaid group practices of the Kaiser Permanente variety, demonstrated that such entities could provide seemingly satisfactory care at 20 per cent less cost than fee-for-service practices. Savings came by reducing hospital admissions and surgical procedures but not by reducing overall access (Luft 1987). As constraints on inpatient use have been extended to care in the fee-for-service sector as well, the financial advantages of capitated groups may have been reduced. More significant, however, is that as the HMO sector has grown, independent practice associations (IPAs) have developed at a much faster rate than prepaid group practices (Miller and Luft 1994). These plans capitate physicians working out of their own office-based practices for particular patients. It is not apparent that IPAs achieve savings in the same way as the large prepaid group practices, and they also lack the advantages associated with a group setting in using physician extenders and substitutes and in developing special preventive and chronic care programs. The IPA is in some sense the reverse of the trend in British general practice (GP) toward the formation of larger GP groups. The American IPA, however, has the advantage of offering patients a wider possibility of choice than group HMOs since IPA networks are much larger than available closed groups. They also provide care in settings that many patients find more personal.

Doctors working in IPAs may be participants in several HMOs and have a mix of fee-for-service and HMO patients. Since IPAs are insurance mechanisms, and not group structures, they do not have the control and quality assurance approaches comparable to those found in large prepaid group structures. Thus, they depend to a larger degree on remuneration incentives, and some withhold considerable reimbursement from primary care physicians when they exceed utilisation standards (Hillman 1987). These incentives very clearly put the doctor and patient's interests in conflict.

Utilisation management (UM) is a more explicit approach than capitated practice for reducing inpatient care and high-cost episodes. Typically, UM is assessed in terms of whether it reduces care in the aggregate and yields savings for employers. In assessing costs, little attention is given to the out-of-pocket expenditures patients and their families assume when care is denied; to the costs to doctors, hospitals, and other institutions in time and personnel in documenting decisions and dealing with UM personnel; to the costs to families and communities when the burdens of care are transferred to them; and to the hassles and demoralising consequences of UM for physicians and the way they see their work (Mechanic 1994a).

The most extreme example of an explicit approach in the American context is the Oregon plan for the Medicaid population, which ranks illnesses and medical procedures in terms of their presumed value. Depending on available funding in any year, a floor is established in which procedures ranked below the floor are excluded from coverage. The advantage of the plan is that it substantially extends care to the poverty population, many of whom were not previously covered. Advocates also saw as major advantages the public character of the decision-making process and the opportunities of the public to participate in setting priorities for coverage. Community participation in the process, however, was limited and highly selective, and such selectivity is inevitable. Moreover, accepting the idea of having persons unfamiliar with illnesses and their consequences making judgements on the value of care requires a high level of credulity.

One of the interesting and less noticed facets of the Oregon plan is its underlying conception of doctor/patient relationships. Medical care is seen as a number of discrete procedures, not as a complex iterative process involving personal needs and circumstances and varying cultural inclinations and tastes. The focus is on cure, not care, and it downplays the humanising aspect of therapeutic relationships seen as opportunities to reduce suffering and influence behaviour. It is particularly ironic that this conception is first tried on the Medicaid population, primarily poor single mothers who have multiple problems. Many physicians will continue to treat conditions that are not covered. Thus, the program will shift substantial costs to physicians. This might be reasonable in some circumstances, but Medicaid reimbursement typically falls well below that of other payers.

Potentials of Prevention

Our intuitions, unfortunately, often clash with realities. Over the years many have argued that making good care accessible to populations would reduce illness and subsequently the demand for care. Experience consistently proves otherwise. As medicine can do more, and is more accessible, demand rises and physicians find more ways to intervene. New emerging technologies will broaden substantially the efforts physicians make, and there is little reason to anticipate the medicalisation of problems that were once considered difficulties of living will abate. The profession has been innovative in developing new services and broadening traditional ones, and new subspecialties continue to develop.

Similar considerations apply to prevention. No one seriously questions the desirability of prevention, but the intuitive notion that preventing illness necessarily saves money is a comforting illusion (Russell 1986). Prevention, however valuable, is often expensive and contributes to increasing cost. The cost effectiveness of prevention depends on a range of considerations including the prevalence of the conditions being prevented, the size of the target population, the cost and efficacy of the preventive intervention, and how frequently the intervention has to be repeated. On rigorous evaluation, some preventive interventions like immunisation and pap smears are cost effective, but many others are not. These preventive approaches still may be valuable, and may be demanded, but we should have no illusions that they will help on the cost side. HMOs often market themselves as being oriented toward prevention, but this reflects marketing strategy more than substantial differences in disease detection and early intervention. Indeed, many so-called preventive benefits like wellness education or fitness programs are initiated to recruit young, healthy enrollees who often want such programs. Such enrollees are low risk and, thus, attractive recruits.

In the aggregate, the growing emphasis on prevention is more likely to increase costs than reduce them. The potential target groups are very large. New approaches such as drugs to reduce cholesterol or PSA screening for prostate cancer, while increasingly popular, are of uncertain effectiveness in enhancing longevity or quality of life (Russell 1994). New sophisticated screening approaches inevitably lead to false positives, taking people down a trajectory of expensive, intrusive and sometimes dangerous interventions (Black and Welch 1993). One can imagine the possibilities for additional cost as cancer susceptibility screening and other such approaches enter the marketplace.

Statistical and Individualistic Thinking

Dialogue on statistical lives is largely free of the emotional trappings that define individual lives. Despite the fact that probabilistic thinking is common in Western culture, probabilities look very different when you, or someone you care about, is the life in question. When ill, and especially when faced with life-threatening illnesses, many patients and their families want all the care that might be beneficial irrespective of whether in the aggregate such care is cost-effective. There are limits to such demands, but within broad parameters probabilities applying to individual lives are seen differently than those in the abstract. Moreover, a strong implicit value persists that in cases where death or serious impairment threatens, rescue and not cost considerations should be the rule (Hadorn 1991). Thus, the principles that policy makers might follow in making macro public policy decisions are not easily replicated at the level of individual cases. It becomes exceedingly difficult to resist providing even very expensive and uncertain experimental treatments should such a capacity exist. When such treatments are resisted by insurers or MC organisations, courts often favour the patient even when the interventions are explicitly excluded by contract. This makes it especially difficult to impose discipline on medical decision making.

The foregoing suggests why implicit systems that set overall constraints but avoid specific allocative rules are likely to work better than UM. UM involves individual denial of care that patients and their doctors often regard as necessary. As UM becomes tougher, conflict and litigation will increase. Similar decisions made flexibly and informally are likely to be more acceptable because physicians can take account of the intensity of preferences and tastes (Mechanic 1992). People have different values about their care, aggressiveness of interventions and even life itself.

An incident that occurred in England some years ago is revealing. Although it was widely recognised there that the intensity of rescue efforts was linked to age, and that aggressive efforts to sustain life among the elderly were not generally made, this understanding was informally administered with little dispute. Perhaps the best documented example was the uncommon use of chronic dialysis for elderly patients with end-stage renal disease, but the understanding appears to have been administered quite broadly. However, when one hospital administrator issued an explicit directive that patients beyond a particular age should not be resuscitated, a national outcry occurred that resulted in a parliamentary debate and the withdrawal of the directive (Stevens 1986).

A similar pattern is observable in the American insurance sector where insurers commonly 'cave in' when patients challenge denials of care. They do so substantially for pragmatic reasons, realising that a legal dispute could lead to precedents far more costly than accommodation to a particular case and that the personal plight of affected patients evokes great public sympathy. As in the malpractice arena, insurers can cut their costs by small accommodations. The process of acceding, however, encourages others to pursue similar claims resulting in a pattern of irrational and inequitable decisions. Many different parties are involved in these decisions, making it especially difficult to forge a coherent social policy (Peters and Rogers 1994).

The flexibility of implicit systems is appealing but worrisome in relation to equity issues. It seems inherently unfair that patients who are better educated, more sophisticated and more insistent should get more care simply because they demand it. All bureaucratic systems built around gatekeepers who control access inadvertently penalize individuals who are less knowledgeable and more docile, and such patients are typically overrepresented among the disadvantaged. Implicit systems alone, without other safeguards, have considerable potential to allocate care in unprincipled ways.

Advocacy versus Allocation

A key aspect of the physician's role is fiduciary responsibility to the patient. Patients feel uncomfortable with the idea that doctors have competing interests that might interfere with advocacy for their patients (Mechanic, Ettel and Davis 1990). It is commonly suggested that placing doctors in allocative roles undermines their major obligation to do everything possible for their patients. Rationing, it is argued, must be done by other authorities while doctors must do all they can within whatever constraints exist (Churchill 1987). Alternatively, it is argued, there is no one in a better position than doctors to determine how finite resources might be distributed to best enhance patient welfare. It is only through considerations of the contingencies of illness that thoughtful allocative decisions are possible, and who understands such contingencies better than doctor and patient (Mechanic 1992)?

Even the most ardent defenders of the physician's fiduciary role recognise the extent to which the realities of life, and the personal needs of doctors to earn a living and gain some leisure, erode the ideal conception. There is now sufficient evidence on the advantages and limitations of capitation and fee-for-service to understand that each payment mechanism carries advantages and risks. What we seek is neutralisation of incentives that erode fiduciary expectations. Such incentives are evident across varying organisational forms (Rodwin 1993). In US fee-for-service, for example, there is growing evidence that doctors who own their own diagnostic facilities – or who have a financial stake in laboratories, imaging centres, and the like – and who refer their patients to them, order more procedures (Thompson 1993). It has not been documented that doing so is necessarily a violation of fiduciary responsibility, but this is a strong inference, and measures have been taken to restrict such arrangements under federal programs.

Alternatively, HMOs in the United States commonly tie substantial remuneration of primary care physicians to adherence to utilisation thresholds. The intent, and the result, is to reduce the services these physicians provide and the referrals they make. In such cases, the incentives directly produce a tension between the physician's interests and potentially those of the patient. The stronger the incentives, the greater the tension, and it should be no surprise that for-profit HMOs use such devices more commonly than non-profit organisations and typically have larger incentives (Hillman 1987). There is no consensus on the limits that should be put on such practices or on the requirements for disclosure to patients about the nature of these arrangements, but both would be advisable.

As organised forms of practice proliferate, the role of the doctor as patient advocate becomes more uncertain. The professional training of doctors and their strong values about autonomy and clinical independence make it likely that such roles could be sustained unless intrusive incentives interfere. It is difficult to define the boundaries, but increasingly doctors complain that medically necessary treatments are being withheld from their patients by insurers or utilisation managers. One protection is to make it obligatory for physicians to inform patients when the insurer or plan withholds services the doctor believes to be essential and to make reasonable efforts to advocate on behalf of the patient (Mechanic 1994b).

In the British National Health Service, general practitioners (GPs) have fought to retain their status as independent contractors. The practical significance of this is not clear, but symbolically the doctor retains a certain moral independence from state authority, and theoretically, advocacy functions are protected. Ironically, few GPs speak out against tough resource constraints or inaccessible services, and if we are to accept Aaron and Schwartz's description (Aaron and Schwartz 1984), they cooperate, although with discomfort, in discouraging patients from seeking further treatment even when efficacious treatments exist. Fund holding provides some realignment of power between GPs and consultants and perhaps some ability to demand more accessibility of specialist and hospital services (Glennerster, Matsaganis and Owens 1994). It does so, however, primarily for one's own patients and not for the system as a whole, possibly resulting in even larger inequalities between rich and poor, advantaged and disadvantaged (Whitehead 1994). This may settle out over time as more doctors become fund holders, but as fund holding becomes more common, the newly felt power of the GP is likely to recede as well.

Controlled Advocacy

There is no obvious way to reconcile the competing goals of constraining health care costs and advocacy to do everything possibly useful. There is substantial waste in the provision of health services, but there are limits to the ability to reduce waste and, in any case, opportunities for new expenditures are almost limitless. Posing the issues in this oppositional way makes solutions appear impossible. Thinking about the issues in terms of levels of care makes solutions more possible.

There are some medical procedures that are so expensive that their availability should be established through an explicit social policy process. In considering the feasibility of supporting such an intervention, attention might be given to the cost per year saved, adjusted for quality; the number of persons in the population likely to be affected; the technical capacity to deliver the intervention with available infrastructure; and related issues. Decisions might be made in favour of selective experimental interventions to acquire more data and experience. If the intervention is to be accessible to only a limited degree, clear rules for allocation are needed. Similar rules already apply to interventions such as organ transplantation that are limited by the lack of sufficient donated organs. One solution is to define subgroups in terms of capacity to benefit and then distribute scarce supply within such groups by lottery or on a first come, first served basis.

A second level of explicit decision making might apply to medical and surgical modalities that are found to be so lacking in efficacy that their use is not justified. The object here is not to limit introduction of new treatment approaches or insist on demonstrated efficacy for coverage. Effort, instead, would be directed to identifying modalities that are repeatedly found to be ineffective but persist because of local custom or inertia. Patients and doctors might choose to have these procedures done, but it would be clearly understood that they would not be reimbursed as part of a guaranteed insurance program.

The vast spectrum of everyday practice, however, would remain as an implicit system operating within budgetarily defined limits. Within these constraints, doctors would be encouraged to advocate for their patients' needs and preferences within a system that regulated the permissible incentives designed to affect physician decision making. Such a system might allow fee-for-service but moderate its incentive to provide more care than necessary by adjusting fees in relation to the volume of procedures. Thus, doctors performing procedures in excess of the norm might receive reduced fees. Alternatively, doctors on salary or capitation could not have their incomes tied to specific utilisation targets, although it might be permissible to provide bonuses earned in the aggregate by groups of physicians who practised in a cost-effective way. The basic idea would be to maintain incentives that encourage thoughtfulness about the cost effectiveness of practice but that are too weak, in any individual case, to distort professional judgement. There are no absolute guidelines, but in this area, judgement, experience and research could help, and a reasonable balance of incentives can evolve over time.

The boundaries between explicit decision making and implicit approaches to practice will also vary with circumstances, the emergence of new technologies and economic conditions. The goal is to define a core area of medical decision making that builds on doctor/patient rapport and opportunities to use the relationship as a therapeutic alliance to affect attitudes and behaviour as well as to respond to medical complaints. Within this circumscribed range of action, UM is not only likely to be intrusive but also may be costly relative to savings achieved. It remains unclear whether UM is needed once budgets have been established or whether the linkage of budgets with thoughtful UM contributes to a fairer and more effective allocation of resources. There seems little doubt that UM, as now practised, has a demoralising effect on many doctors. UM, practised within a collegial group and combined with thoughtful review of practice standards, can be a powerful educational device. Too much emphasis on the regulatory aspects of UM can make it difficult to exploit educational aspects.

Controlling expenditures for care is the relatively easy part of the task. Doing so in a manner that achieves good health benefits and public approval is far more difficult and problematic. There is a great deal of dissatisfaction with care structures, but many people are reasonably satisfied with their physicians and the personal care they receive. There is a danger that in addressing structural issues we intrude on some of the aspects of care patients most value – the ability to select their doctors and medical settings and to negotiate their care with a practitioner who is seen as their agent. Whatever health insurance reforms occur in the United States or the United Kingdom, patients will basically focus on whether they have reasonable access to a range of modern treatment modalities and whether their needs can be comfortably managed in the context of traditional relationships with their doctors. Without such assurances, medical care will remain a troubled and politically unstable arena.

References

Aaron, H., and W. Schwartz. 1984. *The Painful Prescription: Rationing Hospital Care.* Washington, D.C.: Brookings Institution.

Black, W. C., and G. Welch. 1993. Advances in Diagnostic Imaging and Overestimations of Disease Prevalence and the Benefits of Therapy. *New England Journal of Medicine* 328:1237–43.

Bureau of National Affairs. 1993. *BNA Daily Report for Executives Special Supplement: Clinton Administration Description of President's Health Care Reform Plan, American Health Security Act of 1993.* Washington, D.C.: Bureau of National Affairs. September 7.

Churchill, L. 1987. *Rationing Health Care in America.* South Bend, IN: University of Notre Dame Press.

Enthoven, A. 1993. The History and Principles of Managed Competition. *Health Affairs* 12 (supplement):24–48.

Glennerster, H., M. Matsaganis, and P. Owens with S. Hancock. 1994. *Implementing GP Fundholding: Wild Card or Winning Hand.* Buckingham: Open University Press.

Hadorn, D. C. 1991. Setting Health Care Priorities in Oregon: Cost Effectiveness Meets the Rule of Rescue. *Journal of the American Medical Association* 265:2218–25.

Health Care Technology Institute. 1994. *Reference Guide for the Health Care Technology Industry.* Alexandria, VA: Health Care Technology Institute.

Hillman, A. 1987. Financial Incentives for Physicians in HMOs: Is There a Conflict of Interest? *New England Journal of Medicine* 317:1743–8.

Luft, H. 1987. *Health Maintenance Organisations: Dimensions of Performance.* New Brunswick, NJ: Transactions Publishers.

Mechanic, D. 1994a. Managed Care: Rhetoric and Realities. *Inquiry* 31:124–8.

———. 1994b. Trust and Informed Consent to Rationing. *Milbank Quarterly* 72:217–23.

———. 1992. Professional Judgement and the Rationing of Medical Care. *University of Pennsylvania Law Review* 140:1713–54.

———, M. Schlesinger, and D. McAlpine. 1995. Management of Mental Health and Substance Abuse Services: State of the Art and Early Results. *Milbank Quarterly* 73 (1): 19-55.

———, T. Ettel, and D. Davis. 1990. Choosing Among Health Insurance Options. *Inquiry* 27:14–23.

Miller, R. H., and H. S. Luft. 1994. Managed Care Performance Since 1980: A Literature Analysis. *Journal of the American Medical Association* 271:1512–19.

Newhouse, J. N. 1994. Open Issues in Financing and Coverage. In *Critical Issues in US Health Reform,* ed. E. Ginsberg, 12-32. Boulder, CO: Westview Press.

———, and the Insurance Experiment Group. 1993. *Free for All? Lessons From the RAND Health Insurance Experiment.* Cambridge: Harvard University Press.

Peters, W., and M. Rogers. 1994. Variations in Approval by Insurance Companies of Coverage for Autologous Bone Marrow Transplantation for Breast Cancer. *New England Journal of Medicine* 330:473–7.

Rodwin, M. 1993. *Money and Morals: Physician's Conflicts of Interest.* New York: Oxford University Press.

Russell, L. B. 1994. *Educated Guesses: Making Policy About Medical Screening Tests.* Berkeley: University of California Press.

———. 1986. *Is Prevention Better than Cure?* Washington, D.C.: Brookings Institution.

Schwartz, W. B., and D. N. Mendelson. 1992. Why Managed Care Cannot Contain Hospital Costs. *Health Affairs* 11:105.

Shy, K. K., et al. 1990. Effects of Electronic Fetal Heart Rate Monitoring, As Compared with Periodic Auscultation, on the Neurologic Development of Premature Infants. *New England Journal of Medicine* 322:588–93.

Stevens, M. B. 1986. Withholding Resuscitation. *American Family Physician* 33:207–12.

Thompson, D. F. 1993. Understanding Financial Conflicts of Interest. *New England Journal of Medicine* 329:573–6.

Whitehead, M. 1994. Is it Fair? Evaluating the Equity Implications of the NHS Reforms. In *Evaluating the NHS Reform,* eds. Ray Robinson and Julian Le Grand, 208-42London: King's Fund Institute.

Part III

Analysis
and
Policy

11

Policy Analysis As an Academic Vocation

Richard Rose

Public policy research arises from a concern with problems of governing in a time of change and uncertainty. Yet there is no agreement about what the subject is. To describe policy analysis as it is in the universities today tells us what is fashionable. As Schumpeter noted, politicians design policies as garment manufacturers make clothes: they produce what will sell (Schumpeter 1942). So too, university committees everywhere have cobbled together syllabi that can be sold to the relevant faculty committee, examining board, and training board or to students. There are big differences within universities as well as between universities about what is taught under the name of public policy and policy analysis.

My own definition is this: *policy analysis relates ideas drawn from the social sciences to problems facing government.* Policy analysis is not a profession with formal qualifications, as is accountancy or chiropody. To paraphrase Max Weber, it can be described as a vocation or calling (Weber 1948). It draws upon a multitude of academic disciplines, and its distinguishing feature is focusing upon problems facing government. In this sense, it is more social than are social science disciplines concerned with abstractions in a 'model' world.

What Is Policy Analysis?

Policy research must be *analytic*, using generic concepts and ideas to go beyond description, historical chronology, the tabulation of numbers or the manipulation of equations for their own sake. Concepts are required before theories because, as a Nobel laureate in physics has emphasised, 'They determine the questions one asks, and the answers one gets. They are more fundamental than the theories which are stated in terms of them' (Thompson 1961). In an era in which quantitative methods are held in high esteem, all the best variables are nominal, for concepts are necessary to give meaning to numbers. To amass information without any concepts is to produce empirical data that will sink under its own weight. Day and Klein's study *Accountabilities* is an excellent example of imaginatively using a concept to gain analytic leverage upon hundreds of pages of notes of interviews with people in health and water authorities, local education and social services committees, and police authorities (Day and Klein 1987).

Universities and governments are each organised into departments, but the departments have very different names. University departments are named after intellectual disciplines, such as economics, politics, psychology or sociology. By contrast, government departments are named after problems as they arise in society: housing, health, transportation and defence. If policy analysis is to be a social science then it must address problems as they are found in society, for policy makers cannot divide their work into compartments that follow the boundaries of university departments.

Policy analysis is thus *interdisciplinary*. An attractive feature to an inquiring mind is that it overcomes the barriers of compartmentalisation that followed the academic professionalisation of recent decades. People who identify with economics or sociology as an academic profession have a different and narrower calling than those who focus on public policy. It is, as it were, the difference between chamber music and opera. One is not better than the other. But to ignore the difference is to confuse one-dimensional analysis with an understanding of the multidimensional world.

A subject that draws its research materials from problems that surround us is bound to be extroverted, looking outside the universities as well as inside books. The two approaches can be complementary. Research sometimes raises questions that are not easily communicated in sound bites to policy makers unversed in an academic literature. Yet the capacity to communicate to nonacademics is no more proof of emptiness than is the capacity to use words as verbiage or turn jargon into mathematical symbols. An analyst with a penetrating mind capable of sifting the significant from the insignificant can be bilingual, not only expressing ideas in the abstract but also applying ideas concretely in terms understood by non-professionals.

In an environment that is visibly in flux, research must address the *dynamics* of public policy. Many problems today are consequences of choices made in the past and even of policies once regarded as successes. Because government makes long-term commitments of laws, money and organisation, any policy will reflect an accumulation of decisions from the less or more distant past. Today's governors are inheritors before they are choosers (Rose and Davies 1994). For example, the jumble of policies that make up social security today was never chosen at one point in time but was formed through a process of accumulation and amendment, augmented by unintended and sometimes unnoticed changes. Understanding the link between past and present also helps to understand how much or how little room there is for future manoeuvre.

Relevance to concerns of government is necessary; the German phrase *Angewandte Sozialwissenschaft* (applied social science) aptly reflects this. Relevance does not depend upon whether the government of the day adopts an analyst's recommendations or whether a recommendation is in keeping with the views of a particular political party. Relevance means that the research relates to conditions in society that are (or could be) the object of government action. If this is the case, then conclusions are potentially applicable. A professor of theoretical physics is not surprised that applied physicists work in the real world. As Herbert Simon has emphasised, an engineer or an architect's a concern with applicability is at the core of his or her concern with creativity through design (Simon 1969).

Public policy is implicitly or explicitly *comparative*. At its simplest, comparison involves past and present, the time before and after a policy has been put into effect. It can also involve comparisons between present and future: what would be different in future if this policy were adopted? (Rose 1991a). Comparison can also take place between two units of government. Comparison often leads to the creation of league tables identifying variation in performance on a given metric. To make comparison requires concepts that focus on what is generic rather than ideographic in two different places. For authors of descriptive case studies, examining a second case or a second country presents great difficulties. For high-flying theorists, the first real country is a problem.

When the same policy is applied throughout a country, comparison across space becomes international comparison. Health policy is a field in which international comparisons are often made because of significant differences between countries in reactions to a common problem. It is also a field in which study is not motivated simply by idle curiosity; it reflects a desire to learn from the successes and failings of other countries. The debate about the Clinton health bill was full of examples of the use and abuse of comparison – and of beliefs in American uniqueness (Marmor 1994; Enthoven 1990). In Britain, it is debatable whether the nation referred to in the National Health Service is England, in which case there are four health services within the United Kingdom, or the United Kingdom as a whole, in which case Scotland, Wales and Northern Ireland can be considered as administratively separate but parallel providers of services (Hunter 1982; Klein 1989). Rudolf Klein's writings on the British health services have shown a subtle awareness of structural differences in degree and kind.

In central banking, there are interdependencies as well as parallels across international boundaries. The problems facing monetary institutions in London, Frankfurt, New York, Washington and Tokyo are not parallel for they are joined together in a network of interdependencies. The expansion of the European Union has given added significance to interdependencies between policies of different national governments in fields as seemingly 'domestic' as education and environmental pollution (Rose 1991b).

Academic social science is often backward looking, explaining what has happened. By contrast, policy analysis is forward looking, seeking to draw lessons for action in the future. *Lesson-drawing* starts by observing that a given policy X has been in operation in place Y and has had Z consequences. The process is partly empirical, for one is examining a policy that is in effect somewhere. It is also partly speculative: under what circumstances and to what extent would the same policy have similar consequences if adopted elsewhere? Social scientists rarely think about drawing lessons; civil servants and politicians do so all the time. Policy analysis seeks to bridge the gap between two very different modes of thought (Rose 1993).

Last but not least, policy analysis is *open*. It is not the closed deductive system beloved of neo-Thomists,[1] which lead to ideological reasoning based on unexamined and unchallenged premises that cannot be altered because mere 'facts' are exogenous or eroded by stylisation. Openness to observation makes it possible to learn more through a sequence of research, cogitation and further observation. It avoids postulating a static goal in which the only issue is the adoption of the most efficient means for maximising goal attainment. Politics makes policies and as politics change, so do policies. Moreover, in a turbulent and open international environment, the environment of policy makers can change abruptly too. As Herbert Simon has observed: 'The real world in fact is perhaps the most fertile of all sources of good research questions calling for basic scientific inquiry' (Simon 1979).

What Is Science?

The poverty of conventional English classical scholarship is revealed by the fact that, as Secretary for Education, Sir Keith Joseph, a student of classics and Fellow of All Souls, Oxford, was unable to recognise the origin of the word *science* in the former title of the British Social Science Research Council. It had its roots in the Latin *scientia* (knowing) and modern scholarship originated in nineteenth-century Germany by the promotion of *Wissenschaft* (science), a term that can be applied to historical knowledge as well as to mechanical engineering. In America, an equally serious error is the assumption that medicine is a science like mechanical engineering and that the social sciences are or can become a science based upon predictions deduced from closed theories.

Policy research must deal with *uncertainty*; in that sense it is a science like medicine. Confronted with a patient showing symptoms of illness, a doctor uses concepts or hypotheses about causes of symptoms to collect data. The information is then synthesised as a diagnosis; identification of symptoms, collection of medical data and conclusions are a probabilistic calculus, not a mechanical certainty. Second, a doctor seeks to prescribe a means of alleviating symptoms or a cure for the underlying problem. The doctor assesses what is most likely to work best in the circumstances diagnosed. But doctors only make statements of probabilities, not unqualified predictions of success (Etzioni 1985).

If medicine is a science, then the study of public policy can claim to be a science too. The object of policy analysis is not the chimera of anticipating or controlling the future but the reduction of ignorance by identifying assertions that are nonempirical, falsifying assertions that might be empirically supported, and verifying characteristics of a problem in a way that reduces uncertainty about the nature and causes of political dissatisfaction and identifies relevant policies that follow from such a diagnosis.

Universities give degrees to scientists following instruction and examination in theories, techniques and applications. Within universities, the highest prestige is usually given to those who are most proficient at theory. There is, for example, a Nobel prize for physics but none for engineering technology. Graduates (and in some fields, nongraduates as well) acquire a professional qualification by taking examinations based in part upon their academic education as well as knowledge of additional applied subject matter. Often, professionals are required to serve a practical apprenticeship working in the field in which they seek to qualify, for example, as a doctor in a hospital, an assistant in a lawyer's office, or as a site engineer. A professional qualification certifies that an individual not only has theoretical knowledge but is also capable of applying this knowledge to problems in the world as it actually is (Rose 1976).

In public policy, the highest prestige is given to individuals who are skilled in applying their skills to immediate problems. An organisation with a legal problem does not want the wisdom of a professor of jurisprudence but the shrewdness of a lawyer who can find a loophole in an awkward document. A head of state does not want to employ military theorists whose books are read world-wide but generals who will win battles and wars. Traditionally honoured professions, such as the law, the army and the church, were and remain ones with theoretical bases for action that are far from clear. To describe such professions as both art and science is irrelevant to clients who judge professionals by results, not by their theories.[2]

The scientific model of problem-solving assumes consensus about goals. Diseases are bad; cures for diseases are good. Propeller planes are slow; jet planes are faster, and faster planes are better. Consensus about goals promotes dialogue among theorists and professionals and greatly reduces friction. A second widespread characteristic of science is that theories are applicable to concrete problems facing professionals. Theories of physics can be used to construct computers, and chemical theories underlay the production of plastics.

Logically, we can identify four different types of scientific activity, depending upon the extent to which there is consensus about goals and applicable theories:

1. Consensual goals and applicable understanding: for example, physics and related branches of engineering such as computer science or electronics.
2. Consensual goals but limited scientific applications: many branches of medicine, such as cancer research, share a consensus about abolishing the disease, but research has not led to results analogous to immunisation for smallpox or poliomyelitis.
3. Applicable understanding but no consensus about goals: theories of nuclear physics have had awesome practical applications – but from the end of World War II there has been disagreement among nuclear scientists about the relative emphasis upon 'atoms for defence' as distinct from 'atoms for peace.'
4. Disagreement about means and ends: psychoanalysts have produced major insights into causes of human behaviour, but the history of the subject has been one of continuing schisms over the fundamentals of theory and about goals in dealing with patients.

The above distinctions support the following hypothesis: *government will make use of scientists and professionals insofar as they demonstrate consensus about objectives and have a technology that is applicable to real-world phenomena.* The hypothesis explains two common observations: government is a very large employer of many types of scientists and professionals, ranging from physical and life scientists to sewer engineers and lawyers. It is unlikely to employ many professionals who dispute goals among themselves and whose applicable knowledge is doubted, for example, psychoanalysts or sociologists. Social scientists can be classified by the same criteria as natural sciences, albeit social scientists are much less likely to agree on goals and the application of their knowledge.

1. Fields in which there is a consensus about goals and a clear understanding about applying knowledge – such as operations research and management science – are peripheral social science subjects at best. A transport minister harassed by environmental groups may not regard a technical analysis of traffic flows by an operations research specialist as a solution to the problem of choosing between building faster road transport (favoured by motoring and business organisations) and protecting the environment by not building (supported by environmental groups). The fundamental shortcoming of a neat technological solution is that it is apolitical, that is, it ignores the fact that politics is about the articulation of conflicting views over political goals.

2. Economists are notorious for disagreeing about policy prescriptions: from a political perspective, the neo-classical paradigm is not a unified theory but an arena in which there is competition between two mainstream parties, liberal individualists with a bias against government intervention and social democrats with a bias in favour. The absence of a consensus about whether inflation or unemployment is the greatest problem of the day does not prevent economists from participating in government. It simply determines which economists are called upon to proffer advice. Whatever the politics of the governing party, there will always be economists at hand with values and goals congenial to the government of the day – and others to attack them (Ricketts and Shoesmith 1990; McCloskey 1985; Rose 1989).

3. In classic public administration, the consensual goal of 'good' government was taken for granted, like good health. A sharp distinction was drawn between administration and politics; practitioners claimed that they had prin-

ciples that could deal with administrative problems and these could be resolved without regard to political issues. Both assumptions are now recognised as inadequate. Studies of policy making recurringly emphasise the intertwining of politics and administration. The absence of theoretical underpinnings for many maxims of public administration is not proof of practical relevance but of woolly thinking. In consequence, policy analysis, which accepts conflicts about political goals, has now absorbed much of conventional public administration.

4. Conflicts about goals and knowledge, applicable or otherwise, have bedevilled sociology since its emergence. The European tradition emphasised grand theories of society in the style of Comte or Spencer. By contrast, many American pioneers were progressives who wished to do good by developing sociological knowledge that could solve America's problems. Armchair theorists following in the footsteps of Parsons have eschewed the intention to change society; those following Marx's injunction to use philosophy to change society now have some explaining to do about the changes wrought by the Soviet Union. Insofar as contemporary sociologists adopt a pure science aim of seeking to understand the world, then the absence of a social engineering capability is no shortcoming to academic status–but it is a disqualification for the utilisation of this knowledge within government. Today, Lipset argues that there is an internecine war in which sociologists are more interested in 'doing' each other than in doing science (Lipset 1994).

A hypothesis about involvement in policy analysis is: Social science is relevant to public policy insofar as it deals with subjects of political controversy and has theories that can be applied to real world phenomena. Striving for theories so grand or so stylised that they have no application to the world as it actually is disqualifies a social scientist from the world of public policy, just as much as does concentration upon apolitical matters of concern to many efficiency experts. The reason why economics is so prominent in public policy analysis is not because it is 'scientific' through mimicking pure physics but because it is both applicable *and* addresses relevant but controversial problems.

Cultivating Qualities of a Policy Analyst

'Running the economy is more like gardening than operating a computer,' once remarked Denis Healey, a former Chancellor of the Exchequer with an unusually broad and deep commitment to many forms of knowledge and reasoning (Mosley 1984). To garden one must understand a lot about a number of disciplines both pure and applied. One must also have practical experience and exercise judgement about what will grow in a given soil and show foresight as well about the long-term consequences of planting a sapling that will someday become a great oak tree.

The creation of a policy analyst is a matter of cultivation in the sense of growth through nurture and acculturation, developing the ability to survive dramatic changes in climate. While the first generation of policy analysts were unqualified in that they did not have a formal degree in the subject of policy analysis, they did not lack cultivation. W. J. M. Mackenzie, for example, was a former classicist turned politics don who completed his training by participating in battles between scientists in Whitehall over saturation bombing in World War II. As a native of Prague and a medieval historian by education, Rudolf Klein could apply skills cultivated initially in understanding alien societies to examine the normally unanalysed preconceptions of contemporary British policy makers, who take for granted that whatever they do must be the only thing that can be done, at least for the moment.

A good academic education is the foundation of a good policy analyst. Since the problems facing government take many forms, an education in anything from archaeology to zymurgy has relevance to public policy in an era in which British government is concerned about whether museums of antiquities are 'businesslike' and fighting battles in Brussels on behalf of the British pint as against the half-litre of Pils.

In policy analysis, history is not studied for its own sake but as an important cause and constraint upon what is happening today. Virtually every policy issue has a substantial history of prior government action; even unanticipated problems such as AIDS can be dealt with by assimilating it to previous epidemics (Day and Klein 1989). As Joseph Schumpeter has emphasised:

> No decade in the history of politics, religion, technology, painting, poetry and what not ever contains its own explanation. In

order to understand the religious events from 1520 to 1530 or
the political events from 1790 to 1800, or the developments in
painting from 1900 to 1910, you must survey a period of much
wider span. Not to do so is the hallmark of dilettantism
.(Schumpeter 1946)

If Margaret Thatcher had understood the rationale of local
authority rates, worked out in the early seventeenth century, she
would not have rushed headlong into the debacle of the poll tax,
and whoever deals with local government finance in the next
Parliament must first understand the messy inheritance of a failed
poll tax.

To understand how public policies work today it is necessary to
have an understanding of contemporary institutions and
processes. Political science, public administration, sociology and
applied economics are each relevant to this end. With only the
descriptive knowledge obtainable from newspapers, television
and participant observation, one cannot understand the connections between cause and effect, which invariably involve underlying influences that the media cannot depict because they involve
abstractions rather than individuals who can be interviewed on
television.

A knowledge of substantive problems facing government is
essential for what can be described as common to all policy issues
is usually so abstract or general as to leave unresolved the most
interesting theoretical and applied problems. Differences between
programmes, for example, defence, health care and agriculture,
are great within government and conversely create cross-national
similarities within a policy area. Specific knowledge of limited
areas of public policy are provided by social science disciplines,
for example, public administration, public finance, social administration and the sociology of education. Yet much teaching concen-
trating upon specific policy areas of government, for example,
health administration, is carried out in former polytechnics rather
than in established universities.

In the United States, the practice of securing more than one
degree frequently leads people to major first in a social science
and then in a substantive field, such as medicine, or in environmental engineering and then in public policy. Most leading
American schools of public policy have a two-year curriculum in
which the first year is spent on generic subjects and the student

has the run of Berkeley, Harvard or the University of Michigan in the second, studying whatever he or she finds of special interest to his or her public policy concerns.

Policy analysis in Britain risks separating generic knowledge – programme implementation in the abstract – from grounded knowledge about programme implementation in education, taxation, military aircraft procurement and vocational training, where radically different structures and policies are involved. Hybrid subjects, such as the economics of the environment or health policy, risk being 'ghettoised' because of concentration upon a specific field of policy or of being 'economised' by emphasising abstract theory at the expense of institutions and history.

Policy analysis is most readily cultivated when people have interests in both academic study and in the problems of society. This may take the form of membership in a local political party, working in public administration, or campaigning on an issue such as poverty or health care. In the technical sense, such interests are 'extracurricular,' but what is learned off campus can be drawn upon in academic study to test the relevance of concepts and the meaningfulness of conclusions. An individual who is not interested in what government does and is not familiar with how politicians behave is likely to be academic in the pejorative sense of the word.

Constraints upon public policy take many forms. Laws are a major constraint. In American government, the Office of General Counsel is an important office in every major government department. The law not only tells policy makers what they may or may not do; it also gives opponents openings that can be exploited in American courts to stop policies or to get even with individuals. In Britain, the analysis of public policy treats laws as a consequence of policy decisions rather than constraining what can be done. The discretion given ministers by statutes further weakens the role of law (Rose 1986). The Thatcher administration demonstrated that law could be used to impose constraints upon local authorities, always more subject to worry about *ultra vires* than their Whitehall counterparts (Page 1985). It also found effective legal means to command and prohibit actions by trade unions. Its opponents have become more aware of the uses of courts too.

Insofar as economics lives up to its name as the 'dismal science,' it is concerned with a hard constraint, the shortage of cold cash that cannot be resolved by the adoption of notional 'real' money values but must be lived (Wildavsky 1992; Caiden and Wildavsky 1974). A study of the literature of budgeting, a specialised and atypical branch of economics and political science, can give a person some idea of what such a constraint means. The lesson is taught inescapably as a set of problems facing students, teachers and civil servants in public institutions.

Political constraints are the stuff of political science. In the United States, the need to get votes in Congress makes the process of bargaining and trade-offs palpable and public. In Britain, parliamentary votes are not usually the chief constraint upon cabinet ministers. Many constraints have reflected the desire of politicians to maintain consensus within the governing party or across party lines. The friction created by Margaret Thatcher, for whom conviction was more important than consensus, is a reminder of just how hostile British politics is to a government determined to use its parliamentary majority to push through legislation that is controversial. Intangibles are hard to learn about from books alone. Budding policy analysts could do worse than to participate in simulations in which they play the part of cabinet ministers, with each assigned the role of advocating a policy change and the others fighting against it from their different corners.

Radical analysts can elaborate the consequences of a given policy that they regard as undesirable. For example, an analyst can show that by specified measures the Thatcher government increased income inequality and denounce the Thatcher government for doing so. Yet this ignores the fact that promoting the well-being of the better off was part of the Thatcher strategy to encourage business, and Labour leaders have never campaigned on a policy of radical income redistribution for fear that it would thereby cost them votes. There is something to be learned from W. J. M. Mackenzie's distinction between personal preferences and analytic understanding: 'I can explain it but I cannot justify it.'

Sizing up a problem requires a sense of proportion. As John W. Tukey once remarked: 'Far better an approximate answer to the right question, which is often vague, than an exact answer to the wrong question.' This can be shown in words as well as numbers: for example, in former Director of the United States Census Richard Scammon's description of the majority of the American electorate as 'Unpoor, unyoung and unblack.' Republicans got the message faster than Democrats and have more often won the White House by building a majority coalition. In Britain, any statement about the problems of millions of people implies that their problems are not faced by tens of millions of people.

Statistics in its literal sense of the study of politically relevant numbers is invariably important. Unfortunately, it is less and less studied in universities, where teaching now concentrates upon inferential statistics rather than upon the measurement of that which algebraic signs are meant to represent. Inputting inadequate quantitative indicators to a complex system of equations can produce pages of printout, but it does not ipso facto produce policy-relevant knowledge. Policy analysts should be taught *better and more* about the art and science of measurement and statistical analysis. Aaron Wildavsky once surprised a group of British academics by explaining that the University of California School of Public Policy taught its students how to write captions to tables. A London School of Economics professor dismissed this as insulting nonsense. No one educated in Scotland, continental Europe or classical Greece would have reacted thus against the idea that an educated person should be able to express him- or herself in both words and numbers.

Connecting different elements of a problem in a causal model requires the ability to distinguish between cause and effect and then create a flow chart showing what must be done to implement a policy. The causal models of policy analysis are inductive and incremental. Additional elements can be added as one learns more about the nature of a problem. Such learning models differ fundamentally from deductive models of economic systems, created by a process of exogenising known causes of difficulties and being closed to the incorporation of additional knowledge. They also differ from the output of a regression equation, which is normally not a model of an operating system but a set of numbers that can inform but not create an operational model.

Policy making is not only about problem-solving but also about coping by identifying elements of problems that are capable of resolution and adapting to situations that cannot be changed. To do this means moving from the past to the future. By definition, the future cannot be known for certain. To accept this does not mean that we know nothing about what is likely to happen tomorrow, for total uncertainty is also unobtainable. Nor can we accept

that whatever is, is right – for example, that whatever is government policy at the moment about sterling or about Northern
Ireland is the only possible thing that could be done. Anyone who
understands bridge or gambling understands how probabilities
influence outcomes. A penchant for mechanical certainty or total
uncertainty does not absolve responsible people from dealing
with the uncertainties of life.

A proposal for action is likely to involve elements already in
place, a few drawn from lessons elsewhere, and some that are
original. A measure of creativity is thus essential to formulate
policy proposals. Creativity cannot be taught from a textbook, but
it can be encouraged and cultivated. A university that made no
effort to do so would be processing rather than teaching students.
Creativity involves speculation: what would happen if. . . . In policy
analysis, it must be 'bounded speculation' (Rose 1993) subject to
budgetary, legal and political constraints, otherwise it is idle or
academic.

The promotion of public policies is an entrepreneurial activity.
The rhetorical and interpersonal skills required are very different
from those needed for doing good policy analysis. The two are not
mutually exclusive: a single individual may be a good analyst and a
good entrepreneur. In a complementary fashion, a single individual may be a bad analyst and a bad entrepreneur. The more interesting cases are people who are good analysts but bad promoters
of their conclusions and individuals who are good promoters but
bad analysts (Marmor with Fellman 1986).

Planting Seeds

Whereas an academic in a seminar can ignore awkward facts by
uttering the magic phrase – 'Let us assume' – a policy analyst must
accept many constraints as given. Yet in time, constants become
variables. In the 1980s British policy making was dominated by a
democratic constraint, the imperatives and vetoes of a popularly
elected government led by Margaret Thatcher, which placed many
recommendations of the great and the good politically out of
bounds. The 1990s are characterised by the absence of Thatcherite
constraints. The election of a Labour government would introduce
new constraints in place of old. Even topics that are regarded as

'too hot' for any political party to handle are not permanently barred from debate or even adoption. In the 1960s Reginald Maudling explained that no government could have a population policy, for that would mean a policeman in every bedroom. In the 1990s, however, population pressures are pushing population policy forward. The window of opportunity for introducing new policies is often shut but not permanently shut – and can open unexpectedly.

In cultivating ideas about public policy, an analyst cannot expect results to follow as predictably as the rotation of the seasons. A policy analyst needs to cultivate what theologians call a sense of 'right time.' In the graphic image of an American lobbyist: 'People who are trying to advocate change are like surfers waiting for the big wave. You get out there, you have to be ready to go, you have to be ready to paddle. If you're not ready to paddle when the big wave comes along, you're not going to ride in' (Kingdon 1984). This is not the only approach to the waters of time. Whitehall also offers examples that Spike Milligan has sung about in 'I'm Walking Backwards for Christmas Across the Irish Sea.' It is often overlooked that if one keeps walking long enough, eventually a landfall is reached.

Policy analysis is a recent arrival in the universities. The old tradition of studying British government is sacerdotal in the Erastian tradition of *Ecclesia Anglicana*. Teachers pronounced eternal verities of British administration that encouraged students to place their trust or wonder in those who ruled on high. The approach could also be found in the BBC's attitude to authority prior to the advent of independent television (Blumler 1969). It was a far cry from policy analysis conceived as *Speaking Truth to Power* (Wildavsky 1979). It was also a far cry from the belief that by interviewing individuals or reading diaries one can learn what has happened on the inside, as in, for example, the published diaries of R. H. S. Crossman. As I know from personal experience when writing my doctoral thesis, Crossman was an incorrigible romancer, mixing truth with invention, ready to change his mind on matters of fact as well as interpretation if it suited his donnish temper.

Failure breeds need. The symbolic turning point occurred in 1974, when Sir William Armstrong, a giant of the old Whitehall system, was overcome by the confrontation between the Heath administration and the miners. Since then, more than one cabinet secretary has had to admit under public questioning that Whitehall procedure justifies being 'economical with the truth.' In an open international economy, the Official Secrets Act cannot prevent reality from finding a way of breaking in, whether from archives in Washington or from actions in Brussels or Frankfurt. The collapse of the pound in 1992 is a spectacular example of the failure of British policy makers to consider what actions might be necessary by foreign governments to maintain a commitment of Her Majesty's government. A latter-day British policy analyst might someday publish a manifesto entitled *Speaking Truth to Weakness*.

The old-fashioned belief that the job of Whitehall was to produce community not policy (Heclo and Wildavsky 1974) can no longer be sustained. The stimulus to search is not the will-o'-the-wisp of optimisation theory but the prod of dissatisfaction. In such circumstances, a policy analyst could do worse than think of Adlai Stevenson's description of Eleanor Roosevelt: 'She would rather light a candle than curse the darkness.' For his part, Rudolf Klein has not only lit many cigars but also illuminated major areas of public policy that would otherwise be overlooked.

Notes

1. A founder of public choice, Gordon Tullock, once remarked to me that the Virginia School of Public Choice benefited because it initially had to recruit PhD students from less prestigious universities, many of which were Catholic. He considered it easy to teach public choice theory to graduate students who, since primary school days, had systematically been taught the Thomist proof of the existence of God.

2. Compare the distinction made between theory and practice in the story told me by a leading Budapest professor when I mentioned the World Bank. A farmer with chickens that were dying went to the rabbi for advice. The rabbi told the farmer to change the door of the chicken coop so that it opened out instead of in. As chickens continued to die, he returned. The rabbi advised the farmer to lower the window in the coop so the chickens would have more daylight. More chickens died. On the third visit the rabbi asked when the chickens were fed. On learning it was at 6, 12 and 18 hours, he advised feeding based on prime numbers – 7, 13 and 19 hours. The rabbi did not see the farmer until six months later at a

fair. When he asked how the chickens were, the farmer dolefully replied, 'All my chickens are dead.' The rabbi exclaimed, 'A pity. And I had so many more good ideas.' When I started to tell this story to policy makers in Warsaw and Vienna, they interrupted by telling me the punch line.

References

Blumler, J. G. 1969. Producers' Attitudes Towards Television Coverage of an Election Campaign. *Sociological Review Monograph* 13: 85–115.

Caiden, N., and A. Wildavsky. 1974. *Planning and Budgeting in Poor Countries*. New York: John Wiley.

Day, P., and R. Klein. 1987. *Accountabilities: Five Public Services*. London: Tavistock.

———. 1989. Interpreting the Unexpected: The Case of AIDS Policymaking in Britain. *Journal of Public Policy* 9(3): 337–54.

Enthoven, A. C. 1990. What Can Europeans Learn from Americans? In *Health Care Systems in Transition (OECD Social Policy Studies No. 7)*, 57–74. Paris: Organisation for Economic Co-operation and Development.

Etzioni, A. 1985. Making Policy for Complex Systems: A Medical Model for Economics. *Journal of Policy Analysis and Management* 4(3): 383–95.

Heclo, H., and A. Wildavsky. 1974. *The Private Government of Public Money*. London: Macmillan.

Hunter, D. 1982. Organising for Health: The National Health Service in the United Kingdom. *Journal of Public Policy* 2(3): 263–300.

Kingdon, J. W. 1984. *Agendas, Alternatives and Public Policies*. Boston: Little, Brown.

Klein, R. 1989. *The Politics of the National Health Service*. London: Longman.

Lipset, S. M., 1994. The State of American Sociology. *Sociological Forum* 9(2): 199–220.

McCloskey, D. 1985. *The Rhetoric of Economics*. Madison: University of Wisconsin Press.

Marmor, T. R. 1994. *Understanding Health Care Reform*. New Haven: Yale University Press.

———. 1986. Policy Entrepreneurship in Government. *Journal of Public Policy* 6(1): 225–54.

Mosley, P. 1984. *The Making of Economic Policy*. Brighton: Wheatsheaf.

Page, E. C. 1985. Law As an Instrument of Public Policy. *Journal of Public Policy* 5(2): 241–67.

Ricketts, M., and E. Shoesmith. 1990. *British Economic Opinion: A Survey of a Thousand Economists*. London: Institute of Economic Affairs.

Rose, R. 1993. *Lesson-Drawing in Public Policy: A Guide to Learning across Time and Space*. Chatham, NJ: Chatham House.

———. 1991a. Prospective Evaluation through Comparative Analysis. In *International Comparisons of Vocational Education and Training*, ed. Paul Ryan, 68-92. London: Falmer Press.

———. 1991b. Comparing Forms of Comparative Analysis. *Political Studies* 39(3): 446-62.

———. 1989. *Ordinary People in Public Policy*. London: Sage Publications.

———. 1986. Law As a Resource of Public Policy. *Parliamentary Affairs* 39(3): 297-314.

———. 1976. Disciplined Research and Undisciplined Problems. *International Social Science Journal* 28(1): 99-121.

———, and P. Davies. 1994. *Inheritance in Public Policy: Change without Choice in Britain*. New Haven: Yale University Press.

Schumpeter, J. A. 1946. The American Economy in the Interwar Period. *American Economic Review* 36 (supplement): 1-10.

———. 1942. *Capitalism, Socialism and Democracy*. London: George Allen & Unwin.

Simon, H. A. 1979. Rational Decision Making in Business Organisations. *American Economic Review* 69(4): 493-513.

———. 1969. *The Sciences of the Artificial*. Cambridge: MIT Press.

Thompson, G. 1961. *The Inspiration of Science*. London: Oxford University Press.

Weber, M. 1948. *From Max Weber*. Eds. H. H. Gerth and C. Wright Mills. London: Routledge and Kegan Paul.

Wildavsky, A. 1992. *The New Politics of the Budgetary Process*, 2d ed. New York: HarperCollins.

———. 1979. *Speaking Truth to Power: The Art and Craft of Policy Analysis*. Boston: Little, Brown.

12

Some Policy Analysis Fallacies: A Nit-picker's Guide

Patricia Day

Vulgar error is the name given to an opinion which, being thought to be false, is considered in itself only, and not with a view to any consequences which it may produce. It is termed vulgar with respect to the multitude of persons by whom it is supposed to be entertained.

– Bentham, 1824

Fallacy is applied to discourse in any shape considered as having a tendency, with or without design, to cause any erroneous opinion to be embraced, or, through the medium of some erroneous opinion already entertained, a pernicious course of action to be engaged in or persevered in. Thus to believe that the persons who lived in early or old times were, because they lived in those times, wiser or better than those who live in later or modern times, is a vulgar error; but to employ that error in the endeavour to cause pernicious practices and institutions to be retained is a fallacy.

– Bentham, 1824

This chapter is about some of the fallacies encountered in policy analysis. It is a fitting tribute to Rudolf Klein in that he sees fallacy as attaching to erroneous opinions already entertained within policy analysis. But before examining these fallacies there is a certain irony to be mentioned, which is that Rudolf Klein is himself victim of a fallacy; that is, the erroneous idea that a division can be made between policy analysis that is done to be useful and that which is not. Rudolf Klein's self-declared purpose is to produce policy reflection and analysis that is primarily understandable and of interest rather than its being of use, useful or usable: in other words, he is for policy art and craft not policy intervention. The contention of this chapter is that while it is both reasonable and legitimate for individual policy analysts to want to work to fulfil different purposes, the differences between the purposes are themselves fallacious. Good policy analysis carried out for whatever purpose has the same checklist of ingredients. But many policy analysts see their own work as having a broad range of uses, and it is considered perfectly acceptable within the trade to aim for both art and policy intervention. The problems of juggling with multipurpose analysis are well documented by academics (Cohen and Lindblom 1979; Lindblom 1990), and policy analysts have long been urged by Wildavsky and others to assume that their work has multiple aims, including analysis in its own right and for its own sake (Wildavsky 1979).

But it is, however, highly unlikely that analysis can be useful if it is not understandable. And it is demonstrably true that the most negotiable research information is first and foremost an interesting read. Its usability is directly related to its potential to stimulate and engage an audience. Thus, the creation of useful and reasonable explanations about politics and policy turns out to be inextricably linked with analysis done purely for art and interest.

Most of us want our research to be authentic, easy to understand, and interesting to other analysts. At the same time, some of us like the idea of our work being used by practitioners. And it is this need to be useful that makes policy analysts most likely to indulge in fallacies. Indeed, the risk of falling into fallacy is highest among those of us who desire to influence policy making (Majone 1989). For the purposes of this chapter, however, I am allowing my need to make useful contributions to policy making to be overridden by my nit-picking tendencies. Hence, I am assuming the role of fallacy observer rather than fallacy maker.

This chapter will go on to discuss in more detail, and give some illustrations of, the circumstances in which fallacies in analytical methods are most likely to occur. There is, for example, a special danger in policy areas that have a particularly high political temperature: in these circumstances the fallacies on which work is being based are often long established and resistant, therefore, to change. I am not selecting any specific Saint Sebastians for mention but will use these policy areas to illustrate some analytical errors. Very simply my strategy is to take on the fallacies themselves, not individual analysts.

Avoiding New Questions and Protecting Old Answers

Any guide to policy analysis fallacies must begin with the ones associated with inappropriate (in all senses) questions and premises since it is one of the key areas of policy analysis failure. A detailed discussion of the case of the policy analysis question can be found in Ellie Scrivens's essay, 'Asking the Right Question,' in which she gives examples of dead ends down which analysts travel on the back of outdated and irrelevant questions (see chap. 13). In addition, she discusses the problems associated with questions that are either too complex or too simplistic (rather than simple). One of the nicest examples she gives of exchanging the 'wrong' question for the 'right' one is that supplied by Rudolf Klein in 1980. Having been struck by the question commonly asked in policy analysis, why some people get so little a share of society's resources, he suggested that changing the question rather than continuing the search for answers might be more enlightening: 'The puzzle, rather is to explain why. . .the most disadvantaged, lacking in both market and political power, get any resources at all' (Klein 1980).

But, as noted earlier, where the main desire of analysts is to feed into a policy agenda, there is a greater tendency to leave old policy questions unexamined and cling fiercely to the premises that help to fuel partisan arguments. Some areas of policy analysis in particular have been so dominated by unchanging answers and unquestioned principles that the idea of asking new questions has been seen as unnecessary if not unworthy by lobbyists. One such area is that of poverty and social inequalities.

But it is not only new questions that have been neglected in this area, it is also the case that poverty has been put forward as the explanation rather than an explanation of other observed inequalities. For example, the notion that there is a direct causal correlation between poverty, social class and ill health has been the unchanging premise on which the poverty industry has thrived. Not only has the poverty lobby managed to keep this hypothesis virtually intact for many years but it has also successfully maintained the idea that inequalities in health between social classes have persisted over time. It is actually only since the mid-1980s that attempts have been made by outsiders to break into the poverty and health inequalities industry in order to create a better understanding of the mechanisms of the relationship. As a response to the poverty lobby in 1991, Rudolf Klein wrote a paper in which he suggested that separating out health policy analysis from that of social and economic inequalities, treating each as autonomous and legitimate areas of policy concern, would be beneficial to both. He set out to demonstrate the advantages of a more disaggregated approach to the study of poverty and health. It was emphasised in his paper that the motives for subjecting the subjects to some intellectual fresh air were not to destroy either of the policy areas but to do greater justice to both: 'The case for greater social and economic equality should be argued on its own terms, as intrinsically desirable, rather than using the health issue to justify it.' He asked also, 'whether health policy should be exclusively driven by a concern about inequality. . .or whether maximising the population's health might not be an equally desirable policy objective, if with rather different implications' (Klein 1991).

There are, in addition, an assortment of studies being carried out that are expressing serious doubts about the traditional approaches to the study of health inequalities.

> There have been many occasions in the history of scientific inquiry when propositions that have initially provided considerable understanding of a particular phenomenon, then become unbending principles that serve to regulate the acceptance of contradictory evidence and the re-evaluation of ideas. And so it is with contemporary explanations of the social etiology of dis-

ease and death and the dominant and guiding principle that it is poverty that causes worse health and earlier death. The principle seems to be applied whether populations are young, middle-aged or old, whether they are male or female, whether they are aggregated by country, by region or by social class, or whether the time period under study is the earlier, middle or latter part of the century. (Baker 1995)

This study also asks questions about patterns over time in death rates for specific illnesses, which throws into doubt the straight causal relationship between poverty and health inequalities as expressed by the traditionalists. For example, there is now some long-range evidence about deaths from lung cancer in northern and southern Europe that suggests that affluence as well as poverty is strongly associated with ill health and death. It is, in fact, only through longitudinal studies of health status that these new correlations emerge:

But some facts, however they are interpreted, cannot be made to fit the poverty principle and require a more flexible approach to be fully understood. Firstly, premature death from degenerative diseases has been linked to relative affluence as well as relative poverty, suggesting that the behavioural risk factors underlying such deaths are not always more characteristic of poorer populations. Take for example premature death from lung cancer for men in Europe. In the 1950s rates of mortality in more affluent countries in Northern Europe, such as Austria, Finland, England and Wales, were more than double those of poorer Southern European countries such as Italy, Spain and Greece. Increasing affluence has brought a decline in rates of mortality in Northern Europe from the 1960s onwards, but a continuing increase in the countries of Southern Europe, so that there is little variation in rates of premature mortality from this cause in these two contrasting geographical regions of Europe. Changing economic trends have brought with them changes in the relationship between socio-economic conditions and premature death. (Baker 1995)

It appears, however, that there is still some mileage to be gained for the poverty lobbyists in promoting straight causalities between ill health, premature mortality, and socio-economic inequalities and ignoring the research evidence of more complex and puzzling associations between health status and socio-economic variables. The *British Medical Journal* (3 December 1994) contained a series of articles on research findings that were presented as evidence for the promotion of policy to deal with poverty and ill health (Smith and Morris 1994; Judge 1994). In one paper, evidence was cited of increased differences between small deprived and affluent areas of Scotland. Another looked at the differences in life expectancy between Dutch men with different levels of education. However, what is most interesting about the editorial summary is that it failed to discuss the obviously more complex and interesting findings about the relationships between poverty and ill health that do not fit simply into the straight correlations being used for political pressure. For example, the results of the longitudinal study on age-standardised mortality of men aged 40 to 64 in different grades of the British civil service provide us with even more disconcerting evidence that health status is not related to poverty as conventionally perceived (Marmot, Kogevinas and Elston 1987). The study followed more than 10,000 British civil servants for nearly 20 years, and the findings were that health status fell with every grade; mortality over a ten-year period was three and a half times as high for men in the clerical and manual grades as in the senior administrative grades. But, of course, people working in the civil service are not in poverty, which makes these findings both complex and puzzling. It appears that hierarchical positions and relationships between groups and individuals are more significant in health status than absolute levels of income.

Marmot's findings, far from bolstering the poverty lobby, suggest that we still have some way to go in the area of health studies: an aggregate of several inequalities under the holdall title of poverty, although high on political salience, needs considerable unpicking in order to make a useful contribution to policy making. For example, the aggregate of low income, alcoholism, and low levels of education may be highly positively correlated with morbidity and mortality, but this tells us nothing about the relationship between the components of this particular aggregate nor does it indicate the direction of the correlation. Other material on the subject of the complex relationship between poverty and health is provided by Fuchs's study of health policy, which stresses the need for clear and disaggregated definitions of poverty as a priority for health policy analysis:

> Let us try to avoid such confusion. This is not to deny that
> people can be poor in ways other than economic. . . .But to the

extent possible, let us strive for clarity. If we mean low income, let's say low income. If we mean education, let's say education. And if we mean alcoholism, cigarette smoking, crime, drug abuse, fragmented families, hazardous occupations, sexual promiscuity, slum housing, social alienation or unhealthy diets, let's say so explicitly. If we constantly re-define poverty to include anything and everything that contributes to poor health, we will make little progress either in theory or practice. (Fuchs 1993)

However, if we assume that the dogged determination to stick to these principles stems from good intentions and that the old-school poverty lobby is concerned with keeping up a high emotional profile and chivvying politicians (Bailey 1983) then we must also assume that they are working on the notion that the ends justify the means. That is, their refusal to unpick old premises and search for new questions is an effort to be useful to policy making. Even if this is so, it is making the assumption that any new thinking and a change in the questions being asked would automatically undermine the case against poverty and social inequalities. Simple messages have more resonance in politics, of course, and the intellectual investment that has been sunk into poverty studies makes any rethinking a painful process. But the irony is that this particular line of analysis leads to specific and narrow prescriptions and may actually prevent the analysts from looking at things that really matter: the tunnel view that occurs when thinking stops is precisely what denies new policy insights.

The Slough of the False Context

The policy analysis fallacy of constructing an artificial context in order to present a current social or political issue as a 'crisis' has several dimensions. It sometimes takes the form of a past raised up as so much better or so much worse than the present (of which the 'crisis' is a part) in order to make unflattering comparisons or raise the temperature of the policy debate. The false context can also be used to create a real-time 'crisis' out of a policy area that is not actually at a critical level. And it can be employed to suggest a future scenario of mayhem in which current policy analysis can be used to influence political decisions. Like the fallacies associated with asking the wrong questions, the false context fallacies are usually to be found within policy areas where the main aim is to feed into the political lobby or to otherwise inform policy making.

One such area is health policy, where there are regular attempts to create an imaginary past: a policy Eden against which to better contrast a present filled with change and uncertainty – a past that makes it all the easier to display current policies as inappropriate. It has been a device resorted to regularly in National Health Service (NHS) policy analysis whenever there have been attempts to make changes in the organisation of services. Making any alterations to what exists in the NHS has been seen as retrograde by health services workers of all kinds, and the public climate surrounding the British NHS has been largely one of conservation and protection. This resistance to change and its motives has, of course, been taken up and examined by Rudolf Klein over the years, and one of his most valuable contributions to health policy has been to demystify both the origins and organisation of the NHS.

Public housing policy is another area in which the fallacies of the better past have been created in order to demonstrate that present policy is in crisis. This need for fallacy can be explained as follows. Since the mid-1980s there has been a shift from the production of social housing by the public sector and local government to the independent housing association movement. This change from state development has, of course, been accompanied by a deliberate transfer of government finance away from the public sector into the independent or not-for-profit sector (Day, Henderson and Klein 1993). But this change represents more than just a different source of bricks and mortar: it actually means a quite dramatic cultural change for housing policy and in particular for the analysts. The switch of central government resources from local government to housing associations has been seen by many analysts in the field as a disastrous policy, and it has galvanised them into producing evidence that public sector housing provision is being killed off (Cole and Furbey 1994) – and, further, that social housing tenants were safer and better treated by local government than they are by quangos [quasi-autonomous non-governmental organisations] and charities. But just how well does their evidence stand up?

Let us look first at the idea that new policies for housing association development are stripping the public sector of its housing functions, a present and future, that is, in which the state no longer has any interest or responsibilities for social housing. Although it is true that the housing legislation of the 1980s has more or less halted schemes for new developments of housing, local authorities are still by far the biggest landlords of social housing. In spite of the not-for-profit housing programmes backed by state finance and in spite of the sale and transfer of large numbers of public sector dwellings, local authorities in 1994 owned 85 per cent of all housing for rent in the United Kingdom: public housing in England and Wales still accounted for about 20 per cent of the total housing stock (the figure in Scotland was 40 per cent). These figures show a continuing large-scale public sector interest in housing even after a decade of policies designed to cut down the local authorities' share of the social housing market. But, in spite of this evidence to the contrary, the line is being maintained by some policy analysts that public sector housing is a thing of the past. They carefully fail to mention that the state is still, by far, the biggest landlord of social housing despite the quite radical changes in national housing policy.

Another claim by the critics of housing policy changes is that tenants have more rights and a better deal under state provision than their fellows in housing associations since democratic rights are naturally associated with, and assured by, the electoral system. The difference being alleged is that tenancies held within the state system have accountable, elected politicians in control while housing association tenants cannot hold their landlords (or the regulators who inspect and impose sanctions and restrictions on housing associations) to account. In other words, housing policies of the 1990s are creating a democratic deficit by handing over development programmes to unelected bodies. However, while it is, in fact, true that the governing boards of housing associations are not elected into office through the political process, the fallacy here is to suggest that the politicians operating at local authority level are automatically, by reason of election, accountable to their electorate and, in particular, to their tenants.

There are good reasons to argue about the concept of accountability and political election – not least because the notion of accountability to an electoral subset, that is, tenants of public housing, is in itself problematic. However, for the purposes of this chapter, I will avoid some of the more complex issues of political accountability and discuss how elected politicians are often, in practice, unable to be accountable either to their electorate or to a subset of voters. And this dilemma of the unaccountable politician is not new. A social scientist carried out a study in the 1970s of the role of local authorities in the scrutiny and regulation of public services. As part of this study, he interviewed locally elected politicians about their role in local government and discovered that the elected members saw themselves as strong on policy making but powerless on policy implementation. They declared themselves to be largely unable to control the way in which public services were actually delivered and managed. In housing, particularly, where there were (and still are) the most complaints, elected members were in no way able to respond to tenants' problems (Saunders 1979). In effect, politicians had very little accountability for the outcomes of local public services.

Until the revival of performance expectations in the public sector in the mid-1980s, the lack of involvement of the elected members in the outcomes of public services went largely unmentioned (Day 1993). The fallacy here is the creation of a housing policy context in which the analysts carefully avoid the evidence of a democratic failure experienced under old policies while emphasising the democratic deficit associated with new policies.

The Alarmist Future

There are several areas in health policy that have been subjected to large doses of negative crystal ball gazing by analysts determined to alert the policy makers and politicians to impending doom. The HIV and AIDS analysis fallacy of the false future does qualify, as do other fallacies described, as an attempt by lobbyists to sustain interest and resource flows into a policy area. In this sense, the fallacy arises out of a routine strategy of employing analytical means to justify policy ends. The protagonists of this doom-laden yet fallacious analysis are involved in a cause in which, presumably, they believe. But how can we explain the perseverance of the lobby in the face of evidence that the input of resources is vastly out of proportion to the tasks at hand? On the one hand, a level of pessimism about the future of AIDS is understandable since it is a disease with an uncertain future and for which no successful treatment has yet emerged. On this account, therefore, prevention services must be continued and a level of health and social services preserved. However, policies for the allocation of resources for AIDS patients have been confounded by predictions of a future of catastrophically large numbers of people stricken with the disease. The figures on actual numbers of AIDS and HIV cases in the United Kingdom since 1982 contrasts sharply with the predictions that were made for and over the last decade. In 1987, with the cumulative total of AIDS cases at approximately 2,000, the Christian Medical Fellowship (quoted in the Office of Health Economics 1988) predicted three million HIV cases in 1991, rising to twelve million in 1994. They predicted 120,000 and 240,000 AIDS cases, respectively, for the same years. The available statistics on AIDS show that the United Kingdom has one of the lowest prevalence rates in the Western world. The cumulative total of all AIDS cases in the United Kingdom between 1984 and 1994 was 9,865.

But in spite of this evidence of a steady but modest growth in the number of AIDS cases in the United Kingdom, resources continue to be allotted to services for HIV- and AIDS-infected people in the United Kingdom, at a rate that ignores the evidence and chooses to assume an unreasonably pessimistic future scenario. As a result, for an observed AIDS prevalence rate of 156 cases per one million of the population in the United Kingdom, the NHS has allocated £230 million for HIV-AIDS services in 1995, with £49 million for prevention in the same year. These ring-fenced resources allocated to AIDS are being distributed to health authorities, some of which do not have sufficient numbers of AIDS cases to use their allocation. In fact, more than 70 per cent of all AIDS cases in England are in the London regions.

In times of limited public spending and strict advice from central government to health authorities to match their spending and purchasing of services to their own populations, it is a bizarre situation. The reasons for this mismatch of resources to apparent need or demand have been discussed at length by various analysts outside the AIDS lobby and do not, therefore, require a large-scale reiteration here. In brief, the pressure for sustained political and financial involvement has come partly from a lobby whose fear of the unknown is genuine and partly from the medical specialisms for which AIDS has meant a revival of fortunes and a new kudos

(Craven, Stewart and Taghavi 1993). One can only hope that the surplus-to-requirements AIDS funding being experienced by many health purchasing authorities is being used creatively for other good causes.

Another policy area prone to the creation of mock contexts in Britain is that of private health care. The most common analytical fallacy is the one where a future is created in which private health care outstrips and outperforms or otherwise presents a real threat to the continued existence of the NHS. This hypothesis or night-mare scenario has been put forward at regular intervals since the 1970s and has been used to harness support and raise political awareness, usually when the NHS is suffering the strains of new policy making. At these times, a future is created in which a large-scale expansion in the private sector of health care is accompa-nied by an equally strong suggestion that the government of the day is plotting to privatise and, therefore by definition, destroy the NHS. That there has never been any evidence anywhere that either of these hypotheses are true does not seem to deter the zealous analysts who subscribe to the theory of the downfall of the NHS. In reality, the private sector of health care in Britain has expanded between 1980 and the early 1990s, but the growth has been modest in relative terms and shows no sign of achieving the pro-portions suggested by the prophets of NHS annihilation. The total number of private acute hospital beds rose from approximately 7,000 in 1980 to approximately 10,000 in 1991. The number of pri-vate hospitals went up from 154 to 216 during the same period. In 1988, part of the doom-laden school of analysis not only predicted a damaging (for the welfare of the NHS) expansion in private health care but, worse, that this growth would be as a result of an increase in the numbers of American private hospitals and beds opening up in Britain. Quite what the implication was of the expansion's being American did not become clear, unless it was that an American expansion had the drama of a truly capitalist invasion.

But for whatever reasons the policy analysts want to set up this particular negative future for the NHS, there were already signs that this private sector take-over was not going to happen, even while the analysts were predicting it as inevitable. The growth of the American market in particular was a very strange prediction indeed, since at the time it was made in 1988, the number of

American groups in Britain was already declining. In the 1980s, American interests had started to give way to UK and continental owners (mainly French), and the number of American beds went down from 366 in 1979 to 266 in 1991.

Like other fallacies associated with false pasts and presents, the private health care fallacy relied heavily for its credibility on a political climate high on uncertainty and low on real information and knowledge. As of 1994, the private health care sector in Britain is well but modest compared to the NHS. It is most certainly not taking over from the NHS as predicted by the school of disasters – and for precisely all the complex reasons that the serious scholars of health policy know and write about. To mention only one such explanation, the British public and private health care systems are not, for example, discrete entities: the medical staff are the same people in both sectors. Moreover, the relationship between the NHS and the private health care sector has been demonstrated to be highly symbiotic.

Finally, one very large drawback to the creation of a private health sector as a threat to the NHS is the other less well-known private health care in Britain, a hidden sector that actually consists of the medications and treatments bought by us over the chemists' counters directly and with no medical intervention. At last count, the amount spent on NHS services annually by the treasury was approximately £30 billion, the figure for private acute care was £1,868 million per year, and the spending we do ourselves at the chemists, together with what we spend on complimentary and alternative medicine, was £3,050 million annually.

Arbitrary Aggregates

There is a tendency within some policy analysis areas to assume or maintain inappropriate categories and groupings of people for research observation in order to structure findings and therefore influence recommendations for political action; it is sometimes even so that these same people are grouped into different categories simultaneously in order to bend the will of the analysts. This fallacy of policy aggregates, which is another variety of the false context, also has its origins in the good but self-deluded intentions of the policy analysts. Some examples of inappropriate aggregates include those that have been suitable in the past but have become outmoded; other examples occur as straight fictions devised by the lobbyists to create or retain public interest and a high political profile in some policy areas; in these situations, the use of mock but emotive aggregations to support policies is understandable since it remains part of the dilemma experienced by analysts who juggle with their desire to feed into a policy lobby and at the same time to fulfil their role as policy researchers.

But to be fair to lobbyists and policy analysts, populations under observation are rarely conveniently discrete entities, and many have their feet in several camps. For example, the two policy areas of the elderly and single-parent families, which I will discuss in more detail later, are complex and traditionally intertwined with poverty and deprivation studies. In this sense of overlapping and linked policy areas, it has been more difficult, both practically and emotionally, to unpick these groups for closer examination. But while the will to scrutinise in detail has long been absent, often for good reasons, the means for examining these groups in greater depth has become possible with the development of information technology; policy analysts can now study their populations with the aid of machines, expand the research categories, and examine them in other shapes and forms. But if the possibilities for research analysis have multiplied enormously, so too has the scope of analytic schizophrenia in some policy areas.

The problems of inappropriate policy aggregations can occur in a range of research situations, but, for the purposes of illustration, I will discuss only two of the main reasons here. First, problems arise where groupings or stratifications of populations are used over long periods of time but are left unexamined for changes in relevance or appropriateness and with no apparent interest or curiosity on the part of the analysts in how things would look if the groups were disaggregated and reformed. Social class is one such aggregation. David Mechanic sums up cogently the dilemmas associated with the use of this most distinguished of policy analysis aggregates in the area of health policy:

> Socio-economic status is linked through a variety of pathways to many important influences on life trajectories. Socio-economic status thus serves as a window that helps identify important points of intervention and remediation. But practicality requires

that we also identify factors more closely associated with health outcomes so that we maximise opportunities to intervene effectively. (Mechanic 1994)

Second, there is fallacious aggregation where unalikes are put together in the misunderstanding that they form a coherent aggregate. In both cases, the aggregations are artificial and errors occur. I consciously use the word *error* rather than *deception* because the aggregationists tend, like the other fallacy makers, to congregate in the policy-analysis-for-pressure group, which wants to be politically useful and support what it sees as worthy causes. Two key policy aggregates that suffer from long periods of aggregation interspersed with occasional bursts of politically useful unpicking of constituent parts are the elderly and single-parent families. Both groups have, from time to time, had their traditional aggregate dismantled by lobbyists who are calculating the political gain of a strategic, sometimes temporary, disaggregation. Let us see briefly why this is so.

The people aged 60 to 65 years and over in Britain have long since been broken down into different age bands for the purposes of social research and policy analysis. This disaggregation is particularly useful for looking at demographic changes within the group, and it helps to calculate the need for extra resources among the very elderly. Much was made in the 1980s and 1990s of the predictions of a growth in the population of people aged 85 and over and their potential need for health and care services and, in particular, the implications of this for public expenditure. Some of this information was used at the beginning of the 1990s in, for example, the policies for community care. As it turned out, the massive proportional increases in the very elderly that were predicted in the 1980s turned out to be fairly small in number. But, of course, the resource implications for the over-85-year-olds are different from those of the 60-to-70-year-olds.

However, at the same time that the analysts have subjected the elderly to this particular scrutiny, they have refused to consider any kind of financial disaggregation of people over 60 and 65, and their disparate need for, and entitlement to, a one-price pension; the only policy concession which has been made to an economically disaggregated elderly population can be seen in the slightly higher state allowances given to the over-75-year-olds, but this is

strictly age, not means, related. So although one policy case for the
elderly is felt to be better served by an age disaggregation, the
lobby for the uniform state pension supports a continued aggregation. By sticking to the unqualified elderly label, all people 60 to 65
years old and over are assured a politically high profile as deserving and relatively poor whereas an analysis of their financial status
could weaken the support for non-means-tested old age pensions.

The case for means testing here is, of course, that the poorer
elderly could get larger pensions than the richer elderly, thus
making the pension a fairer and more cost-effective exercise. The
case against financial disaggregation of the elderly is that means
testing, in itself, is undesirable and divisive. Both of these statements are true and are part of the classic, never-to-be-resolved
policy dilemma of trying to target resources while attempting to
avoid stigmatising recipients of state monies and services. It is an
example of where policy aims are fair in some senses and unfair in
others. However, for the time being, an aggregation of the elderly
remains the preferred option for most policy analysts.

The policy aggregate of the single-parent family produces further schizophrenic tendencies among analysts than those associated with studies of the elderly population. More than most other
policy areas, the single-parent family lends itself to quite dramatic
leaps between aggregates and to charges, therefore, of arbitrary
groupings. It is a policy area that benefits at times from a massive
aggregation while at other times it best suits the political cause if
single parenthood is broken down into several discrete categories
that demonstrate the need for different policy interventions.
Single parents, like the elderly, are sometimes indistinguishable
from the poor and otherwise socially deprived, but as a policy
area they have the added danger of being able to create social
stigma through analysis. Because of this, analysts have needed to
be extra fleet of foot as they move between aggregate groups and
subgroupings. For example, it served the single-parent lobby well
for some time to allow the image of the group as uniformly poor
and socially deprived to stand unquestioned. And it was only after
the image of single-parent families as victims of society became
less clear-cut that the lobbyists saw it as politically expedient to distinguish divorced single parents from the less socially acceptable
category of never-married single parents. The problem with this
fresh analysis was that it unexpectedly showed the latter category

in an even more unflattering light, as parents who never intended to be anything else but single. These findings did not enhance the public or political support for this policy area and served mainly to drive up requests for even greater disaggregation – unfortunately, from critics rather than lobbyists. Disaggregation, in this instance, damaged rather than supported the credibility of the single-parent family: at the very least, the policy area was injected with an unwelcome level of scepticism over the plight of single parents. Disaggregation, in fact, gave rise to the suspicion that single parents and their children are possibly highly disparate types of people with a variety and range of financial and social states. This idea not only threatens to break the solidarity of a policy area and its supporters but has the potential for divisive stigmatisation of never-married women who produce children.

After this disastrous experience of disaggregation, the policy analysts are trying once again to restore the political image of the aggregate group as worthy and deserving. The problem is that the single-parent family may be unable to be reinstated as a single entity and unpicked policy area. After the separation of the group into subgroups with very different lifestyles and economic circumstances, there may be no way to restore its original policy image.

There is no doubt that disaggregation in policy analysis is both exciting and frightening in prospect. On the one hand, it can provide information and new insights that will lead to a more accurate targeting of resources, and it can be used to add weight to arguments for increased resources. On the other hand, the disaggregation of a policy area can produce information that has the power to take away public sympathy and political support for established policies.

Summary

This is a critical chapter but its tone is not intended to be downhearted. However, we do have to tell ourselves a few cautionary policy tales. First, we must recognise that, in spite of itself, policy analysis is persuasive rhetoric – all the more reason to be aware, therefore, of our own tricks as well as those of others so as to avoid being carried away by them. Second, it is essential that we produce an intellectual map that marks the fallacy traps, particularly in policy areas that are most susceptible to error. We must remind ourselves that policy analysis will only stick if we can demonstrate its safe ground. This chapter is a contribution to that end as well as a tribute to Rudolf Klein.

I began the discussion with Bentham and his definitions and descriptions of the different kinds of fallacies that we can fall into when we try to persuade others. I will finish with Aron and his arguments in favour of taking our policy theory and practice with copious drafts of doubt and scepticism - or in Rudolf Klein's language, making sure our search for answers does not stop us from asking questions:

> The secular religions dissolve into politico-economic opinions as soon as one abandons the dogma. Yet the man who no longer expects miraculous changes either from a revolution or an economic plan is not obliged to resign himself to the unjustifiable. If tolerance is born of doubt, let us teach everyone to doubt all the models and utopias, to challenge all the prophets of redemption and the heralds of catastrophe. (Aron 1957)

References

Aron, R. 1957. *The Opium of the Intellectuals*. Translated by Terence Kilmartin. London: Secker and Warburg.

Bailey, F. G. 1983. *The Tactical Uses of Passion: An Essay on Power, Reason and Reality*. Ithaca, NY, and London: Cornell University Press.

Baker, D. 1995. Poverty and Disease: A Postcard from the Edge (editorial review). *Journal of the Royal Society of Medicine* 88: 127-9.

Bentham, J. [1824] 1962. *The Handbook of Political Fallacies*. Ed. H. A. Larrabee. New York: Harper and Brothers.

Cohen, D. K., and C. E. Lindblom. 1979. *Usable Knowledge: Social Science and Social Problem Solving*. New Haven and London: Yale University Press.

Cole, I., and R. Furbey. 1994. *The Eclipse of Council Housing*. The State of Welfare. London and New York: Routledge.

Craven, B. M., G. T. Stewart, and M. Taghavi. 1993. Amateurs Confronting Specialists: Expenditure on AIDS in England. *Journal of Public Policy* 13:3.

Day, P. 1993. Social Housing Policy from the 1960s to the 1990s: Old Issues – New Machinery. Paper presented at the Housing Studies Autumn Conference, University of Reading. Fall.

———, D. Henderson, and R. Klein. 1993. *Home Rules: Regulation and Accountability in Social Housing*. York, UK: Joseph Rowntree Foundation.

Fuchs, V. R. 1993. Poverty and Health. In *The Future of Health Policy*, 51–64. Cambridge: Harvard University Press.

Judge, K. 1994. Beyond Health Care. *British Medical Journal* 309: 1454–5.

Klein, R. 1980. Models of Man and Models of Policy: Reflections on Exit, Voice and Loyalty Ten Years Later. *Milbank Memorial Fund Quarterly/Health and Society* 58:3.

———. 1991. Making Sense of Inequalities: A Response to Peter Townsend. *International Journal of Health Services* 21(1):175–81.

Lindblom, C. 1990. *Inquiry and Change: The Troubled Attempt to Understand and Shape Society*. New Haven and London: Yale University Press.

Majone, G. 1989. *Evidence, Argument and Persuasion in the Policy Process*. New Haven: Yale University Press.

Marmot, M. G., M. Kogevinas, and M. A. Elston. 1987 Social/Economic Status and Disease. *Annual Review of Public Health* 8:111–35.

Mechanic, D. 1994. *Inescapable Decisions: The Imperatives of Health Reform*. New Brunswick, NJ: Transaction Publishers.

Saunders, P. 1979. *Urban Politics: A Sociological Interpretation*. London: Hutchinson.

Smith, G. D., and J. Morris. 1994. Increasing Inequalities in the Health of the Nation. *British Medical Journal* 309: 1453–4.

Wildavsky, A. 1979. *The Art and Craft of Policy Analysis*. London: Macmillan.

13

Asking the Right Question

Ellie Scrivens

Rudolf Klein has written widely and eloquently on many subjects. In so doing, he has shed light on policy questions and problems, many of which would have remained unexamined had he not tackled them. In a number of cases, he has predicted changes in situations long before policy makers and academics have recognised their significance. But he has arrived at these conclusions by adopting his own particular approach to policy problems, one that questions conventional wisdoms and assumptions and in many cases requires policy analysts to question the basis of their own work. He shares with Heclo a scepticism of complexity: 'The simplest seeming questions are ones that can embarrass a political 'scientist' most: How do things happen? What makes things happen?' (Heclo 1994). Klein's main enthusiasm has been for examining the origins and effects of welfare policies and questioning the role of institutional power and internal organisation. His academic approach has been catholic, borrowing theories and ideas from many disciplines as and when appropriate.

The 'nose' for spotting an interesting policy area is undoubtedly something with which Rudolf Klein was born. The formulation of the interesting question is a craft that most academics can only envy. He is aided in his task by a lack of inhibition about questioning the theories accepted by many social scientists. In the Heclo mould, his interest and entertainment, for both himself and his readers, derive from looking for something interesting.

'Understanding is not enhanced if one begins by asking, "What theory of methodological schema do I have and how can it be applied here and there to historical situations?" Instead one should begin by asking, What interesting question do I want to answer and what are the most appropriate ways of trying to answer it?' (Heclo 1994).

Thus, a typical Klein approach to analysis begins with asking not why does something happen, as most social scientists would, but why do analysts assume certain outcomes when there is evidence that does not support the thesis. For example, in his examination of public expenditure, Klein began by asking the simple but rarely explored question: why do analysts postulate a direct causal link between rising public expenditure and inflation? He pointed out, 'when governments step on the accelerator of public expenditure, the engine of inflation does not automatically rev up' (Klein 1985, 196-221). Klein then begins to lay out for the reader the different hypotheses that have been used to explain the relationship and shows that these all emphasise economic rather than political factors. The explanations, so beloved of policy makers 'fail to take account of the complexity of the social, political and institutional factors that help to explain and mediate between spending and inflation' (Klein 1985, 196-221). The Klein analysis is not directed at proving a point about public expenditure but at questioning the limitations of the traditional explanatory models. Can they be improved, can our understanding be furthered if we look outside the traditional limited forms of analysis?

Underpinning Klein's question based approach to analysis is always a recognition of the need to ask simple questions, paring away the complexity to address, not the answerable, but the askable questions. A favourite starting point is to look for the puzzle or the paradox: 'The puzzle, rather is to explain why. . .the most disadvantaged, lacking in both market and political power get any resources at all' (Klein 1980b, 416-29); 'The puzzle of the emergence of private practice' (Klein 1979b, 464-90); 'The puzzle is (against all odds) the welfare state has survived – but is being reconstructed' (Klein 1990b, 501-23; 1991, 275).

The spotting of the puzzle frequently requires revision of the common form of construction of the question. So, for example, in 'The Goals of Health Policy: Church or Garage,' Klein rejects the ambitious definition of health policy, restricting himself to a narrow definition that focuses on the goals of the health care delivery system, the aims of the designers and managers, and the criteria used for judging the system's performance. The justification for this approach is that it is all too easy to lose sight of 'what can be expected of individual institutions: that blame diffusion will lead to a blurring of responsibilities' (Klein 1993a, 136-40). Or as he puts it more simply, 'what should be the policy goals of the NHS, recognising that the contribution of any health care system to "health" – at least as conventionally measured by mortality and life expectancy is very limited.' Similarly, he asks, 'It is therefore worth trying to analyse why. . .the political economy model in Britain has failed in what should be its prime function: expressing social priorities in the allocation of resources' (Klein 1974b, 1-14). 'But [he goes directly to the heart of the matter], how does it actually work? Does the system of central direction and planning in fact allow a more parsimonious and effective use of resources? How does the ideology of the political economy model health service – an instrument designed to mould the service to the needs of the community as a whole rather than any particular section of it – work out in practice. (Klein 1972, 112-25) Or, put another way, the Kleinian question is simply: if the health service can't do much about health, what is it realistic to expect it to do?

Throughout Klein's work can be found a fascination with the institutions of government, not only their structure but also their ability to continue regardless of the changing environment in which they exist. This is combined with a curiosity about the political forces that can, or cannot, shape policy. What, in fact, is it reasonable to expect policies designed by political systems to tackle?

> Let me illustrate this [issue] by looking at the debate about poverty. This is a debate essentially about inequalities in income [and opportunity]. But as soon as we define it in these terms, it becomes apparent that when we ask why inequalities have persisted so stubbornly, we are asking why it is politically so difficult to re-distribute income: a question not about the design of specific social policies but about the political feasibility of achieving certain policy aims. (Klein 1980a, 24-34)

Klein has used the tool of pointing the finger – sometimes of fun, sometimes of blame – at policy analysts who appear to be too committed to their own assumptions about how the world works or to a too narrow view of their subject. In looking at the success of capitalistic welfare states, he points to a paradox in the academic literature. His three composite theorists, the neo-Marxist O'Goffe (O'Connor, Gough and Offe), the welfare statist Marmuss (Titmuss and Marshall), and the New Right Hayman (Hayek and Friedman) are compared in terms of how well they argued the future of the welfare state. 'Take O'Goffe's assertion about the conflict between the competing claims of political legitimation, capital accumulation and consumption. What evidence is there to support the assumption that this is somehow peculiar or unique to capitalism. None' (Klein 1993c, 7-17). His criticism is directed at the limited approach adopted by analysts who have concentrated solely on endogenous variables, failing to recognise other criteria that would have been generated by a wider analysis. 'Similarly, the evidence of parallelism between capitalist and communist welfare states tended to be overlooked. . . .It is therefore difficult to resist the conclusion that the under-prediction of crisis reflected both the linguistic incompetence and the ideological predisposition of most of the scholars in the field.'

Klein has demonstrated the need to use different forms of analysis when investigating different situations. Rather than seeking a single model that will explain phenomena, Klein urges a more eclectic view: 'This paper has raised many questions without answering them. This is because, to return to the main theme, all the modes of explanation seem to be useful to varying degrees in different situations. There is no reason for assuming, a priori, that any one theory should have equal explanatory powers irrespective of the situation to which it is being applied' (Klein 1974a, 219-36). 'But how helpful are the various theories when applied to a specific field of activity? To ask whether a theory is "helpful" is to concede that it is not specific enough to be tested in a rigorous manner' (Klein 1974a, 219-36).

However, although explanatory models are used as the basis for debate, Klein has tried to develop a more rigorous approach to the activity of policy analysis itself. It is an approach that builds understanding on the basis of questioning and comparing existing levels of knowledge. In short, he has been searching for a method that will permit more wide-ranging consideration of factors and issues but that also offers better explanations of events and developments. 'The various tools of explanation are too helpful in a sense. All seem to explain something; none explains everything.

Collectively, they make up a useful analytic tool-kit; individually they are far from being universal in their application' (Klein 1974a, 219-36). One approach is to 'map,' unravel, unpick the traditional explanations:

> This paper is in no sense a statistical analysis. The method used is different. The first part of the paper reviews selectively some of the main explanatory modes developed primarily in the American literature on public expenditure, with only tangential references to the British experience; the second concentrates on a more detailed and specific analysis of British public expenditure in the light of this ground clearing discussion. . . .The starting assumption of this paper is, therefore, that where a variety of analytic tools is required when it comes to trying to explain something as complex as changes and movements in public expenditure, where a seductively quantitative face conceals some tough, unyielding questions about what the figures signify. (Klein 1976a, 401-32)

The argument driving this analysis is that simple outcomes like the extent of public expenditure reflect many policy decisions. No single explanation can account for the observed outcome.

> But what our analysis does suggest is that the limitations of each mode of explanation largely reflect the fact that each is anchored in a particular definition of the relevant universe, when it is the interaction between the societal, political and governmental systems taken together than large determines the outcome. . . .The problem then is not to decide which is the single most useful mode of explanation but how the various approaches should be fitted together. (Klein 1976a, 401-32)

What Klein demonstrated was that another analytic method used to explain policy needed to be developed. He has cautioned against the simplistic examination of the past. 'Health care policies tend to be shaped by wider societal trends. The danger is that in extrapolating past reactions we may be missing out on more important, if wider and therefore more difficult to pin down, trends such as changes in the technology of service organisation and delivery' (Klein 1987, 5-12). He has argued instead for a multi-faceted view of policy analysis:

> Instead of studying one issue in depth, it reviews a number of policy areas, deliberately using broad brush strokes. Instead of concentrating on the black-box of the decision process itself –

on the activities of the politicians, civil servants and lobbyists –
it looks at the policy areas and the policy outputs and relies
almost wholly on deducing inferentially what goes on in inside
the black box. This method has a number of advantages. It is
not conflict centred, and so allows non-decisions as well as decisions to be examined. It encourages, indeed compels, an analytical and abstract approach, so hopefully leading to a
classification of the problems, actors and outcomes which may
permit comparisons both within the NHS and across other services. (Klein 1974b, 1-14)

Comparative analysis has been a primary tool in Klein's analytical armoury. He has argued strongly the benefits of comparisons –
and the dangers. 'Comparisons are essential if one is to achieve an
understanding of one's own national health care system. Logically,
it is impossible to make a statement about cause and effect within
a national system without checking it out against the experience
of another country' (Klein 1991, 275). The significance of comparative studies in the Kleinian analysis is that it offers an alternative
truth against which to test our assumptions about what is the
'right' explanation. 'Before we can make a statement about cause-
and-effect in a particular society – or a class of societies – we
surely have to be able to test it against a counter-factual.
Otherwise, we are operating in a solipstic universe' (Klein 1993c,
7-17). And this has lead Klein to the conclusion that comparisons
must form the basis of social policy analysis: 'The comparative
method is not just a luxury add-on to the study of social policy, but
an essential component if we are to avoid repeating O'Goffe's
blunder in over-predicting the crisis of the welfare state in the
West while under-predicting its collapse in the East. . . .Even when
there was evidence of the failure of the communist regimes in the
welfare field – notably that provided by rising mortality – it tended
to be neglected in comparative social policy studies'. (Klein 1993c,
7-17)

Having argued the case for comparative analysis, he is highly
critical of the lack of analytical approaches in this field. His criticism is focused on the lack of objectivity of most analysts under-
taking comparative analysis: 'There is a lingering tendency to use
comparative studies as a search for ammunition in domestic political battles' (Klein 1993c, 7-17); 'selective perception is the original
sin of comparative studies' (Klein 1991, 275-91); 'comparativists
suffer from an occupational disease, a highly developed capacity
to find what they were looking for' (Klein 1991, 275).

Klein's comparative analytic approach calls for identification of the characteristics calculated to enhance understanding. 'Comparative studies have to be explicit about the criteria being used: the spheres of analysis as it were. Second, analysis has to be anchored in an understanding of the specific historical origins of national institutions, and of their economic, social and political context' (Klein 1991, 275). This necessitates the identification of similarities rather than differences between national health care systems. And Klein argues the case for a question-based approach to comparative analysis: 'The source of confusion is that much comparative health care research is data rather than question driven.' Analysts are forced to use the data available, mostly that relating to costs, rather than seeking data to answer questions about the relative efficacy of health care and treatments. Klein refers to this mode of comparative analysis as learning or prescriptive. It leads ineluctably to the recognition that health care systems cannot be considered in isolation from the societies that they inhabit.

Klein has attempted to develop a method of examining the world that blends the general and the specific:

> The above account of the 1974 to 1976 crisis is by no means a comprehensive history of events; it simply presents the context of analysis in order to define the questions which require further investigation. Some of these are general in kind, and applicable to all fields of policy study. How, for example, do we identify the precipitating factors which convert a dormant political issue into an active one? Others are more specific to the field of health services. How, for instance, do we account for the emergent influence of the trade-unions during the crisis, and does this mark a shift in the balance of power within the health care system to the disadvantage of the medical profession. In turn, does such a shift (assuming there was one) reflect a more general structural shift in society? (Klein 1979b, 464-90)

And:

> The aim of the analysis in the previous sections has been twofold. First, it has been to delineate the particular practical problems encountered in the British NHS in trying to achieve a satisfactory balance between centralised control and some elements of community and worker involvement. Second, it has been to demonstrate, using a more theoretical perspective, that these problems do not just reflect the special local situation of

the NHS but also point out some more general dilemmas. (Klein 1979a, 70-94)

He argues that policy analysis requires a broad canvas. For example, in his analysis of the existence of private practice in the NHS, he suggests that it is impossible to explain the phenomenon without recourse to an examination of the total environment in which the policy makers were operating.

> And the puzzle can only be resolved by placing the issue for private practice in the larger context of the political and economic situation in which the in-coming Labour Government found itself in 1974. . . .One clear conclusion to emerge from this analysis of the 1974 to 1976 crisis over pay beds in Britain is that to study the politics of health care issues in isolation is to risk mystification or misinterpretation. . . .This would in turn suggest that the usefulness of different theoretical perspectives depends on the nature of the puzzle being tackled. (Klein 1979b, 464-90)

So theoretical perspectives should be carefully selected to underpin analysis. But equally Klein's approach demands that there are criteria for judging how a policy has evolved. 'The academic study of social policy as a discipline must be the process of argument about the criteria of evaluation' (Klein 1982b, 133-40). The intellectual challenge of this kind of activity then is in devising instruments of measurement – quantitative and qualitative – that will allow the assessment of the 'extent to which goals are realised.' For example, a criticism frequently levelled at the British welfare state is its inability to achieve equality. Yet Klein points out that this was never a policy goal. And, once again, Klein reiterates the need for criteria to assess the way in which a health care system develops. The criteria must be 'independent of historical legacy of assumptions and ambitions built into existing institutions' (Klein 1993a, 133-40). According to Heclo,

> we need to show that there is a way of getting from 'here to there' between bulky historical 'forces' and the micro world of human actions. . . .Thus, if we find a strong relationship between changes in economic conditions and certain kinds of election outcomes, it is not very informative to construct accounts of political development as if there were a self-contained world of macro-economic and political relations peopled only by aggregate variables. (Heclo 1994)

Klein has a well-developed sense of the interactions of the macro and the micro (Klein 1974a, 1-14; 1993b, 309-11). The macrodecisions and their accompanying theories concentrate on the distribution and organisation of power; microtheories concern the processes of policy making. This is spelt out in his paper on dimensions of rationing where he draws attention to the constraining influences of decisions taken at different levels of the organisation on each other. 'So when we talk about priority setting we are really discussing the complex interaction of multiple decisions, taken at various levels in the organisation, about allocating resources' (Klein 1993b, 309-11). Klein argues that the microworld needs to be described in terms of structure and power:

> So far the emphasis has been on the political influence of the trade-unions in the NHS. This method of analysis inevitably draws attention to the importance of structural factors, or the role played by organised labour in a particular society. But this is to neglect the possibility that the influence of the trades-unions may also be based on their industrial strength. . . .If the situation is analysed in terms of industrial power within complex organisations, then both the failure of the medical profession to prevent the Labour Government from taking up the pay beds issue and its ultimate success in compelling a compromise become comprehensible. (Klein 1979b, 464-90)

His analytic method calls for an understanding of organisational factors and in particular organisational and social values. 'While structural factors may be a necessary precondition for change, organisational factors may explain the problems involved in carrying out new policies' (Klein 1979b, 464-90). But he also warns of the need to step back from the immediacy of the situation under analysis. 'Thus, when we talk about structural factors limiting the possibilities of change within health services, it would often be more accurate to talk about the social values which constrain state hegemony, and embody a concept of freedom opposed to the abuses of both market and bureaucratic power' (Klein 1979b, 464-90).

His method therefore calls for an analytical technique that examines the interaction of many complex organisations.

> Structural change, by promoting the growth of organised labour, has created a situation where there may be more pluralistic bargaining. But in future it will no longer be possible to

analyse pressure groups politics in terms exclusively of the relationship between governments and the medical profession. The
problem rather, will be to analyse the interaction of a whole
complexity of organised interests. In other words, the paradoxical conclusion is that structural and pluralistic theories of policy
making are mutually supportive rather than exclusive. It is structure which shapes the universe and provides the value-language
of pluralistic bargaining. But it is the interaction of the various
interests involved, not the structure, which determines the outcome of any particular policy dispute. (Klein 1979b, 464-90)

The organisation and the development of institutions have
formed the major cloth that Klein has used to cut his policy analysis. A central fascination has been the tension between the forces
of administration – centralisation versus decentralisation, control
versus entrepreneurship. Klein weaves into this fabric the repeating patterns of consumer choice, the functioning of markets and
the development of new institutional forms to cope with changing
environments. He continually questions the structure of accountability, its definition and translation into practice, by identifying
the balance of power between the individual actors involved in
any political decision making process.

> Firstly, what should be the balance between the managerial and
> representative principles in the selection of members?
> Secondly, can the members of the authorities, however selected,
> be expected to play their part without adequate training?
> Thirdly, can they be expected to monitor the performance of
> their officers without access to independent advice. (Klein 1971,
> 363-75)

Power is a key explanatory variable that Klein feels has been
neglected by British social policy analysts in particular: 'for the
British tradition of social policy has been conspicuously strong on
prescription but short on any theory of power' (Klein 1980a, 24-
34).

> Inevitably the policies adopted will reflect the perceptions of
> the policy makers – in particular – the dominating model of
> health care – and the power of different pressure groups in the
> health care policy arena; any policy prescription which ignored,
> for example, the ability of the medical profession to veto
> change threatening its own interests (real or perceived) would
> be totally unrealistic. (Klein 1982a, 95-128)

Policy creation for Klein is a process of debate reflecting the values of the actors and their interests. 'Objectives do not set themselves: they are the product of organisational processes. Criteria are not self-evident: they are selected and shaped by the values of the organisational actors' (Klein 1982c, 385-407). 'What really matters is how that debate is structured: how far it promotes reasoned, informed, and open argument, drawing on a variety of perspectives and involving a plurality of interests' (Klein 1993b, 309-11). A major theme of Klein's work has been to detect a number of significant changes in the debate that appear to be changing the health service universe and that will therefore require new developments in the approach of policy analysts. He has pointed to the adoption of the language of consumerism, which is radically changing views about the nature of public accountability (Klein 1990a, 127-33). It is also changing views of the health care system 'from seeing it as a church to seeing it as a garage. . . . What if the demands of the consumer do not match expert-defined needs? Do we then stick to the traditional view that needs always trump demands? Or do we reverse the doctrine, and argue that demands should have precedence over needs?' (Klein 1993a, 136-40).

The Role of Policy Analysis

Although Klein has evolved a view that policy analysis is about debate, he has been swift to argue that there is a real role for policy analysts in the late twentieth century. Its origins are indeed in the arena of policy consensus: 'Typically, policy has been made by setting up expert committees – usually dominated by a medical membership – to report on specific policy problems. Thus the emphasis has been not so much on policy analysis as on achieving a policy consensus among those representing the very professions that would have to implement any decisions made.'

But he argues, in more recent decades there has been a need for objective analysis to inform the policy debate.

> In the mid 1960s however, policy analysis, if of a very rudimentary sort, began to creep in. There were a number of reasons for this. First there was the change in the general policy making environment: long range planning was becoming fashionable –

an example is the rolling five-year projection of government spending plans that followed the Plowden report on the management of public expenditure and there was growing pressure on individual departments to justify their claims for extra resources in an intellectually more sophisticated way. (Klein 1976b, 459-75)

He has strongly criticised those who would turn policy analysts into service researchers. Service research, in his view, is 'primarily supportive research – that is ... a means of helping those in charge of making and executing policy to carry out their functions more efficiently. It implicitly rejects the critical role of analysis, which surely involves not only examining ways of implementing policy but also challenging (if necessary) the assumptions of the policy-makers' (Klein 1976b, 459-75). He has vociferously argued the case for independent policy analysts to challenge policy makers – to redress the balance and to explain to the world what is happening:

Policy analysis is not self generating: nor can it be introduced into the political system simply because it is felt to be a necessary piece of intellectual equipment in the pursuit of that elusive holy grail of policy making – rationality. . . .Before analysis can be expected to take root, it must be able to demonstrate that it actually has something useful to contribute. (Klein 1976b, 459-75)

Hence, Klein's apparent irritation with academic policy analysts, too wedded to their own theories and their own assumptions and too keen to support policy makers in their own value bases. 'The fault line does not run simply between discipline, or curiosity-driven and policy-concern-driven studies. There is no inherent reason why an interest in policy issues – or even a strong bias toward a preferred policy solution should necessarily lead to selective perception' (Klein 1991, 275-91).

But to do this requires rigorous analysis, based upon the sort of approach he has advocated.

Social policy needs a very different sort of theorising: one that is based not on large and often vacuous generalisations about the nature of capitalist or any other kind of society but on a rigorous analysis of the policy conflicts in particular societies and of the criteria used to justify specific choices. Diagnosing contradictions, i.e. conflicts, in societies does not get us far. Investigating how different societies tackle those conflicts –

their institutional capacity for so doing, the structure of power and the arguments used in the process is likely to provide far more illumination. (Klein 1993c, 16)

But like policy, policy analysis must also find a way of dealing with debate. 'Evaluation involves a constant, unending and probably unresolveable dialogue between arguments about criteria and assessment of impact' (Klein 1982b, 133-40). For Klein, the workable definition of policy analysis has to recognise its malleability within the political environment:

> It is an argument which will be shaped by both the substantive nature of the policy arena and by the characteristics of the organisation concerned. On the one hand, it will reflect the nature of the goods produced. On the other hand, it will reflect the structure of the organisation: the power, legitimacy and authority of the different actors involved in the argument. (Klein 1982c, 385-407)

And the emphasis on debate has thrown up the need for better language in policy analysis. A constant theme has been the need to develop an improved vocabulary for dealing with policy questions.

> The major gap in policy-making studies seems to me to be the failure to develop a basic descriptive vocabulary as the first step towards developing analytic theory. . . .Hence, in my view, the most urgent requirement in policy-making studies – whether these are analytic or prescriptive – is to develop a more precise vocabulary capable of delineating policy environments, areas and issues with more accuracy than is at present possible. (Klein 1974a, 219-36)

In 1987 Klein wrote: 'Debate about health care is often dominated by a sort of mid-Atlantic economist's vocabulary. This obscures the crucial point that the United States and Western Europe have very different political, legal and institutional traditions for dealing with the relationship between the public and private spheres of activity and that the words themselves tend to have a different meaning' (Klein 1987, 1802-1900). Klein has attempted to widen the vocabulary of policy analysis by creating some workable definitions that open up ideas to more rigorous analysis.

> It is therefore perhaps best to think of 'public accountability' in the NHS in a rather less technical sense than that in which it is usually used and as a shorthand, instead, for a number of

related concepts. Accountability in the context of the NHS should mean, I suggest, the acceptance of the responsibility publicly to explain and justify policies, to welcome rather than stifle discussion of priorities and objectives, and awareness of and sensitivity to public needs and finally, a willingness to admit to and remedy errors. (Klein 1971, 363-75)

For most policy analysts there is a bifurcation of their field into analysis of policy and analysis for policy. Although Klein has contributed much to the debate about policy futures, his approach is firmly grounded in the analysis of policy. He has frequently offered visions of future policy conundrums but has always fought shy of predicting the future. 'It is difficult to anticipate how they [political parties] would react in unpredictable circumstances. To do so would mean making heroic assumptions not only about the future economic and political context of policy making, but also about the role of the various interest groups involved in the health care policy arena' (Klein 1982a, 95-128).

Klein neither uses nor seeks a rational outcome in his analysis. His perspective on policy making is shaped by a belief in competing forces and continual dialogue between interested parties: 'To evaluate, appraise or assess the performance of an organisation is to engage in debate. It is a debate about how the objectives of the organisation should be defined, about the criteria to be used to measure performance and about the interpretation of information' (Klein 1982c, 385-407). Similarly, he argues, 'Objectives do not set themselves; they are the product of organisational processes. Criteria are not self-evident: they are selected and shaped by the values of organisational actors' (Klein 1982c). 'Information does not automatically yield conclusions: data acquire meaning only when there is already an agreed policy paradigm' (Klein 1982c).

For Klein, the fascination of policy analysis is in the continual struggle of forces for dominance – with little hope of any resolution. 'So the ongoing debate about the structure and organisation of Britain's National Health Service represents a necessary dialectic, and one which is likely to continue without any final resolution. Different aims of policy – embodying different values, all desirable in their own right but not necessarily compatible with each other – pull in different directions' (Klein 1979a, 70-94). 'The conclusions drawn from any developments will depend on political evaluation. In turn, the political evaluation will be informed by the underlying assumptions about the desirable direction of policy: in other words, it will depend on which of the two basic, polar models dominates the assumptive worlds of the policy-makers' (Klein 1982a, 95-128). At each policy turn, a new set of simple questions can be directed at policy makers to keep them on their toes.

References

Heclo, H. 1994. Ideas, Interests and Institutions. In *The Dynamics of American Politics,* eds. L. C. Dodds and C. Tillson, 366-92. Boulder, CO: Westview Press.

Klein, R. ——. 1993a. The Goals of Health Policy: Church or Garage. In *Health Care UK 1992/3,* ed. A. Harrison, 136-40. London: King's Fund Institute.

——. 1993b. Dimensions of Rationing. *British Medical Journal* 307: 309-11.

——. 1993c. O'Goffe's Tale, or, What Can We Learn from the Success of the Capitalist Welfare States? In *New Perspectives on the Welfare State in Europe,* ed. C. Jones, 7-17. London: Routledge.

——. 1991. Risks and Benefits of Comparative Studies: Notes from Another Shore. *Milbank Quarterly* 69(2): 275-91.

——. 1990a. From Status to Contract: The Transformation of the British Medical Profession. In *Health Care Provision under Finanical Constraint: a Decade of Change,* Royal Society of Medicine Services International Congress and Symposium Series No. 171. ed. H. L'Etang, 127-33. London: Royal Society of Medicine Services Limited.

——. 1990b. Research, Policy and the National Health Service. *Journal of Health Politics, Policy and Law* 15(3): 501-23.

——. 1987. Towards a New Pluralism. *Health Policy* 8: 5-12.

——. 1985. Public Expenditure in an Inflationary World. In *The Politics of Inflation and Economic Stagnation,* eds. L. N. Lindberg and C. S. Maier, 196-221. Washington: Brookings Institution.

——. 1982a. Private Practice and Public Policy. In *The Public/Private Mix for Health – The Relevance and Effects of Change,* eds. G. McLachin and A. Maynard, 95-128. London: Nuffield Provincial Hospitals Trust.

——. 1982b. Evaluation and Social Policy. *Evaluation and Programme Planning* 5: 133-40.

——. 1982c. Performance, Evaluation and the NHS: A Case Study in Conceptual Perplexity and Organisational Complexity. *Public Administration* 60 (winter): 385-407.

——. 1980a. The Welfare State: A Self-Inflicted Crisis? *The Political Quarterly* 51(1): 24–34.

——. 1980b. Models of Man and Models of Policy. *Milbank Memorial Fund Quarterly/Health and Society* 58(3): 416–29.

——. 1979a. Control, Participation and the British National Health Service. *Milbank Memorial Fund Quarterly/Health and Society* 57(1): 70–94.

——. 1979b. Ideology, Class and the National Health Service. *Journal of Health Politics, Policy and Law* 4(3): 464–90.

——. 1979c. Universities in the Market Place. *New University Quarterly* (summer): 306–20.

——. 1978. Normansfield: Vacuum of Management in the NHS. *British Medical Journal* (December 23–30): 1802–900.

——. 1977. The Conflict between Professionals, Consumers and Bureaucrats. *Journal of the Irish Colleges of Physicians and Surgeons* 6 (January): 88–91.

——. 1976a. The Politics of Public Expenditure: American Theory and British Practice. *British Journal of Political Science* 6: 401–32.

——. 1976b. The Rise and Decline of Policy Analysis: the Strange Case of Policy Making in Britain. *Policy Analysis* 2(3): 459–75.

——. 1974a. Policy Problems and Policy Perceptions in the National Health Service. *Policy and Politics* 2(3): 219–36.

——. 1974b. Policy Making in the National Health Service. *Political Studies* 22 (March): 1–14.

——. 1972. The Political Economy of National Health. *The Public Interest* 26 (winter): 112–25.

——. 1971. Accountability in the National Health Service. *The Political Quarterly* 42(4): 363–75.

Part IV

Envoi

14

Between Worlds:
An Autobiographical Footnote

Rudolf Klein

The point about being an insider is
that you can't see anything as it really is.

– Julie Burchill, film critic

The experience of having a festschrift dedicated to one is unsettling. Reflecting on it prompts anxious introspection and carries the danger of emotional self-indulgence. A celebration of one's past achievements is (in career terms) a memento mori: a reminder that intellectual productivity depends on animal spirits and that energy diminishes with age. From now on, the entries in the c.v. are going to become slimmer, year by year; the output of papers will inexorably diminish; the invitations to conferences in cities with good opera houses will gradually dry up. A festschrift also prompts uneasy questions. Having always prided myself on operating as a *franc-tireur* – an intellectual sharpshooter, not associated with any of the big battalions – have I now joined them? Have I – the thought jars but must be faced – become a respectable elder statesman of the academic trade? What have I done to deserve (with all the ambiguities of that word) this collection? Melancholy is, however, more than balanced by a sense of exhilaration. This volume, as I see it, is less a celebration of my work than of the friendship I have earned among colleagues over the years: a tribute as much to their tolerance of my idiosyncracies as to my own achievements. There is something very cheering about the thought that so many friends and professional colleagues have thought it worthwhile to contribute to this volume. I am extremely grateful to all of them for rescuing me from the temptations of self-pitying melancholy on the occasion of my sixty-fifth birthday.

There remains a problem about this volume. If only I had stuck to my first interests as an undergraduate and followed in the path of my Oxford tutor Michael Wallace-Hadrill, this could be a collection of essays by distinguished medievalists. If only I had persevered with the topic suggested to me by my postgraduate research supervisor, A. J. P. Taylor, I might well have become the world's leading expert on the diplomatic history of the Dardanelles between 1894 and 1896, and there would have been no difficulty in assembling contributions around this theme. In retrospect, I am extremely glad that I did neither. But in either event, a review editor – although he or she might well have had doubts as to whether the book was worth noting – would have had no difficulty in finding a specialist competent to deal with the volume. In the case of this festschrift, though, the focus is not quite so clear. Most of the essays deal with one aspect or another of health policy and politics. But their perspectives are very different. Should the book be reviewed by a political scientist, by a philosopher, by an economist or by someone actively engaged in the health policy field? The answer is not self-evident, and my sympathy goes out both to prospective review editors and to possible reviewers.

This footnote is therefore written partly in an attempt to suggest that the multiple perspectives of this volume have some sort of logic insofar as they accurately reflect the strengths (and weaknesses) of my own approach to the study of public policy. The contributions to this volume mirror what my friends would call (I hope) my intellectual pluralism and what my critics would describe (I suspect) as my intellectual dilettantism. To call this approach a strategy of inquiry would be both pompous and inaccurate. If I have moved between different worlds – 20 years in journalism, 20 plus years in research institutes and universities – and if I have never pledged allegiance to a single academic discipline or topic of inquiry, it is not because of deliberate choice. It is, rather, the result of circumstances and, no doubt, of personal temperament. As an immigrant I have never felt the need to compensate for my foreignness by becoming an epitome of conventional Englishness (á la Leslie Howard) but rather have seen the status of naturalised citizen as a privileged opportunity to be a detached observer of events: in effect, to have the best of both worlds. Similarly, I have always seen myself as a contemporary historian trying to understand my country of adoption rather than as someone producing policy prescriptions. Prophecy, it has always seemed to me, is the occupational disease of young journalists and ageing academics.

The sense of surprise that an immigrant has – the shock of the new – was reinforced in my case by my career in journalism. For journalism is (at its best) an attempt to convey to the reader – or viewer – something of the excitement that a new experience brings. It has to be a controlled, disciplined sense of excitement: the corruption of journalism lies precisely in the temptation to be carried away by words or images and to capture the audience's attention by exaggeration or overdramatisation. The ideal journalist has to combine the characteristics both of a naive child who is constantly surprised by the oddity of what goes on around him or her and of a world-weary sophisticate who can put what is happening in context and perspective. When the sense of surprise dulls – when world-weariness takes over, as one sees the cycle of events repeating itself – the time comes to quit journalism: which is one reason (among many) why I did.

There is another characteristic of journalism that is worth noting in trying to explain the relevance of experience in Fleet Street (as it still was in my day) to developing a particular style of policy analysis. Particularly in the case of those who are engaged in commenting on and interpreting current affairs, there is a delicate balance to be struck. On the one hand, there are the dangers of seduction, of being sucked into the world of politicians and civil servants. There are few things more flattering than being rung by the Chancellor of the Exchequer, as one sits pounding out an article on a devaluation just announced by the Treasury, to explain precisely why he has chosen a particular parity. How difficult it is to respond to such confidences by criticism in the next day's newspaper. Similarly, lunching ministers may corrupt the host more than the guest by drawing him or her into the inside world of politics.

On the other hand, though, there is the danger of aloof contempt, of seeing politicians as blundering buffoons, when they are not self-seeking careerists. If journalists start to see themselves as public prosecutors – as the Robespierres of the media, charged with cross-examining the politicians to destruction – they are likely to present a caricature of political processes and their prophecies of public alienation from politics will become self-fulfilling.

So the challenge to journalists is how to explain the difficulties of political decision making – the necessary compromises, the limited scope for manoeuvre, the inadequacies of the available policy instruments – without ever becoming the apologists of those in power. It is a challenge that calls for both empathy with the actors in the policy process and critical detachment in interpreting the shards of evidence and the competing versions of what 'really happened' provided by self-interested actors. And it creates a sense of ambivalence insofar as one often wants to be both an insider and an outsider.

When I became reincarnated as a university professor in my middle forties – after a period in quarantine in a research institute – I therefore started my new life, as I came to realise, with enormous advantages. Without realising it, I had received the best training possible for investigating the process of policy making and implementation – the main focus of my interests in subsequent years. I had learnt that the best way to make sense of events was to read everything available – parliamentary debates, white papers, newspaper reports – and then to try out the story on the participants: to test the novel that emerged from the evidence on the characters in it. Equally important, I had learnt that ministers and civil servants – once they knew that the interviewer had done his or her homework and could be trusted – were quite ready to trade information, to match their version of events against those of others. Academic timidity and incompetence rather than official secrecy, I realised, helped to explain the lack of policy research in the United Kingdom when compared to the United States. Thus, when I started my academic career in the late 1970s I was astonished to find that the Social Science Research Council (since rechristened the Economic and Social Research Council) deferentially refused to fund any studies of government without first getting the official permission of the Whitehall department concerned. Clearly, the thought that it might be possible to get politicians and civil servants to talk informally – sometimes across a lunch table – had never crossed the minds of the funders. Things have improved since, but even so I have never dared, alas, to put the cost of such lunches in my research applications, though it would be money well spent. Not surprisingly, therefore, some of the best accounts of how British institutions and politics actually work have been written by expatriate or visiting North Americans – like Anthony King and Richard Rose, Hugh Heclo and Aaron Wildavsky – who do not share the inhibitions of their native colleagues. Similarly, in the field of social and health policies, our understanding of the policy process would be much poorer but for the work of Harry Eckstein, Keith Banting, Ted Marmor and Dan Fox. There are, clearly, advantages to being an outsider.

The catalogue of names of those who have contributed over the decades to our understanding of British institutions also underlines the extent to which anyone interested in policy analysis has been dependent on ideas imported from North America. Indeed the very notion of policy analysis was somewhat alien in the British context: policy analysis, we were sharply told at a conference held in the 1970s to explore this new concept, was what civil servants had always done. There was no need to invent a new academic discipline, just as there was no need to invent institutions like a British version of Brookings in which this new art might be practised: Ralf Dahrendorf's enthusiasm for launching such an institution ran onto the rocks of the conservatism of the London School of Economics. Certainly policy analysis has never become institutionalised in British universities, in contrast yet again to North America. My own attempt to launch a master's degree modelled on the US example turned out to be a miserable failure, with few takers. Perhaps this does not matter. Policy analysis is a vague enough concept, and it may be that what is really valuable about it – the notion that different disciplinary perspectives can be combined to analyse policy problems, processes and options – has been largely accepted in practice. And in the process Britain has avoided the danger – so evident in the United States – of seeing policy analysis dominated by economists.

American ideas also helped in the transformation of social policy as an academic area of study that has taken place over the last 20 years or so. Symbolically, all professors of social administration have become professors of social policy, a change of title in which, I like to think but cannot be sure, I was the pioneer. It marked a deliberate repudiation (at least in my own case) of the Titmuss tradition that had hither to been dominant in the universities. Titmuss's own work was marked by a rare generosity of spirit and was also, in many respects, ground breaking. But when translated into the common currency of academic teaching and research, it meant that social administration had become the study of the existing institutions of the British Welfare State. It was critical of the shortcomings of the Welfare State – the failure to eradicate poverty in particular – but its critique was based on the same intellectual framework that had created the institutions. When the global stagflation crisis of the mid-1970s destroyed the assumptions on which policy had been built – that the welfare state could go on living off the ever increasing dividends of economic growth – the Titmussian tradition had no answer except to rally to the defence of the inheritance and to denounce every attempt at modification as a betrayal of the past.

The study of social policy as it developed in the 1980s and 1990s represented an emancipation from this traditionalist framework of thought as well as from an excessive reliance on sociology and a watered-down form of Marxism (the two were often synonymous in the 1970s). Instead of seeing the world through the filter of the British Welfare State's institutions, we started looking at those institutions from a variety of critical perspectives – many of them provided by American academics. By drawing on the work of philosophers like Rawls or Rae, often as translated for us by Albert Weale and others, we were able to reflect critically on what kinds of equalities we were concerned about. By using the insights of the new political economy, as expounded by Sam Brittan among others, we learnt to think of governments as intent on maximising their chances of reelection, rather than necessarily trying to maximise welfare, and of markets as instruments of discovery rather than of exploitation. By learning about the economics literature, we extended our vocabulary of analysis to include such concepts as opportunity costs, incentives and interests. By developing the comparative study of social policy, we discovered that in many respects other countries were doing better, that it was perfectly possible to have a welfare society without having anything that looked like a Beveridgean welfare state. Social policy became an intellectually demanding and more rigorous discipline precisely because it was not a discipline but an invitation to scavenge for useful tools of analysis wherever these were to be found.

The development still has a long way to go. Many of those in the trade do not share my sense of exhilaration at the new perspectives that have been opened up but still see academic social policy as a society for the preservation of inherited institutions. If the intellectual centre of gravity has shifted greatly, the emotional bias remains largely unchanged. The instinct is still to see change as a threat. When my colleague Patricia Day and I gave a cautious welcome to the government's reforms of the National Health Service in 1991, we found ourselves isolated and in danger of excommunication. There are still words and phrases that tend to set many social policy knees jerking: markets and private health care are two such. Supporting any of the policies introduced or proposed by Mrs Thatcher's government was an activity that could be indulged in only by consenting adults in private, prepared to run the risk of being caught in flagrante delicto by the thought police of the academic social policy community.

My own heterodox views in all this – as an aesthetic egalitarianism sceptical about many of the institutions of the welfare state – represented, I suppose, a coming together of two worlds, those of the British social policy community and of the Hapsburg Empire diaspora. It was from the former that I drew my raw material; it was from the latter that I drew most of my ideas. Let me illustrate. Of the many conferences on the international crisis of the welfare state that I attended during the 1970s and 1980s – before we discovered that the welfare state had an unsuspected capacity for adaptation and survival – one of the best took place in a small hotel overlooking a lake in Switzerland. Among those present were Peter Flora and Hal Wilensky, as well as some of the contributors to this volume. It was successful precisely because of the mix of disciplines, perspectives and nationalities represented. But, going round the table one evening, we discovered that we all hailed, either as first- or second-generation migrants, from the former countries of the Hapsburg Empire – even though not everyone was Jewish. Maybe displacement can encourage detached analysis, although there are some notable exceptions.

Better policies, on this view, are the by-product of better understanding. In contrast, a rush to prescription, shortcutting the laborious process of arguing about words and evidence, risks perverse outcomes. Which is why I insisted – defying my editor – on giving the title *Only Dissect* to the collection of my own papers over the decades that forms the companion to this volume. If we don't learn about anatomy, let alone physiology, how can we set about changing the body politic?

But the role of a detached observer, moving between different worlds, carries its own occupational risks. If the prescriptive approach to social policy can lead to a mindless utopianism about the potential for improving the world, the analytic approach can degenerate into a nihilistic agnosticism about all solutions. Here, I think, the only remedy is – as in journalism – to keep alive one's sense of childlike wonder, to retain one's capacity to be surprised and excited by events. If detachment turns to indifference about what is happening – if one loses one's ability to respond to change by seeing it as an opportunity for research and exploration – then it is surely time to take up petit point embroidery or to start breeding canaries.

One of the many shocks that awaited me when I moved to the University of Bath as professor of social policy in the late 1970s – shortly afterwards becoming Head of a School of Social Sciences with 40-odd staff members drawn from a mixed grill of disciplines – was precisely the discovery that most academics lacked the capacity to be excited by anything except their own domestic politics. Previously, I had only met the high-flying academics whose articles I had edited when on the *Observer* or the members of the Hapsburg diaspora. Nothing had prepared me for my encounter with the foot soldiers of the social sciences: the marginal members of what was then a marginal university still struggling to emancipate itself from the taint of a humble past. No doubt it would have been different if I had been a natural scientist. The pace of laboratory science imposes, I suspect, its own discipline and sense of urgency on its practitioners, in much the same way that deadlines and competition for space create discipline and competition among journalists. But who has ever heard of a race to publish results in the social sciences? The publishing schedules of most social science journals are measured in months – sometimes even years – and hardly encourage immediacy. Here the death of *New Society* has left a gap still waiting to be filled.

Nor does the culture of the social sciences encourage its practitioners to react swiftly to changes in the environment. Social scientists tend to be theory-fetishists. For many of them the world is a quarry for material to illuminate theory; the notion that theories are merely disposable tools for exploring the world, to be discarded if they don't work, would strike many of them as strange. They are reluctant to see themselves for what they are – craftsmen who (if they are well trained and skilled) can help to illuminate what is happening in the world around them – and tend to suffer from delusory visions of themselves as the critics of society. Unlike natural scientists who want to find out how things work, social scientists all too often concentrate on what doesn't work. Reputations are built on identifying failure rather than success, and accentuating the negative tends to be the theme in the social science hymnal. So, for example, we know a great deal about the factors that precipitate people into poverty but remarkably little about how others manage to escape from it.

The new world of academe therefore struck me as strangely introspective: self-obsessed yet lacking in self-awareness. How could it be that academics, whose trade it was to study other professions (such as doctors) never analysed their own culture and left it to the novelists to hold up a mirror to them? Similarly, I thought that the generally held interpretation of the principle of professional autonomy was self-indulgently unrealistic. Did professional autonomy really mean that teachers should have a lifetime's freehold of their courses, however badly they taught them and however little students might be interested? I rather doubted it, a scepticism that caused some resentment among my colleagues. Given external threats and pressures – the abolition of tenure, reductions in budgets and staff numbers, increases in the student population – the tendency was always to dig in to defend the past, rather than to anticipate challenge and seek ways of adapting to the new environment in which the universities (like all other institutions in Britain) were working. And naturally it was the most radical academics – the 1960s revolutionaries – who turned out to be the staunchest defenders of the status quo. It was not a comfortable time to be in a university, far less to be urging the case for innovation and change – even though it taught me much about how all professions, and not just doctors, tend to defend their turf and resist demands for public accountability.

I must not exaggerate: the journalist's training puts much emphasis on capturing the reader's attention (in contrast to the academic who, usually wrongly, assumes interest) and tends to betray one into using bright colours when subtler shades are called for. My social policy colleagues who came together at Bath – perhaps because, like me, they did not see themselves as defined and bound by a discipline – proved congenial collaborators and friends. The university as a social collectivity, if not its architecture, mellowed as it gradually climbed up the ladder of my esteem; the ritual arguments diminished and resistance to innovation crumbled, as growing domestic commitments and the pressure of rising student numbers meant that my colleagues no longer had the time or energy to indulge in bloody-mindedness as a form of recreational activity. As I gratefully escaped from the rising burden of filling in ever more forms for ever multiplying assessment exercises by transforming myself into a part-time research professor, so it seemed that the shock of the new had worn off: the culture of the academic world had changed and so had I. If I had not become fully assimilated, I had at the very least become anaesthetised to the sheer oddity and comedy of academic behaviour.

So I end by returning to the worries set out in my first paragraph. Over the last 20 years I have always thought that my interest in the health care policy field was simply a by-product of other (wider) concerns – about public accountability, about the role of regulation, about the influence of professional power and so on. The National Health Service (NHS), I always argued, was simply a useful laboratory for exploring such issues. But now I find myself monumentalised in this volume as an *authority* on health care policy, a rentier living off the dividends of past investments in the accumulation of intellectual capital. It is a role that I do not cherish. A festschrift, I believe, should not be a tombstone commemorating past achievements but a signpost on the road to future achievements. So I will take this publication as a prompt to start thinking about moving into new intellectual fields in order to renew a sense of surprise before it becomes blunted by an overlong exposure to the same environment.

Contributors

Samuel Brittan is principal economic commentator and assistant editor of *The Financial Times.* His most recent book is *There is No Such Thing as Society* (1993).

Patricia Day is senior research officer at the School of Social Sciences, University of Bath, England. Her most recent publication is 'Accountability,' which appeared in *Learning from Innovation: Housing and Social Care in the 1990s,* edited by N. Deakin and J. Doling (Birmingham: Birmingham Academic Press, 1993).

Daniel M. Fox is president of the Milbank Memorial Fund. His most recent book is *Power and Illness: The Failure and Future of American Health Policy* (Berkeley: University of California Press, paperback edition, 1995).

Peter Hennessy is professor of contemporary history at Queen Mary and Westfield College, London. His most recent book is *The Hidden Wiring: Unearthing the British Constitution* (London: Castle, 1995).

Rudolf Klein is professor of social policy and director of the Centre for the Analysis of Social Policy at Bath University. He has recently updated his book on the politics of the NHS, which was first published in 1983 and revised in 1989. The 3d edition is called *The New Politics of the NHS* (London: Longman, 1995).

Julian Le Grand is the Richard Titmuss Professor of Health Policy at the London School of Economics and professional fellow at the King's Fund Institute. His two most recent books are *Evaluating the NHS Reforms* (with Ray Robinson) (London: King's Fund, 1994), and *Quasi-Markets and Social Policy* (with Will Bartlett) (London: Macmillan, 1993).

Theodore R. Marmor is professor of public policy and management at Yale School of Management and professor of political science at Yale University. His most recent book is *Understanding Health Care Reform* (New Haven: Yale University Press, 1994), a collection of his essays. Currently, he is working with Tom Hamburger on a book dealing with the fate and aftermath of the health reform stalemate.

Jerry L. Mashaw is Sterling Professor of Law at Yale and the author of a number of books on public policy, including studies of disability, auto safety, administrative law, and, with P. L. Harvey and T. R. Marmor, the American welfare state. He is now writing a book on positive political theory and American reform.

Robert Maxwell is chief executive of the King's Fund. His most recent publication is *What Next for London's Healthcare?* (London: King's Fund, 1994).

David Mechanic was Visiting Fellow at the King's Fund Institute, United Kingdom, in 1994–95 where he studied reforms in the English National Health Service and worked on health care rationing issues. His most recent book, *Inescapable Decisions: The Imperatives of Health Reform* (New Brunswick, N.J.: Transaction Publishers, 1993), makes the case for a new approach to health care that is more sensitive to behavioral factors and to preventing illness and limiting disease. Dr Mechanic is René Dubos Professor of Behavioral Sciences and director of the Institute for Health, Health Care Policy and Aging Research at Rutgers University.

James Robinson is associate professor of health economics in the School for Public Health, University of California at Berkeley. His research interests focus on the development and application of institutional economics to the health care system, especially vertical integration, complex contracting, and payment incentives. His policy interests center on health maintenance organizations, integrated delivery systems, and organized purchasing of health care as components of a managed competition approach to market and organizational reform.

Richard Rose is director and professor of public policy in the Centre for the Study of Public Policy at Strathclyde University. His most recent book is *Inheritance in Public Policy: Change without Choice in Britain* (with P. L. Davies) (New Haven: Yale University Press, 1994).

Ellie Scrivens is professor of health policy in the Centre for Health Planning and Management at Keele University. Her most recent book is *Accreditation: Protecting the Professional or the Consumer?* (Buckingham: Open University Press, 1995).

Richard Smith is editor of the *British Medical Journal*, chief executive of the BMJ publishing group, and professor of medical journalism at the University of Nottingham.

Albert Weale is professor of government at the University of Essex. His latest book is *The New Politics of Pollution* (Manchester: Manchester University Press, 1992).

Index